SETON HALL UNIVERSITY

3 3073 10381472 7

Old People, New Lives

Jennie-Keith Ross

Old People, New Lives
Community Creation
in a Retirement Residence

The University of Chicago Press
Chicago and London

SETON HALL UNIVERSITY
McLAUGHLIN LIBRARY
SO. ORANGE, N. J.

Jennie-Keith Ross is associate professor of
anthropology at Swarthmore College. She has
done extensive field research in France and has
written many articles for professional journals.

The University of Chicago Press, Chicago 60637
The University of Chicago Press, Ltd., London

© 1977 by The University of Chicago
All rights reserved. Published 1977
Printed in the United States of America

82 81 80 79 78 77   9 8 7 6 5 4 3 2 1

Ross, Jennie-Keith.
  Old people, new lives.

  Bibliography: p.
  Includes index.
   1.   Retirement, Places of–France–Paris region–Case
studies.   2.   Aged–France–Paris region–Case studies.
3.   Community.   4.   Social Structure.   I.   Title.
HQ1063.R67   301.43′5   76-8103
ISBN 0-226-72825-0

HQ
1063
R67

Dedicated with love and thanks
to my mother and father,
Romayne and Paul Hill

Contents

Preface

The questions I'm most often asked about my research in a French retirement residence are "Wasn't it depressing?" and "That's not really anthropology, is it?"

No, it wasn't depressing to live for a year with old people when I was twenty-six. Like learning to participate in any unfamiliar setting, it was a challenge; it was stimulating, difficult, funny, sometimes exhausting, but not depressing. Frankly, I didn't expect it to be. The first old people I knew, my grandparents, were powerful, interesting, central characters in my life. This may not have sent me out looking for old people to study, but it did mean that when new kinds of retirement housing suggested an intriguing research problem, I didn't hesitate to pursue it.

Yes, it is anthropology to map an unknown social world, even in a Parisian suburb. Aging, with the powerful negative charge attached to it by American culture, is in fact a subject particularly in need of the cross-cultural and emic perspectives of anthropology. We know very little yet about the cultural dimensions of aging, and less about how aging looks to the old.

Many people contributed to this book. The field work was supported financially by a post-doctoral fellowship and research grant from the National Institute of Mental Health (MH-37442). Moral support and intellectual stimulation for my first anthropological work on aging came from Paul Bohannan; Remi Clignet gave me encouragement and advice during the planning of the French research. Ethel Shanas kindly introduced me to her friends and colleagues in France; and Dr. J. R. Huet was my guide into the world of French gerontology. The study of Les Floralies would not have been possible without the permission and assistance of Jean-Paul Guerillon, former director of the Résidence Les Floralies, of Yves Pergeaux, former director general of the Caisse National de Retraite des Ouvriers du Bâtiment et des Travaux Publiques, and of Olivier de Moussac, director of the Centre de Gérontologie Sociale.

The staff members at Les Floralies were also hospitable and helpful.

Before choosing Les Floralies as a research site, I consulted many people about the range of housing available to old people in France, and also spent six weeks visiting residences throughout the country. I am very grateful to the people who helped me during this process, especially Dr. Balier, Association de Gérontologie du 13eme Arrondissement; Mme. Cendron, Centre de Gérontologie; M. Clement, Fondation Nationale de Gérontologie; Mme. M. O. Lahalle; M. Mauvais, Caisse Interprofessionelle de Prévoyance des Cadres; Suzanne Pacaud, Directeur Scientifique au Centre National de la Recherche Scientifique; M. Paul Paillat, Institut National d'Etudes Démographiques; Mme. Petit-Lievois, UNIOPS; Mlle. Revol, Chef du Service, Association des Résidences pour Personnes Agées; Mlle. Dauce, Head Nurse, CNRO residence at Nantes; M. Thoreux, former Director, CNRO residence at Reims; M. Petitbon, CNRO residence at St. Etienne; M. Laborie, Director, CNRO residence at Bordeaux.

Some aspects of this research have been reported in other publications. A briefer analysis of socialization into the residence appears in "Learning to be Retired: Socialization into a French Retirement Residence," *Journal of Gerontology* 29 (1974):211–23. I appreciate the permission of the Gerontological Society to reproduce table 6 from that article. Bases of happiness in the residence are discussed in "Successful Aging in a French Retirement Residence," in *Successful Aging*, ed. Eric Pfeiffer (Durham: Duke University Press, 1973). The relationship between social organization inside Les Floralies and in the wider society outside is analyzed in "Life Goes On: Social Organization in a French Retirement Residence," in *Late Life: Communities and Environmental Policy*, ed. Jaber F. Gubrium (Springfield, Ill.: Charles C. Thomas, 1974). A shorter examination of conflict in the residence appears in "What Did You Do During the War? Community Conflict in a Retirement Residence," in *Community, Self and Identity*, ed. James Preston and Bhabagrahi Misra (The Hague: Mouton and Co., 1977). Sandra Barnes, Sheila Johnson, and Irving Rosow made very helpful comments on an earlier version of the book.

Jim Tresize typed the original manuscript, and believed it would become a book; Marguerite Clifford cheerfully worked on revisions. Pauline Federman, secretary of the Sociology-Anthropology Department at Swarthmore College, made her usual important and gracious contributions to my work.

A special quality and degree of thanks go to the residents of Les Floralies and to Marc Howard Ross. The old people let me into their lives and, in addition to everything else reported in this book, taught me that life can go on until death. I would enjoy thanking them by name, but to protect their privacy, they are all referred to by pseudonyms. Where detailed descriptions might be embarrassing, specific personal characteristics and past experiences have also been slightly changed to prevent recognition. Marc shared the field work, analysis, and writing; each stage was happier and better done because of him.

Probably the most surprising finding of my study was that, except for their being old, little about these old people was surprising. Their friendships, fights, and love affairs, their in-jokes and strategies for coping with common problems are only striking because we don't expect old people to go on living like everyone else. The old people I knew at Les Floralies used courage and ingenuity to continue living like human beings; and their availability to each other was a major resource in this struggle. I hope my account of the conditions that promoted the creation of their community will raise the chances of its happening again.

1 Community Creation

Introduction

The physical fact of new buildings labeled "retirement village" or "adult community" first provoked my curiosity about social life inside these new walls. Could older people living together make the names a reality? Could old age become a basis for community?

The first answers I heard to these questions came from younger people: a resounding no. Fogey farm, waiting room for death, geriatric ghetto were a few of the epithets used; and there was inevitably a comment on the horror of children "putting" their parents away in these places. The equally emphatic positive response from the old people I met on my first visits inside these residences suggested that spatial separation was far from the only barrier between young and old. Deep differences in perceptions of old people and of their wants and needs defined another kind of difference across the generations. Younger people saw the residences as an emphasis of passivity and dependence; old people were *put* there. Older people described the same setting as making continued independence possible. People of an age to have old parents assumed that older people wanted to live with their children; older people said they wanted above all to maintain an independent household. Younger people saw large numbers of old people living together as a horrifying cumulation of their collective sickness and tendency to live in the past: a dreadful museum of decaying individuals frozen into their previous social roles. Older people talked about the relief of having special facilities to insure physical care and security, about mutual aid when sickness occurred, and about the possibility for more active social participation in the present than they could have hoped for in at least the immediate past. Considering these contradictory responses, the physical boundary of separate residence might also represent protection from the less tangible barrier of negative attitudes. Could a

community of the old offer insulation from the stereotypes, preju-
dices, and misunderstandings of younger people whose ideas about
aging are usually dominant in the wider society?

The first residences I saw happened to be in California; but
neither they nor the responses of their occupants are simply
additional West coast oddities. More friendships, more social
activity, more help in emergency, and higher morale are consistently observed in settings where old people are available to each
other as potential friends and neighbors: in public housing, in
retirement communities, villages, and hotels, and in "normal"
apartment buildings with a high proportion of older residents.
Community is emphatically used to describe the bonds among
older people in situations as diverse as a life-care home for
Sephardic Jews, a blue-collar trailer park, a condominium of
garden apartments for the well-to-do.

The reverse situation has also been documented. Older people
who find themselves close in space to younger neighbors do not
necessarily become close to them in other ways. The old people, in
fact, often make considerable efforts to locate other people their
own age for friendships and help in emergency.

Some older people in some situations have created communities
in which they live satisfying social lives. Given the painful social
role, or lack of one, facing old people in most industrial societies, it
is obviously important to ask when and how and for whom age is
likely to become the basis of community. We need to know not just
that these communities exist, but under what conditions and
through what processes they develop. These questions are directly
relevant, first of all, to millions of older people in many modern
societies, where separate housing arrangements for the retired and
for the elderly are an increasingly common addition to the social
repertory. Because of the unusual visibility of these settings, the
new roles and life styles developed in them will have consequences
even for the many old people who do not live in them, and for
future old people who learn from them new ways of looking at
retirement and old age. Very few younger people in modern,
industrial societies still have a clear view of the entire life cycle
through everyday contact with individuals of many ages. Highly
visible clusters of the old and retired may do more to define these
frighteningly ambiguous roles than the often invisible old people
next door.

As an anthropologist faced with unanswered questions about

social life in a new kind of residential setting, my reaction was the classic one: I decided to move in. The method of participant observation (the technical term for "moving in") is based on participation in a social context as a means of observing it. Participant observation is most necessary for just the kind of problems presented by residences for old people. Judgments about the presence of community, analyses of its development, and comparisons of its organization to that of the society outside require the kind of holistic perspective offered by this method. Since these situations are new, they are also unknown. Like the exotic "native" societies where anthropologists first developed participant observation, residences for old people are also immune to many other techniques, such as survey research, until an initial period of participant observation has discovered not the answers but the questions appropriate to the new setting. Because the participant observer is the research instrument, the quality of observation obviously depends, at least to begin with, on his or her opportunity to observe. So the method is most effective for relatively small populations.[1] Most of the new residential settings for older people involve a small enough number of individuals, usually a few hundred, that an observer can have frequent, personal contact with everyone.

Where to move in was the next question. Armed with a problem and a method, I had to choose a place to work. My training as an anthropologist also suggested that, at least for the first time I used it, participant observation would be most successful outside my own culture. The same principle applies in photography: it is easier to see clearly that which is not too familiar. Photos are better—and observations more accurate—when the newness of a scene sharpens vision. As the eye becomes trained, it learns to focus just as clearly on the familiar. The distance enforced by a foreign setting should become a tool to be brought back home and used to understand what was once too close to be seen. Work with older people in another culture should be the basis for clearer understanding of aging in America. In addition, given the appearance of residences for old and retired people in many industrial societies, questions about social life inside them should eventually be considered cross-culturally, so that effects of age-homogeneity can be clearly separated from consequences of particular cultural contexts. Study of a residence for older people outside the U.S. is a first step in that direction.

The specific choice of France as the location for this research was based on much more practical and immediate considerations. There is a broad range of housing for older people in France. I speak French, and through American colleagues I was offered initial contacts with French gerontologists and French retirement programs. Although I did my homework about aging in France, my research focus was not on French old people, but on the possible development of a community by old people in an age-homogeneous residence. There is an atmosphere of Frenchness about the descriptions which follow, from the wine bottles on the tables to the inexorable interpretation of daily life in political terms. However, my central conclusions about patterns of community creation and of individual socialization are intended to be distinct enough from this ambiance to provide a basis for general hypotheses about community, old people, and communities of old people in other settings. The residence I chose for study, and the reasons why, are discussed in detail in the next chapter. Before diving into daily life at Les Floralies, however, it is necessary to discuss the concept of community that I went to observe.

Concept of Community

Community is a key concept in all the major questions of this study. Under what conditions does community develop in a residence for old people? What is the relationship between patterns of social life inside and those of the wider society outside, for instance in terms of the significance of age itself as a principle of social organization? How do people learn to participate in this new kind of community?

Community at first seems to need no definition; the word is so widely used, surely everyone knows what it means. But this is the very reason why it needs explicit definition. The concept is used in so many different ways and has so many different meanings that, without careful discussion, it cannot be the basis for orderly investigation of a problem. While for some people the absence, or "eclipse," of community is an identifying characteristic of complex societies, in contrast to simple or primitive ones, other researchers doggedly go about the business of doing "community studies," observing what these settings are, by some definitions, supposed to lack. Another way to consider the range of phenomena to which this term is applied is to ask what the west end of Boston, a trailer park in northern California, and a band of Pygmies in the Congo have in common.[2]

In the voluminous discussions about community—what was it, what is it, what could it be—three major themes consistently appear: territory, we-feeling, and social organization. Territory is quite literally the fundamental aspect of most definitions of community. Although living in the same place is never presented as a sufficient basis for community, it is necessary to all but the most symbolic uses of the term. We-feeling is a sense of distinctiveness, of shared fate, of things in common, in short a feeling that "we" is the right word to use to describe a collectivity of individuals. A widely shared we-feeling is the characteristic essential to almost every usage of the word "community," from the narrowest to the most metaphorical. It emphasizes the way people look at their own social world, and often appears most clearly in the oppositions individuals make between themselves and some outside "they." The we-feeling is also very obvious to a newcomer who does not yet belong and whose differentness can be summed up as "he's not really one of us." The sense of shared fate is expressed in concern that actions taken by individuals in the collectivity, or things done to them by outsiders, could have consequences for everyone: either "people like that give all of us a bad name," or "that could happen to any one of us." This sense of commonality can have many sources: ethnic background, shared traditions, threat from the same enemy, a variety of common needs, interests, or problems.

Those who see community vanishing from the modern scene often point out the multiplicity of groups to which most individuals might refer as "we," and argue that since few of these memberships overlap, they cannot provide a basis for community.[3] Others point to the persistence of community, either claiming that this multiplicity means people now belong to many communities or stressing the studies which indicate that even in major, urban centers in industrial societies, the ties of kinship, class, friendship, age, and residence typically overlap.[4]

The social rather than spatial aspects of living together are central to other discussions of community. In this sense, community implies patterned, as opposed to random, social contacts. Mutual expectations about interaction, and the interactions themselves, are regular enough to be identified as roles. The boundaries of various groups and categories are mutual knowledge. Community members share general norms about the way people ought to behave—views which are often quite distinct from what they actually do. They also have in common beliefs—things they consider true, if not always desirable—about the workings of their social world.

Since territory, we-feelings, and social organization are present in all but the most metaphorical (e.g., "community of scholars") occurrences of the term, they can be combined into a useful composite definition. Although presence or absence of a shared territory is a simple either/or judgment, both we-feelings and patterned organization of social life can be evaluated in more-to-less, higher-to-lower terms. The higher the overall level of these characteristics, including the presence of territory, the greater the degree to which community is present. Especially for investigation of the creation or development of community, this kind of definition is useful, as different aspects of community may develop at different rates, and may be affected by different factors.

For the study of community formation, the territorial aspect of community is the least interesting, because it does not develop over time. The timing of its appearance in relation to the other aspects of community, however, does vary, in particular between planned and unplanned cases of community creation. When community emerges among a collection of individuals who did not intentionally set out to create it, the process typically begins because they already live together in a defined space: urban squatters are an example. When a group of people set out to create a community, on the other hand, they want to do so, and make efforts to obtain a territory, because they already share some degree of we-feeling and social organization: utopian experimenters are the classic case.

Development of Community

Community creation as a process can be summarized as the definition of new social borders, the insertion of new boundaries on a social map. The external border of a community may be marked by gates and fences or by feelings of distinctiveness. The development of social organization, on the other hand, traces borders inside a community. Shared understandings about these internal borders in turn reinforce the boundary between insiders and the outside world.

Even in the smallest, most stable examples of community, individuals often do not participate directly in or feel allegiance directly to the entity defined as their community. The social ties that intertwine into a community are most immediately with others who share some characteristic such as age, sex, kinship, occupation, politics, or neighborhood. The process of community creation consequently involves the definition of borders around the subgroups which mediate participation in the community, as well as borders which separate the community from the outside.

The original process of community creation is a subject for speculation, with only fragments of archeological evidence or comparisons with nonhuman primates as shaky footholds for an evolutionary perspective. In historical times, however, community formation has been observed in diverse settings: on a national and international scale where political scientists, in particular, have tried to understand what explains success or failure of attempts to create nations or to integrate them into larger communities;[5] in the slums of many cities where squatters sometimes build not only shelters but communities; and in utopian experiments, where community becomes the tangible model for a dreamed-of better world.[6] Although all of these experiences differ from a residence for older people in certain ways, they all offer evidence from natural experiments in community formation. Even across the difference in levels, and the distinction between planned and unplanned community formation, certain factors will guide our analysis of community formation at Les Floralies, and will make possible understanding of what happened there as an example of a more general process, rather than as that unfortunate anthropological speciality, the unique case study.

Factors which affect the developmental aspects of community formation—we-feelings and social organization—can be divided into those which are present or not present among a collection of individuals at the beginning of the process, and those which may or may not develop over time. When the individuals involved are not intentionally trying to create community, the process of community formation begins when they find themselves living together in a shared territory. Background factors can then be observed from the beginning of their common occupation of this territory; the other factors may or may not appear as they continue to live together.

Since Les Floralies, like many separate housing arrangements for old people, is not an example of intentional community creation, from here on when I refer to the process of community formation I will mean the unplanned type which begins with the presence of shared territory. This does not mean that certain factors which have been observed to affect community formation as an intentional goal are not applicable to Les Floralies. Many factors drawn from studies of utopias, for instance, were observed after the participants already shared a territory. Other factors, such as those derived from attempts at international integration, are described as having a general effect on we-feelings, regardless of shared territory, and can certainly be applied to that more limited case. There are many background characteristics which can be identified early: social and cultural homogeneity of the individuals; the alternatives they perceive to living where they are; the sacrifices necessary to living there; the amount and irreversibility of investment required to live there; the size of the collectivity; the leadership skills available within it; and the material and social ties which may pull individuals away from the potential community. Shared symbols; levels of participation in internal activities; proportions of social contacts shared inside the territory rather than with outsiders; degree of interdependence among residents; their perceptions of threat from the outside; participation in communal, unpaid work; and the definition of status in internal terms—all are factors which may develop with time.

Background Factors

Homogeneity

Wherever the community formation process has been observed, the common cultural and social background of the people involved is pointed out; they share characteristics that are visible and salient to them. Stated as a proposition, the greater the homogeneity of the individuals involved, the more likely they are to share we-feelings, and the more likely they are to develop common institutions.[7] We could obviously turn the relationship around, and propose that the lack of homogeneity would be a block to community development. Support for extending this proposition to potential communities of older people comes from the fact that older people who have more local social contacts, more local friends, and higher morale when they live near others their age also share additional characteristics such as social class. Older people living together should be more likely to form a community if they have more in common than age. Or, the other way around, tendencies for common age to promote community may be blocked by interference from other differences, such as social class or ethnicity.[8]

Lack of Alternative

Both urban squatters and utopian experimenters are more likely to feel a sense of shared fate the more tied each one feels to the common situation. If few alternatives are evident, then each individual is more likely to feel that his or her own destiny is bound up with that of all the others.[9] Utopians who feel there is nowhere else they can live the good and right life, and squatters who feel there is nowhere else they can live at all, share a kind of all-in-the-same-lifeboat commitment to each other which is a powerful basis for both feelings and structures of community. Similarly, older people who find themselves together in special housing arrangements certainly often share the feeling that they have very little alternative to being there. Sometimes with gratitude, sometimes with resentment, they frequently express the feeling that these are the only places where they can live in independence and security. In many cases, health, finances or urban renewal make these the only places they feel they can live at all. The lack of space in special housing, usually emphasized by waiting lists, also promotes the feeling that there are very few alternatives not just to special housing in general, but to the specific project or high-rise or village in which the older person is living. If this is not the only place he or she was admitted, it may be the only one he or she could afford.

Investment and Irreversibility

Successful utopian experiments, those which create stable communities, tend to have in common the fact that members must make a substantial investment in order to belong.[10] The explanation seems to be in line with the psychological theory of cognitive dissonance: making a substantial investment, especially if it is irreversible, stimulates commitment to the community as a means of justifying the investment. In the utopian examples, the investment is often financial, as new members turn over their money and property to the group and often do not get it back if they leave. There is typically also a substantial investment of time and energy demanded, which leads to an either/or, in-or-out kind of residence requirement. Since only those who make the necessary commitment are allowed to live in the utopia, there can be no nonresident members. "Commuters" to the community might threaten the commitment of those who make the greater investment of full-time participation.

For many older people, the decision to move into a home or a residence, or even into a retirement condominium, has these qualities of important and nearly irreversible investment. Assets must often be liquidated, either because welfare rules set a minimum for admittance to public housing, or because the fees of a private setting require almost all the individual's resources. Most special housing for older people also has the in-or-out kind of quality of the successful utopian experiment; to benefit from the independence, security, or leisure opportunities which the setting offers, it is almost always necessary to make the commitment to live there.

Also consistent with the theory of cognitive dissonance, and demonstrated by initiation rites of all kinds, is the tendency of successful utopias to involve sacrifice and struggle. The difficulty of entering the group, and often things which must be given up in order to join it, are other kinds of investments which lead the new member to see his or her membership as precious because its cost was high.[11] Reminiscences about those hard early days then often become a way of expressing togetherness in the community. In both French and American homes, residences, villages, and condominia, I have heard proud stories about those tough early days, or about the pangs of leaving furniture behind, which suggest just those kinds of initiation and sacrifice which create a sense of belonging in utopias and secret societies.

Material Distinctions

Giving up individual property is often required in successful utopias as a way of minimizing material differences that might pull individuals away from commitment to the community.[12] Although the reason is usuallly hygiene or lack of space, rather than any intention to create community, older people moving into special housing arrangements are often faced with the impossibility of bringing major belongings. They also often find themselves in a situation where the differences in physical housing are minimal compared to those used as status signals in ordinary neighborhoods.

Social Exclusivity

Successful utopias also typically try to break down sexual or emotional exclusivity by weakening couples and families.[13] If the importation of many sexual and kin ties into a new residential setting is seen as a barrier to formation of communal sentiments, then much separate housing for older people is unusually free of this kind of obstacle.

Leadership

Leaders may pull individuals into participation in an emerging community and may also become symols of it. The presence of people with leadership ability is a background factor which can of course be observed in residential settings for older people as well as in squatter villages, in utopias, or on the international scene.[14]

Size

The last background factor is the size of the population involved in the process of community creation, which seems to help determine the speed with which the entire process takes place. In a small population, where relationships are face-to-face, development of both the attitudes and institutions of community is likely to happen faster than elsewhere, because the entire process will be so highly visible.[15] Since many residences for older or retired people include only a few hundred individuals, there is a potential for relatively rapid community development.

Emergent factors

Participation in Community-Wide Events and Decisionmaking

Another set of factors observed to promote community formation in a variety of settings must be investigated over time, since they cannot be identified immediately and may or may not appear as a group of people live together in a defined residential space. Both the quantity and the quality of the contacts these people share will affect the possibility of their becoming a community. In terms of quantity, for instance, successful utopias are more likely to have many group meetings; often all members meet together every day.[16] Studies of urban squatters also show that the level of participation in community-wide activities is related to strength of we-feelings.[17] Two psychological principles seem to be involved here. First, the strain toward cognitive consistency could explain the relationship between participation and commitment to a community by looking at participation as another kind of investment in the group, which will lead the individual to value it and be concerned about it because of what it has "cost" him or her. Second, the "participation hypothesis," which has been extensively investigated in small group situations, suggests that a particular kind of participation (that is, in decisions affecting the group) will promote feelings of satisfaction with it and of solidarity among its members. Therefore the more potential community members share in decision-making, the stronger their attachment to it should be.[18]

The general level of participation in community-wide events is often high in housing for old people. The activities may be bingo games, common meals, religious services, or pot-luck suppers, depending on the setting; the important thing is that participation is widespread, regular, and frequent.

Although extensive participation in decision-making is seldom planned for residents of age-separate housing, it has often developed or been demanded. Resident "revolutions," usually aimed at unreliable or paternalistic management firms, have occurred in several retirement communities. Factions battling over control of internal politics appear in almost every residential setting for old people about which we have information. As Communists versus Socialists, Greeks versus Turks, conservatives versus liberals, one Baptist Church versus another, factions translate past identities into alignments on present issues inside the new community.

Proportion of Kinds of Contact

The proportion of kinds of social contact which are shared among residents of the territory in question is another quantitative measure of their likelihood of becoming a community. The more kinds of activities they share among themselves the more likely their contacts are to become the basis of a distinct social organization and the stronger 'we-feelings' they are likely to promote.[19] Participants in utopian experiments which succeeded in creating communities, for example, typically spent more than two-thirds of each day with other members, which implies that a wide range of social contacts is involved.[20]

Old people living together often share more kinds of contact with each other than with anyone outside. When they leave the community, they usually go together; and guests coming in are often shared with other residents. Many kinds of ties, such as help in sickness or emergencies, are maintained both with outsiders, such as children, and with inside friends and neighbors.

Interdependence

The quality of what people do together also affects their potential as a community. Kenyan squatters who support themselves by producing and selling beer, a cooperative effort, have in common with commune members who feed themselves with joint farming, or nation states which form a common market, a perception of mutual need and interdependence.[21] All of these cases suggest that the greater the extent to which individuals see themselves as interdependent, the more likely they are to have a sense of shared fate and to develop the predictable patterns of social relationship which define a distinct social organization.

Help in sickness or emergency is the most consistently reported and most intensely valued kind of interdependence among older people living near each other. Homemade food, handmade clothing, recipes, rides, plant and pet care also typically circulate in complex networks of reciprocity.

Work

Quilting bees, house-raisings, even taking turns at doing the dishes, are all examples of the idea that communal, unpaid work is a kind of participation especially valuable for promoting sentiments of community. Comparison of successful with unsuccessful utopian experiments, for instance, shows a striking tendency for communal work to go along with creation of stable communities.[22]

Making plastic wastebaskets or knitting socks to sell for mutual benefit, writing get-well cards, watering the garden or repairing the plumbing, older people in very diverse settings work for their communities without pay.

Threat

Relations with the outside have powerful effects on the development of community inside a territory. Threats from outsiders are cited so often as a source of internal cohesiveness that threat has become a kind of classic variable in discussions of group solidarity. Threat certainly appears as a factor in community creation in cases ranging from the bulldozers which menace most squatter settlements to the religious persecutions from which American utopians have sought refuge or the harassments some long-haired commune members suffer from their neighbors today.[23] However, as a factor promoting community formation, threat must be thought about in terms of level. Extreme examples such as concentration camps are a reminder that if threat is too great, it suppresses rather than promotes group sentiments which might become a basis for community. Threat can certainly also be at too low a level to be a catalyst for community. Moderate amounts of outside threat, enough to be seen as important, and yet on a scale that makes action seem worthwhile, should promote community formation.

Security is mentioned appreciatively by old people in many separate residences and is a major reason for their entering them. Afraid for their physical safety in the world outside, they are eloquent in their descriptions of the reassurance of door-guards or fenced and patrolled territories. The potential of help in emergencies is also reassurance against the deep and widespread fear of being hurt or falling ill alone.

Importation of external values and sources of prestige can pose another kind of outside threat to community creation by impeding the development of a distinctive social organization. Successful utopias, for instance, are characterized by a status system defined in internal terms.[24] Internal sources of prestige are an explicit part of many utopias, which are created with the purpose of escape and reform. However, given the logic of its influence on border definition, the spontaneous development of internal sources of status should be a positive factor in the formation of less intentional communities.

By defining participation in the immediate social situation as the major source of prestige, communities of age peers do render harmless many of the status rules that guarantee most old people a place at the bottom of the wider society. Easy access to activities and to other people in these settings makes physical frailty and limited incomes much less restricting on participation. Someone who would be just another old person, physically weak, socially dependent, and powerless, can become popular and influential as tournament winner, elected leader, good square dancer, or talented transmitter of local information.

Symbols

As people live together, they may develop shared responses to certain symbols of their life together: events or individuals may become new symbols, or symbols from common past experiences may be translated into terms relevant to the present. Affective symbols uniquely associated with the emerging community will be a source of the sense of shared fate and distinctiveness that I have labeled we-feeling.[25] Legendary "good residents" or successful agers, along with their opposites, appear in reports of old-age communities, as do assorted conflicts and celebrations that have become important markers on a shared map for current social relations.

Older people in separate residential settings are potential community members. The background factors which provide a basis for community formation are often present. To understand the process through which older people living together might become a community, it is necessary to observe the operation of these other, emergent, factors over time. The formation of a community in a residence for retired French construction workers is the subject of this book.

Les Floralies had been open eight months when I arrived. During the year that followed I observed the process through which this collection of old people, unknown to each other, and thrust into a situation relatively unknown to the entire society, created an engaging, active, complex social world—a community in every sense of the term. The residence, to begin with, had to a high degree all of the background factors identified as sources of community in other settings. The bulk of this book is a description and analysis of the other factors—kinds and degree of participation, distillation and translation of attitudes and symbols—which furthered the formation of a community.

Les Floralies as a Community: Background Factors

Because the new setting they entered was residential, the people who came here automatically acquired a territorial basis for community. They were eligible to live in the residence because of their work in the construction trades. They were an extremely homogeneous group in terms of occupation, as well as ethnicity, education, income and, of course, age. All residents except one were over sixty-five. Common physical, social, and historical age provided common problems, and techniques for coping with them in the present, as well as common symbols and experiences from the past.

Moving to Les Floralies was for most people a decision motivated by lack of alternative. For many, the letter telling them about the possibility of living at the residence represented an extraordinary, unhoped-for solution to problems of expropriation, loneliness, failing strength, and poverty, combined with a strong desire to preserve independence.

The decision, on the other hand, was a painful and difficult one, and was seen by almost everyone as irreversible. Privacy and an independent household are high values in France, and the vague notion of a collective life was frightening. In France, as in the United States, the idea of special settings for older people evokes images of the poor farm and the old folks home. Overcoming fears of entering the residence was a difficult process, made more difficult by the need for almost everyone to apply for social welfare in order to pay the fees. This required turning over assets, except for 10 percent of previous pensions as pocket money, and also involved an investigation of children's finances to see if they should pay a share of the costs. The bureaucratic struggle, the agony about imposition on children, and the perceived irreversibility of "going on welfare" added to the difficulty of the decision to come to Les Floralies. In the terms used to discuss utopian communities, the decision was a costly one which required an important and irreversible investment, both psychological and financial.

Apartments at the residence are fully furnished, so that there is room for only a minimum of additional objects. This restriction of possibilities for displays of ownership, as well as the extremely limited budgets of almost everyone in the residence, provided some of the restraint on material distinctions observed in many success-ful utopian communities. The dyadic ties which are considered a threat to community formation by many utopian planners are also mainly absent here. There are fourteen married couples at Les Floralies, and one kin pair, an aunt and her niece. Six more couples met in the residence, and are recognized as couples only in the eyes of other residents, not in the legal terms relevant outside Les Floralies. These ties, rooted in participation in the residence, seem to me to bolster bonds of community rather than threaten them. In this sense they are more similar to the distinctive sexual arrangements (celibacy or free love, fictional sibling ties) of many utopias than to the ties of married couples who arrive in the residence after many years together. One of the most dramatic evidences that utopias try to create something that has never existed in the real world is their attempt to break down the subgroup ties which in natural communities are the link between individuals and the community as a whole. Utopian experiments aim at tying the individual directly into the entire community, and they very often stumble on the obstacle of what apparently are very deeply rooted habits of social participation via intimate ties to kin, sexual partners, and friends.

Since Les Floralies represents a case of unplanned community formation, it is probably more reasonable to expect it to follow the pattern of natural rather than utopian communities: the definition of sub-groups should appear as part of the community creation process. However, the utopian examples do suggest that the importation of many exclusive subgroup ties from past life outside the new setting might be a hindrance to community formation, while the development of these ties inside the emerging community would not only increase its emotional salience for many individuals but also add to the shared experiences and understandings which make the community a distinctive locus for social life. From this point of view, Les Floralies has a relatively low number of kinship, sexual, and friendship ties derived from the past, and a relatively high number defined in terms of present life in the residence.

Les Floralies was planned to house about 150 people; when we left, there were 127 residents. It certainly has the characteristic of small size, and its social relationships are face-to-face.

Several individuals with exceptional leadership skills provide the last of the background factors for community formation. The president of the Residents' Committee, the leader of the opposition faction, and several other militant faction members who will appear in action in the following chapters, are talented, energetic leaders who both pushed and pulled others into participation in residence activities and also became themselves symbols of the emerging community.

The residents of Les Floralies now participate in a community. This book describes that community and the way it was created, compares it to other collectivities of the old and retired, and proposes the significance of their existence for other older people, who are so often excluded from community in the modern world.

2   Les Floralies
The Research
Setting

The Residence

The change of scene for new arrivals at Les Floralies is both social and physical, total and abrupt. Their participation in a society of old people begins as they climb into the car with a group of other new residents. The short ride takes them from the crowded walk-ups of working class Paris or the country village atmosphere of its surrounding suburbs to a fourteen-story glass and concrete residence. Its setting also radiates newness: an expressway, multi-story office buildings, and an instant neighborhood of low-rent high-rise apartments next to a modern shopping center. Bagnolet is an old suburb, just across the eastern city limits of Paris; residents say that peaches from Bagnolet orchards were favorites at the court of Louis XIV. But its character is changing rapidly. The steep, narrow streets, the medieval church and the outdoor market are gradually being encircled by new industrial and commercial sectors.

The residence was built by a retirement fund called the Caisse Nationale de Retraite des Ouvriers du Bâtiment et des Travaux Publiques (CNRO), the national retirement fund for construction workers. Because labor unions in France are focused on political orientation rather than on occupation, organization of a retirement fund for the construction trades required joint efforts by various unions as well as of management groups. The CNRO was created in 1959 to provide pensions on an employer-employee contribution basis. It was also decided to pay pensions to already retired workers, such as the people in the residence, who had of course never contributed to the scheme. When questionnaire and interview studies of the retired members of the CNRO revealed that housing was a critical problem for these individuals, the directors of the fund began plans to build a series of retirement residences in various regions of France. The first one was opened near Bordeaux in 1964; there are now ten CNRO residences in the country.[1]

Retired CNRO members in the Paris region received letters

telling them that there would be a residence in Bagnolet. The people who responded with interest were visited, at first by the future director of the residence, and later, when he was too busy, by someone else from the CNRO. It seems clear that at this time the problem was to convince people to enter, rather than to choose among eager volunteers. Reasons for coming to Les Floralies were often negative: people had lost a home through urban renewal; they were suddenly alone because of the death of a spouse or had recently faced the fear of loss because of a serious illness; some were unable to keep up their housekeeping and dreaded losing their independence by moving in with children; or they were already living with children and unhappy. For these people the letter and the visit from the CNRO presented an unhoped-for possible solution, often not clearly understood in all its implications of life in a community of the old, but more attractive than the all too well understood alternatives. For a few, the move to the residence had a more positive basis, usually the overwhelming comfort which it offered. The first group of about thirty residents arrived at Les Floralies in December 1968.[2]

Nearly all of those who decided to enter had to apply for national welfare assistance, since their own pensions were not sufficient to pay the thirty francs per day (about six U.S. dollars), which was then the cost for an apartment, all meals, recreational facilities, and the services of a clinic. The process of getting the welfare pension often took several months; and it was always much longer for those with children, whose incomes might require them to pay part of the cost, than it was for the childless. Of the 127 residents, only fifteen could afford to pay their own expenses. The others turned over their assets to the welfare program, which paid their costs at the residence and gave them back 10 percent of their original pensions as pocket money.[3] The average monthly value of this 10 percent was twenty-five francs (about five U.S. dollars).[4]

Almost everyone here was either a construction worker or the wife of someone in the construction trades. These former jobs ranged from ditch digging to master mason. Many women also worked, usually as maids or as sewing machine operators in a garment factory.

In return for selling the land on which the residence was built, the mayor of Bagnolet asked for the right to place ten old people from the town in Les Floralies. During our stay, there were ten residents who were sponsored by the town and had not necessarily worked in construction.

"Be sure to sit in the middle of the chair," is likely to be the first piece of advice a newcomer hears as he or she enters the residence. The lobby is furnished with colorful, modern chairs and tables. Most of the chairs are low and tend to tip; many have no arms. Residents become skilled at cautious landings and take-offs, and they are careful to warn unsuspecting visitors. The room is divided into several areas by steps which change the floor level; all the doors are glass, and there is a glass wall next to the garden outside and another inside to divide the lobby from the entrance to the elevators. The first effect on most visitors or new residents expecting the traditional old people's home is startling. The bright, airy space could be the lobby of a modern hotel, or a waiting room in a new airport.

The first-time visitor to the residence of course also expects to see old people. Another source of the surprise most people feel when they come here for the first time is that there are often no old people in sight. Residents spend very little time in the lobby, except just before and after meals when a small group usually sits for about a half hour in the chairs nearest the door to the dining room. If there are people sitting in the lobby at other times, they are likely to be newcomers and not established residents. New arrivals often assume that the lobby is a place to meet people, and during their first days in the residence they come downstairs a little nervously, sit alone sometimes for several hours reading magazines and chatting with passing staff members until they realize their mistake.

What they eventually discover is that the arena for public contacts is not the lobby, but the dining room. It is the one place where everyone in the residence sees everyone else at least once a day, since all members of the community are required to eat at least the noon meal there. Round tables for four are arranged in two rooms partially divided by a fish pond. Since there is only one entrance from the lobby to the dining area, as people come in or go out they walk by many of the tables. Greetings and gossip circulate this way before and after meals. The room becomes a living map of social contacts every noon as people move from one handshake to another and eventually settle down at their own places. The places at table are considered permanent by the residents, although the staff makes occasional efforts to encourage people to move around. Being established at a table is the most important sign of incorporation into social life at the residence, and people change tables only under the influence of a forceful new attraction or of exploding hostility. Social ties to table partners are often quite strong, and a place at table also represents a person's location in community information networks.

Most of the people in the dining room are women, 81 of the 127 residents. Some couples arrive arm-in-arm or show by courtly help with a chair or serving food that they are "together." There are fourteen legally married couples in the community and six others who are considered couples inside the residence although they are not married. A few residents come into the dining room on someone else's arm for a different reason: because they have difficulty walking or seeing, neighbors or table partners help them from the elevator to their place. The average age here is 75; the youngest person is 61, a woman married to an older man; the oldest is 91. (See table 1 for a summary of social characteristics.)

Table 1	Social Characteristics of Residents	
	Average age	75
	Female	64%
	Male	36%
	Marital Status:	
	Married	22%
	Widowed	69%
	Divorced or single	9%
	Receive government assistance to meet costs of living in residence	90%
	Have children	47%
	Average length of time in residence	12 months

NOTE: The figures in this table are based on data for the total residence population of 127 in July 1970, when the residence had been open for nineteen months.

There are other signs that this is not an ordinary restaurant, that the people arriving for lunch seem at home here. They carry drawstring bags or cloth envelopes with their own napkins, and often a little jar of some favorite condiment such as mustard or vinegar. Many of them are comfortable in soft carpet slippers. Aprons or smocks are typical clothing for women, and most of the men are wearing wide suspenders and well-worn shirts and pants. As the greetings subside and the meal progresses from the first glass of wine through detailed commentary on the food to the final drooping hand-rolled cigarette, the impression grows that these are workers having their noon meal at home or in a habitual cafe. The room is noisy as people eat with enthusiasm, argue, joke, and tease the waitresses. The hands which gesture to illustrate a story show the signs of hard work; the language vibrates with Parisian slang and juicy vulgarity.

The public aspect of contacts in the dining room is remarkable because most social life in the residence takes place in private space. All members of the community live in independent apartments, and perhaps the overriding shared value here is that each person has the right to be, and takes pleasure in being, "chez soi"—at home—in his or her own home. The apartments are on the second, third, and fifth through thirteenth floors. Most apartments have a kitchen and a bathroom; those on the second and third floors are reserved for people whom the staff feels are unable to do their own housekeeping and bathing, and therefore have no kitchen, and a toilet but no bathtub. Each corridor has thirteen rooms, two for couples and the rest for single residents. The couples' rooms have a separate bedroom and are located at the two ends of each hall. The other apartments are studio-style, one room with a bed which is covered with a tailored spread to look more like a couch in the daytime. Although the rooms are completely furnished, residents create a great variety of atmospheres in them: the smoke-filled den; the grande-dame opulence of hot-house plants, signed photographs, and a feather boa draped over the mirror; the cozy comfort of doilies, teacup collections, and embroidered linen.

The side of the hall without double rooms has at one end a common room with a sink, ironing board, and garbage and laundry chutes. The two lower floors have in addition a room with a bathtub. There are elevators at both ends of every hall, and people usually ride up and down with others from their half of the hall. The division of the corridors in half is also emphasized by swinging glass doors placed in the middle as a fire safety measure.

The hallways are dim, since the lights, like those found in most French apartment buildings, respond to a button which puts them on for one minute and then automatically shuts them off again. Since so much of social life goes on behind closed doors, the halls are also typically empty. Residents protect their privacy by keeping their doors closed except to invited guests or visitors who knock. Invitations to visit are common, and a drink before or a coffee after a meal are popular reasons for a relatively formal invitation. About one-third of the residents also cook dinner in their own apartments instead of going to the dining hall. If they do this, they are given the food they need once a week instead of getting their meal already prepared downstairs. Almost everyone who has a kitchen prepares breakfast in his or her own room. The half-dozen men who do not—some, but not all, from the floors without kitchens—come to the dining room for café-au-lait and bread and butter every morning.

People often speak possessively and with a sense of identification about the floor they live on. I was told many times how well everybody on their floor got along, or how everyone on their hall was particularly nice. Certain floors also have definite images to people who did not live on them. The thirteenth is frequently referred to as Communist; the fifth, many people say, has residents who are particularly close and helpful to each other. Residents are also concerned about guarding privileges of their hall for themselves. At one point, the director experimented wth a new system of distribution for breakfast supplies by putting coffee, chocolate, sugar, and other items in the laundry room on each floor. Residents could then take what they needed and sign for it, instead of ordering everything once a month. A great many people were extremely upset about this experiment, and organized a petition against its trial even on a temporary basis. People from other floors, they insisted, could not be trusted not to sneak up or down and take "our" food. These images of different floors are the kind of shorthand over-simplifications which people in communities use to reduce the complexities of social living to a manageable order. The presence of one well-known person, for instance, often gave a floor its possible identity, although the others who lived there might not have the same political ideas, or even be particularly friendly with that person. Friendships consistently crossed floors, so that although each hall was seen as a distinct territorial unit by residents, these spatial boundaries were not barriers to social contact.

The significance of proximity on a hall for social ties is reduced by the relatively greater importance of the dining room as a scene of social contact. Since lunch is the major public social event, the contacts made there are for many people more central to social life than greetings exchanged in the hallway. Room location also almost never represents social choice, while a place in the dining room typically does. When residents arrive they of course have very little basis for choosing a room in terms of social preference. In addition, they are not given a wide choice of rooms. The nurse usually asks them if they want to be up high or down low, with a view of the city or of the garden. Most new residents see one of two rooms and make a choice, sometimes influenced by the color of the curtains and upholstery. These choices, of course, will be more limited as the residence fills up. People also very rarely change rooms. During a year, I observed three room changes, one resulting from widowhood, one from illness, and only one because of personal conflicts with neighbors. Table changes, on the other hand, do occur, and without exception reveal shifts in social relationships, either positive or negative.

There are other clearly defined territories in the residence. The first day I spent at Les Floralies I was taken with great secrecy up the stairs from the thirteenth to the fourteenth floor. "This isn't for us," my new neighbor explained as she showed me around two elegant dining rooms, a compact kitchen, and several lounges. This was evidently not her first trip there, as she knew precisely how to operate stoves and open sliding walls or cupboards. She even provided details of a meal which she claimed the "big shots" had eaten there several months before. Since Les Floralies is near Paris, where the CNRO had its national headquarters until 1972, it was planned not only as a residence, but also as a place for meetings and for the entertainment of important visitors. The occasional arrival of well-dressed strangers who were whisked up to the top of the building and fed special meals prepared in the fourteenth-floor kitchen led to diligent investigation by residents to discover who they were and what they ate, and to the strong impression that this was forbidden ground, "not for us." Several months after our arrival, the fourteenth floor began to be used occasionally for residents' activities, such as the sewing club. Residents at first were very excited about this change, but eventually they began to feel that this floor was part of their territory and used it more casually for playing cards or for showing visitors the view.

The CNRO also provided a wing of the building for offices of their research organization, and for a large auditorium. Residents definitely did not think of this as part of their space, and when the weekly movies were shown in the auditorium, there were always a few spectators confused or lost on the way. Most residents did not know what the research organization was, and had only an extremely vague idea that there were CNRO offices of some kind in the building. This wing has three floors, and on the third there are several guest rooms and apartments for the director, the financial manager, the head nurse, a secretary, three nurses' aides, and a chef's assistant. The handyman/chauffeur also had an apartment on the first floor near the kitchen. Staff members who did not live in the residence included four waitresses, a laundress, two cleaning women, two cooks, and an accountant. A doctor made daily visits to the residence, and his wife came once a week to teach the pottery class.

The clinic, above the dining room, connects the two wings of the building. Residents go to the clinic to visit sick friends or relatives and also to see the doctor. During his office hours, there are often six or eight residents sitting in chairs in the hall. The clinic is a familiar part of the community building to most residents.

Every afternoon after lunch, a group of men go to the fourth floor, where they sit huddled around their cards, cigarettes glued to lower lips, concentrating on *belote*. The fourth floor is reserved for various recreational activities and has no apartments. One lounge is seen as the property of the men who play cards. There is also a terrace garden, a library, and a lounge with a television. In the evenings, a group of about twelve regulars watches programs here.

The residence is never locked. The one "run-away" walked out the front door with his suitcase in broad daylight; he left a note in his room that he was going to live with his mistress in Paris. The bus for Paris stops in front of the building, and it is only half an hour's ride to the middle of the city. The new shopping center at Bagnolet is two blocks away, the old downtown area about four, but en route to these is a steep hill which is especially hard to climb in winter. Since only one resident owned a car, and one a motorized bicycle, the residents either used public transportation (which was often a limited possibility because of very small budgets), walked, or waited for rides from friends or relatives.

Several men began every morning with a walk to the cafe in the shopping center, where they drank a glass of wine, bought the newspaper, and once a week placed a bet on the horse races. Women often went down the hill to the twice-weekly outdoor market or around the corner to the supermarket. "Even if I only buy three lemons, I feel I've done my shopping," was the way one neighbor explained the pleasure of carrying on this routine, even though lack of money made the purchases very small.

Research Begins

When my husband and I moved into an apartment at Les Floralies, our arrival was in many ways similar to those of other new residents: momentous for us and highly visible to others. Since I would be doing the research, I went through the official first-day activities alone. The six residents on the elected Social Committee were the first people I met. They invited me to the usual aperitif with which they welcome new arrivals. The director introduced me very briefly and as the Committee watched with polite, but puzzled, smiles, I wrestled with the problem of explaining what I was doing there. Explaining myself and my research seemed suddenly appallingly difficult. How would they feel when I said I had come to study them? How could I avoid the superiority, the impersonality, the threat to privacy often suggested by that proposal? Many people had advised me to avoid these difficulties by not saying anything about a study, by taking a role in the residence which would allow me to observe without identifying myself as a researcher.

Deception was not appealing ethically; it also seemed impractical, since discovery would certainly be more of a threat to my research than any fumbles I might make in presenting myself honestly. The roles available were also very limited, since at twenty-six I could not masquerade as a resident or even as a visiting retired person from America. The only possibilities were positions on the staff, such as waitress or hostess, which offered very restricted kinds of contact with residents. Members of the CNRO research organization had also expressed concern that the fact that my research was sponsored by the U.S. government might make residents distrustful. Others pointed out gloomily that these people were uneducated and generally suspicious of anything to do with answering questions or filling out forms.

As I nervously explained that I was interested in older people, and especially in what they thought about this kind of residence as a solution to some of their problems, to my great relief, heads nodded and people kept smiling. The members of the committee apparently did not find it surprising that someone thought they were interesting enough to learn about. They seemed all too aware that old people have many problems, and they also knew that the residence was an exceptional attempt to ease them. The idea that the only way to understand people is to live with them, which was my on-the-spot explanation of participant observation, also got an enthusiastic response.

The president, looking official in a suit with a vest and a gold watch chain, began immediately to explain in lecture-style detail the complexities of CNRO history and organization. After a few minutes the vice-president, a small, springy man with a bushy mustache, jumped up to interrupt with corrections. The director steered the group toward their regular business meeting, and my introduction to the committee was over. The next step was for them to introduce me to the rest of the residence.

Like most newcomers, I first saw other residents, and was seen by them, in the dining room. The first meal I ate with one of the women from the committee. Throughout the rest of our stay, I changed tables every day. At first, this required repeated introductions and explanations, but soon people were used to the pattern, and only complained if they felt I had been away from their table for too long. Participant observation is difficult in a modern apartment building where there are few public spaces, and more so in a society where privacy is so highly valued. The dining room was consequently as crucial to my research as it was to social life in the residence.

Two neighbors helped us move into a two-room couple's apartment on the thirteenth floor. The nurse had offered a choice of two apartments, and knowing nothing about any of the floors, I chose the thirteenth because of the view. It was a lucky choice. This location in space turned out to have important consequences for access to the social realities of the residence. The most significant social borders in the community are those defined by two factions, one clustered around the president and the other focussed on a woman who lives on the thirteenth floor.[5] The characteristic which is used to identify potential recruits to one side or the other is political allegiance: Mme. Dupont's group is pro-Communist; the president's group is anti-Communist, including both Socialists and Catholics. These political allegiances at first marked the border between the factions inside the residence. As time passes, the role of these factions in the socialization of new arrivals, and in the patterning of social life inside the community, is the basis for their redefinition into internal terms. The opposition continues, but the labels on the border are progressively being redefined by events and loyalties inside the residence, rather than in the wider society— in the present rather than in the past.

Research in a polarized community is always a tightrope act. Too clear-cut an identification with either group would have made contact with members of the other one extremely difficult, and yet close involvement with the factions was obviously essential to understanding this community. Since the thirteenth floor had a Communist image because Mme. Dupont and several other faction members lived there, our location provided a necessary balance to my early and frequent contacts with the president and other members of the committee, most of whom were his supporters.

It was possible for us to have an apartment in the residents' section of the building because the community was not full when we arrived. About eighty people lived there when we came, and over forty more moved in while we were there. The community had still not reached its planned capacity of about 150, mainly because of delays in processing the welfare applications of people who wanted to come but needed public assistance to pay the fees. The fact that it was not full was one reason I chose this residence for research. We were able to live in the community, and a significant number of new people were guaranteed to arrive and learn how to live there during the year.

The location of Les Floralies was also attractive for research because it was close enough to Paris, where all the residents had spent their working lives, to make possible investigation of their contacts with friends and family in terms of choice. We made a kind of gerontological tour of France in order to choose a site, and many residences recruited their population from such a wide area that the old people were too far from former neighbors and kin to make possible any reasonable discussion of their choices about maintaining contact.

In the first few weeks, I participated in every possible aspect of community life, as I tried to outline a map of social relations. Access to organized activities was easy: committee meetings once a week, a weekly sewing and knitting group, daily work with volunteer residents in the kitchen, the laundry or the research office, and the afternoon *belote* game. These activities, as well as the meals at different tables led to invitations to aperitif or coffee in people's apartments. Neighbors invited us too, and the head of the Communist faction became my knitting teacher, which required frequent visits.

My husband Marc had an office in Paris, where he went every day to work on a book he was writing. His routine coming and going made us seem more normal to our neighbors, since it was logical to them that he should go off to work while I stayed home. He ate lunch in the dining room and visited people on weekends, and was soon well known in the residence. He became more involved in its daily life when he broke his arm and stayed home from the office for three weeks.

The essence of politics in this community was expressed for us when a woman at my lunch table explained to me the political nature of the injury to Marc's arm, which occurred during a basketball game in Bagnolet, a community well known for its Communist loyalties. "They broke his arm because he's American," she explained. When I protested that he was playing *on* the Bagnolet team, she said "of course then the others broke his arm because they don't like Communists."

Marc's photography interest led us to a very effective way of meeting more people. At a birthday party for the first resident to turn ninety, Marc took pictures of everyone in the dining room. We then offered them to the residents, who signed up for the ones they wanted, which I delivered to their rooms. This was not only a natural way of visiting almost everyone, and learning all their names, but in addition their spontaneous and explicit comments about other people in the photographs were excellent leads for discovery of friendships and conflicts.

A group of new residents arrived about three weeks after we did, and I went with the chauffeur, the nurse, and the vice-president to pick them up at their homes. I went this way to meet almost everyone who arrived during our stay. Sharing the emotional journey to the residence included me in the bond which often develops among those who arrive together. I never needed an excuse to drop in on them, and they were always eager to talk about the progress of their adjustments to the residence. I generally kept in close touch with them during their first months, and also interviewed them formally about their impressions of learning to live in the community.

About four months after we had moved into the residence, a new player appeared at the *belote* table. At this point, I was familiar enough with daily routines in the community that his appearance presented a serious puzzle. Why was he there? Had he developed a friendship with one of the other players? Was his wife friendly with one of theirs? As I plotted strategy for eating lunch at the new player's table, chatting with his wife at the pottery class, and checking the game carefully in the next few days, my husband pointed out with some amusement that the very fact that M. Lafarge's presence at the card table was such a challenging new piece of data was good evidence that I had accomplished the goal of the first phase of the research. Basic social routines and relationships had been charted, and, if anything, at this point I risked getting lost in the pleasure of refining the scale of my map unnecessarily. It was time to use this map of social organization in the community for investigation of more specific questions: the socialization process, the role of the factions in it, and consequences of this role for their redefinition; the persistent conflicts which both reinforced and redefined factional borders; the relationship between social organization inside the community and that in the wider society, especially as reflected in sources of social status.

To shift to this new, more specific perspective, we left the residence for a week. Removed from the absorbing detail of daily life, I re-read my original research design and reviewed books and articles about community and about the social life of older people. Then I rewrote the research plan in light of what I knew about Les Floralies.

We went back to the residence with the outline of the interview with new arrivals and of a questionnaire about contacts with family and friends inside and outside the residence and about attitudes toward the community and life in general. The questionnaire was administered in June 1970, after we had been in the residence for ten months. Detailed daily note-taking continued, but now with a focus on conflict and on social status. As soon as I had a hint that a conflict was simmering, that situation took priority over anything else, as I spent all my time moving back and forth between the two sides, watching and listening, to follow the development as closely as possible.

We also devised a scheme for recording systematic judgments about social status and other characteristics of residents, such as the clarity of their political identity, their participation in group activities, or the importance of the community to them.[6] We did this coding in April 1970, after eight months in the residence. For each characteristic, my husband read the names of every resident, to which I responded with a score of high, medium, or low. This simple coding system helped me avoid the tendency of participant observers to rely too heavily on a few eager, and often marginal, individuals and also alerted me to information I did not have while I still had time to get it. The system also made possible statistical correlations between my observations and responses to the questionnaire. In the chapters which follow, I will specify the sources for various kinds of data as they are presented. Results of the questionnaire are referred to explicitly as such. Numerical statements described as based on my observations come from the coded judgments.[7] Other descriptions are derived from my daily journal.

"I can't possibly answer questions like that. I just can't tell you those things!" The finger pointing at the questionnaire was trembling. All the darkest warnings about survey research in this context seemed to be justified. As I looked at the offensive questions—how many children do you have? brothers? sisters?—Mme. Moulins continued talking. "I can't tell you about my family. They disowned me when I left the Communist Party. And children, what misery! Intercourse with my husband was always too painful for me; his penis is so big. So you see, I can't tell you about all those troubles." I wrote down, in full view of my confidante, all this information which she has said I could not have. As we continued through the questionnaire, it became apparent that she was uncomfortable about putting these facts on an official-looking piece of paper but didn't mind at all telling them to me, even if I wrote them down or marked them directly on the questionnaire. She had never seen a questionnaire before and became more and more excited as we went through attitudes about life and judgments of her own personality characteristics. It seemed to be a highly personal experience for her, a conversation between us about things of deep interest to her, which she usually never discussed. We spent a mutually enjoyable afternoon, and I left pleasantly full of home-made liqueur and information.

There were very few absolute refusals to do the questionnaire. One couple had recently answered questions from the welfare department about their family, which had led to very painful relations with their children who were subsequently asked to pay a part of the expenses at the residence. They were unwilling to take any chances of a repeat of this experience. One man who was very marginal in the community refused, I am convinced, because most other people agreed. He also insisted that his girlfriend refuse, although she was visibly very anxious to do it. She agreed to see me three times, but always backed out of doing the questionnaire at the last minute. Most of the residents who are missing from my questionnaire were either sick or away from the community during the time I administered it. The opposite nature of these two reasons for missing responses is reassuring in terms of possible bias; in addition, a check of characteristics of those who did and did not complete the questionnaire shows no significant differences.[8]

When we first decided to live in a residence for old people, my husband and I agreed to rent a separate apartment for occasional escape. After several months at Les Floralies, we realized that we had never spent a night in our secret apartment, which simply provided housing for various visiting friends. We had already learned a lesson about the egotism of young people who assume that youth and physical vigor give a monopoly on the complexities and satisfactions of social life.

3   Participation in Community

Introduction

Some residents at Les Floralies roll up their sleeves and work; they peel vegetables or iron sheets or weed the roses. Others join groups for recreation, to play cards or sew together. Some people have social contacts which are less public and less formally organized: they visit friends for a drink or faithfully offer an arm to someone who has trouble walking to the dining room. Still others barely move from a chair, but by watching, listening and skillful interrogation of passersby, become such valuable sources of information that their immobility is irrelevant; people come to them to find out what is happening.

Social participation at the residence, as in any community, takes many forms. The patterns which emerge in this participation reveal the regularities of social organization essential to community. Residents distinguish various spheres of activity, roles, and categories of people, going far beyond, and often counter to, staff efforts to influence social life. Work roles are sharply separated from taking part in activities considered leisure. Workers take their jobs very seriously; they feel that people *ought* to work at Les Floralies and that the residence must be protected from individuals who criticize and try to take advantage. As one staff member learned, any attempt to impose the obligations associated with work on residents taking part in what they consider a leisure activity, is met with stubborn and resentful refusal. Formal, organized activities like the sewing club or pottery class are also seen as distinct from more private, informal social contacts. Some residents have, by choice, a very active social life almost exclusively through informal ties.

Communists do not think residents ought to work at Les Floralies; anti-Communists think everyone who can work should. The anti-Communist supporters of President Beliveau are more likely to take part in formal, organized activities than are followers of Mme. Dupont, leader of the Communists. The first look at social organization offered in the following section of this chapter already shows the emerging definition of a factional border. Most formal activities have taken on a factional identity, and informal contacts are channeled within these borders. The introduction of a pottery class gives a microcosmic view of the way an activity intended by the staff to include "everyone interested" acquires its factional aura and also becomes segregated by sex. Although sex does not define as sharp a social border as politics in the residence—and fewer social contacts cross political than sexual lines—men and women have some different ways of participating in its social life.

The kinds and levels of participation which have been associated with community formation in other settings also appear in this chapter. The general level of social participation at Les Floralies is high, and the residents share with each other a high proportion of their total range of social contacts. Many of their relationships involve interdependence, especially when one partner is ill or handicapped. Many residents work. Community-wide events such as parties or special entertainment are almost universally attended; and every resident sees everyone else at least once a day at noon in the dining room.

Work

M. Beliveau, president of the Residents' Committee, comes downstairs to the kitchen every morning at 7 a.m., puts on an apron, and begins grating carrots or slicing potatoes. Four other residents, all women, stand around a separate table, washing or peeling vegetables and chatting. M. Beliveau's position as a man, and as president, are emphasized. He is the only one who uses machines for grating or chopping; he always works alone at his own counter even if he is doing the same job as the others; he stands nearer the chef and carries on the most conversation with him.

Groans of concern about getting it all done by lunchtime greet a particularly difficult job such as washing spinach. The workers feel a strong sense of responsibility to finish, and assume that if they don't do the job it won't get done. Although they complain about how much they have to do and how difficult some of the work is, they quickly align themselves with the chef and his assistants on the receiving side of complaints about the food which come from other residents.

Eating is a sacred sport in French working-class households, and these women had learned to be expert at choosing good food for very little money. In addition, one of them had sold vegetables from a push cart in the old central market of Paris. They recognize mistakes by the buyer immediately and comment on them in acid detail. Tough carrots or rotten mushrooms produce a combination of concern about community finances and a slightly pleased sense of superiority toward the young business manager who does the buying.

"I work for gerontology," Mme. Thibault said to introduce herself when we met at my first aperitif with the committee. Gerontology work is a daily job for seven women who collate and staple papers for the CNRO research organization and occasionally for the administration of the residence. Mme. Thibault is the leader of this group. She gets the assignment and is responsible for carrying it out with her crew. Tall and raw-boned, she strides to the workroom, notebook under her arm, with great purpose and pride. The women especially enjoy the fact that they work with papers, which seems a great step up from the sewing machine sweat shop work or domestic cleaning most of them did before retirement. Some of them also read the papers as they work, which leads to memorable discussions of theories or observations on aging. An article on the beneficial effects of sexual activity after sixty-five, for example, set off a discussion about the technical difficulties of intercourse with an old man. The raucous debate had reached the possibility that laundry starch might be the answer, when one of the women suddenly stopped and said, "but Mme. Ross is here, what's she going to think?"

When the gerontology workers do a job for the residence office, they often have advance notice of a meeting or an entertainment as they staple the announcement. The room where this work goes on is a lively, noisy place, mainly because of three strong-minded, vocal women who are good friends with each other and with Mme. Thibault. More accurately, they were good friends at the beginning of our stay, but grew farther apart as personal disagreements became politicized until the work group split completely along factional lines.

Soon after arrival, most new residents see the vice-president at their door with his tool kit, and watch with relief as he bustles around the apartment making minor repairs, putting putty in a loose window frame, adjusting a stubborn drawer. His helpful contacts with new residents are a source of political support for M. Clere, who greatly enjoys being a leader in the community. He is not unaware of this pleasant side-effect, although he describes his own motives for working as strictly altruistic. However, one of his first reactions to an election defeat which was a stunning surprise to him was to threaten not to help anybody anymore, "since this was the way they thanked me."

There are several other independent workers in the residence, a plumber, a heating repairman, an electrician. Residents ask them to come when there is a problem, and most of these workers have a waiting list of requests. Many people contact them directly, but if they go to the adminstration with their complaint, it is usually turned over to these residents anyway. They all prefer to work alone, rather than with the staff handyman, who, they say, bosses them around. "A little something"—usually a drink, sometimes cigarettes or something special to eat—is always offered at the end of the job, although these workers are never paid.

Another independent worker, and probably the best-known in the community, is the mailman. He collects the mail in the office, sorts it by floor, and delivers it every morning to each apartment.

A short woman, bent under the weight of a large watering can, appears every morning in the dining room to take care of "her" plants. She worries about all the house plants in the residence, and makes her daily rounds to water them. The large garden outside the lobby is the territory of a man who is extremely deaf. He has trouble carrying on conversations, and can no longer listen to music, which was his favorite recreation. His tufts of white hair, pointing in all directions, bob in and out behind the plants in the rose garden for hours at a time. From the windows of the fourth floor two other residents are visible every afternoon in the terrace garden. She is energetic and voluble, talking about the condition of each flower, making plans about plantings for the next season, pushing her wiry grey hair back into its knot as she gestures. He is tall, quiet, always wearing a beret and holding the last crumbs of a hand-rolled cigarette against one lip. He digs and carries, pushes the wheelbarrow, following her instructions. It is well known in the residence that the fourth floor garden is their responsibility. They invite visitors to take a tour, and as the plants are inspected, she explains that she and M. Villers met each other inside the residence and have set up one household out of their two apartments. She always mentions also that she is one of the few residents who pay the entire cost of living in the community themselves, without any help from l'Aide Sociale.

A small bar was opened in the residence lobby in June 1970.

Several women take turns working here two at a time, serving aperitifs and soft drinks, and washing the glasses, before lunch and dinner every day. Another resident has become a volunteer waitress in the dining room by gradually doing more and more to help serve and clear the tables in her corner of the room. She also includes in her role a boisterous flirtation with the men she serves.

In the basement of the residence is the laundryroom, where four residents, one couple and two women, especially enjoy working because it is far away from other people and "a person can work in peace." They each go several days a week, but often one at a time, to help the employee in charge of laundry. They are very fond of the laundress, who is a grandmother and is also from a working-class background very much like theirs. They work as peers, with this staff member grateful for their help and not at all in the role of boss. They complain together that there is really too much work for one person, and agree that it's just a good thing the residents are there to help. These people also have their own special insight into the private lives of some other members of the community. Although the laundry is mainly responsible for bed sheets and kitchen linen, those who live on the "semi-invalid" floors, especially the men, send their personal laundry here also. Staff members who live in the residence also have their laundry done, or use these facilities to do it themselves, as we did during our stay. Discussions in the laundry therefore include comments on the incontinence of some residents, as well as on the style and condition of the underwear of staff members or the anthropologist.

"Isn't it terrible? What can I possibly do? We'll never get done," Mme. Prevot mutters as she hurries between the tables of women making paper flowers. They began in November making paper flowers to decorate the dining room for Christmas. Mme. Prevot had worked in a tiny factory making flowers out of paper and cloth since she was thirteen years old. She mentioned this in a conversation with the director, who suggested that he buy materials which she could make into flowers for Christmas. Consequently she views him as the boss for whom she must produce enough flowers in time for the holiday deadline, and she literally wrings her hands as she watches the slow progress of the other women trying to learn to twist paper and wire into roses. Mme. Prevot thought I had special talent for this job and often ambushed me in the dining hall to ask me to help. I found out after Christmas that she and her closest friend had sneaked back at night to redo the flowers which did not meet her standards.

From its beginning this group had predominately members from the Communist faction, since they were recruited personally by Mme. Prevot and her friend, both Communists. It became progressively "purified" of anti-Communists as the election conflict, which climaxed in early December, brought politics so much to the surface of daily life that the group apparently could not persist in a state of coexistence. The Communist flowermakers finally cold-shouldered the others out altogether.

Serving on the Residents' Committee is also thought of, and grumbled about, as work—at least by its six elected members. The perceptions of others are more variable. Depending on their political attitudes, other residents view committee members as dedicated and helpful, selfish and power-hungry, or deluded by their own sense of importance into thinking they have influence in a situation which is really controlled by the administration.

The committee became highly visible as a result of the December election battle, a bitter factional conflict. Many residents who had never taken it very seriously began to think about the committee differently after seeing the earnestness with which popular and respected individuals fought each other for the positions. One of the conflicts which reverberated out from the elections was focussed on an attempt by the pro-Communist losers of the election to organize a separate leisure committee. The fact that the "real" committee, lead by President Beliveau, was able to defeat this proposal in spite of the director's enthusiastic support, greatly bolstered perceptions of the committee's influence. In the months following the elections, the combination of greater visibility and greater credibility as an influence on residence affairs led to a broadening of committee functions. Originally vaguely defined as a social committee concerned with recreation, the group became involved in making decisions about a wide range of issues: should a Mass be said in the residence? should there be public funeral arrangements? The committee also gradually assumed a role in conflict resolution, as residents came to them with problems to which more informal sanctions did not seem appropriate. Intervention in several conflicts also fostered an image of the committee as an intermediary between residents and the director, so that for an increasing range of problems, many residents felt that they ought to pass through the committee instead of going to the director's office on their own. As we will see in the chapter on factional conflict, although there is a widely shared perception that the committee does in fact play this interstitial role, it is by no means universally approved. Members of the Communist faction, which lost its representatives in the December elections, greatly resent this situation.

Thirty-four residents (27 percent) have a recognized, persistent work role, according to my observations. They have developed certain attitudes in common, and tend to have higher status in the residence than those who do not work ($r = .34$, $N = 121$).[1] Work roles have existed since the first days of the residence. However, the number of roles and the number of residents involved have increased for several reasons. The first work shared by residents was the preparation of a now legendary Christmas dinner, for which staff members and residents peeled potatoes together. The president has worked in the kitchen ever since. The fact that many of the first workers were committee members—M. Beliveau, Mme. Thibault, M. Clere, Mme. Cassard—probably both made work visible and gave it its factional and status connotations, all reasons why other residents were recruited into jobs. When new residents arrive, they observe work activities and often find that these are easy ways to begin participation, since working has an aspect of being helpful which allows the new person to feel he or she is offering something instead of simply appearing in a more social group and hoping nervously to be accepted. New people also bring new skills, so that if they work, they create new jobs, such as flowermaking.

The distinction between work and leisure activities is made not only by these workers but also by other residents. The workers talk about their responsibilities as something done for the residence, and assume that if they don't finish the vegetables or the flowers in time, the job won't get done. They typically put some staff member, whether he or she likes it or not, in the position of boss, and then indulge in complaints about lack of understanding from the "boss" and ingratitude from the other residents they serve.

Some workers think they should be paid, and give examples of other retirement residences where this is done. Others simply think that people who work should have priority for participation in trips or entertainments when the number who can take part is limited. Some stress the reciprocal nature of what they do for the residence, since they are "grateful for all the residence has done for them." These people are likely to point out the disgrace of the many residents who don't do anything and just let others work for them.

Residents who work are more likely than others to feel that everyone who is capable should work; that residents are *not* always ready to help each other; and that residents do *not* have a right to demand what they want (as is shown in table 2).[2] Working seems to stimulate feelings of distinctiveness: workers are different from the majority of residents who are seen as not helpful to each other. Working also seems to promote identification with the residence as a whole and the way things are done there; workers feel demands are inappropriate, I think, because they see them as being directed at themselves by other residents.

Table 2   Possession of a Work Role, by Attitudes about the Residence

	Possession of a work role
The capable ought to work	.37** (64)
Residents help each other	−.21* (66)
Residents have the right to make demands	−.48** (64)

Sample sizes in parentheses
*Significant at the .05 level
**Significant at the .001 level

Other residents also distinguish work activities from leisure, although their attitudes toward workers vary. Some people admire them and say that if they themselves were in better health, or did not have a spouse to take care of, they too would find a job. Mme. Dupont, on the other hand, vehemently refers to work in the residence as exploitation, because the old people are not paid and the use of volunteers takes jobs away from young workers who otherwise might have been hired at the residence. Her closest and most militant supporters share these opinions. Other members of the faction take a kind of "no taxation without representation" attitude toward working. They say there is no reason to work since we don't have any say over what is done with the results. "Since Beliveau and his gang control the residence, let them do the work."[3]

However, since some supporters of Mme. Dupont do work (for instance, Mme. Prevot and her friends who made flowers), there is no correlation between factional allegiance and *actual* participation in residence work.[4] This apparent contradiction between attitudes and actions has several sources. First of all, people work for many reasons: to pass the time; to regain a status lost with retirement; to enjoy the social contact; and, of course, to be helpful. Working often provides a pleasant sense of being an insider, because a job gives behind-the-scenes knowledge about something in the residence, from what Sunday dinner will be, to advance warning of a general meeting, to news of someone in the clinic. Some work offers an unusual amount of contact with the staff, who are an excellent source of all kinds of information which give the resident extra currency to use on the gossip exchange. Work is also fun. The fact that it is clearly distinguished from leisure is no contradiction to its being a source of greatly enjoyed social contacts and group memberships. For a member of the Communist faction, perceptions of working for more "selfish" reasons are much less contradictory to the anti-work ideology than is the idea of working to contribute to the community. Second, the ideological stance of a faction leader may take priority over other motivations for the most militant supporters, but it does not have equal importance for everyone who is identified with the faction. Faction membership means different things to different individuals: some are far more involved and more political than others. The close-up look at experiences of new residents discussed in chapter six reveals that as individuals become more engaged in the Communist faction, they are likely to drop out of work activities. Mme. Prevot will appear as a clear example. The exceptions to this pattern are individuals who work at highly independent jobs which do not imply a sense of participation in the organized activities dominated by the other faction.

Formally Organized Leisure Activities

Residents take part in leisure activities because they enjoy them. Participants have no notion that what they are doing is helpful to the residence, and no sense of responsibility to anyone for consistent participation. Although in some cases staff members introduce the possibility that a leisure activity could benefit the community—for example, through the sale of objects made in the ceramics class—this is not a primary goal or even a strong interest for the participants. Any awareness that a staff member is trying to make residents feel they ought to go to an activity which they define as leisure, or to include in it something they can see as work, elicits resentment and almost always refusal.

"I hadn't played cards for twenty-five years before I moved in here," one *belote* player told me. He is one of the regulars who meet after lunch everyday at two tables in the fourth-floor lounge. M.

Beliveau is one of these players, and other members of the group often stop by his table in the dining room to say they'll see him soon, or will be late, or can't make it that day. The players know each other well as partners and opponents, and there are many references, not always complimentary, to familiar styles of play: the notorious over-bidder, the under-bidder, the expert, the cheat. Each man also has his own way of putting the cards down as the tricks are played, slapping them aggressively, lowering them in a slow, suspenseful arc, or sliding them unobtrusively toward the pile with a last-minute triumphant turn.

M. Beliveau's table includes only members of his faction, and is a very stable group. The second table includes one Communist, one Cuban, and one man who is considered bizarre and difficult to get along with because he often becomes incoherent after drinking and tells long complicated stories about being married to a midget circus performer who is now imprisoned in Poland. This table does not play every day, and does not represent the kind of close group that the president's has become. A new player, M. Simon, was added to the latter during our stay, and his appearance gives a preview of the factional filtering process which is discussed in detail in chapter six. When M. Simon came to visit Les Floralies, like many visitors he met the president. A short conversation was enough for M. Beliveau to decide that the newcomer was not a Communist, and so M. Simon was asked if he played *belote*. As he is an avid player, he joined in a game the day of his visit. When he moved into the residence, he immediately became part of the Beliveau table, although this meant that there were often five players for the four-person game. The extra man always waited and watched and finally traded places with a player rather than cross over to the other table.

The card game is a male enterprise. The players swear and tell risqué jokes. The appearance of a woman in the lounge usually stops the game, as the players silently wait to see if a wife has come to carry off her spouse for some domestic chore. Once or twice during the year four women played at a separate table, but women residents never played in the men's game. Men say that women only know how to play simple *belote* and not the complicated no-trump and all-trump versions which are included in the men's game. Some couples make up foursomes for *belote*, but they always play in each other's apartments, never in the men's fortress on the fourth floor.

Before the sewing group moved its weekly meeting to the

fourteenth floor, the card-players used to complain about the "invasion" of the fourth floor by women. A regular core of about fourteen women, and sometimes more than twenty, do their sewing and knitting together every week. Tea, coffee and cookies, paid for by the residence, are served, and a few extra people always arrive in time for refreshments. This group was at first called the *ouvroir*, a word often used in reference to a workroom in convents where poor women do sewing or mending in exchange for some kind of assistance from the nuns, or where richer women do the same work as an act of charity. Many residents did not know exactly what *ouvroir* meant, but for those with an idea, the word had an institutional resonance which they strongly reject. Residents are very sensitive about emphasizing that they are in their own homes, not in an institution. Use of the word "sheltered," for example, to refer to residents in an official document was enough to provoke an angry protest to the Residents Committee.

Sewing club became the new name of this activity at the insistence of the wife of the CNRO executive director when she decided to come every week to cut out dress patterns. This change not only removed the religious and poorhouse echos of *ouvroir* but also more accurately reflects the women's definition of this activity as leisure rather than work. They bring their own sewing and knitting, and come to enjoy company and refreshments while they do what otherwise they would do at home.

After M. Guerillon had encouraged the ceramics class to make pots for sale at a show, the sewing club was invited to embroider place mats and tablecloths for the sale too. As the head nurse—who organized the club and who sees herself as its leader—made the rounds of the tables offering the printed embroidery patterns, she was visibly startled and displeased with the chain of refusals. Neither flattery nor half-joking insistence got any results except "I have to finish this blanket for my great-grandchild"; "embroidery hurts my eyes"; "I have so much to do at home." This unwillingness to participate in the project is easily explained: about half of the regulars in this group are aligned with the pro-Communist faction and tend to see work for the residence as exploitation. The few "volunteers" who finally accepted the job were all members of the other faction, and included one woman who particularly likes embroidery and is known for her special skill, the always willing Mme. Thibault, and several new residents who are typically especially vulnerable to persuasion from staff members. Mme.

Barret, who is disliked and rejected by most other residents, was unwilling to do the work but was also unwilling to give up totally the possibility of approval from the nurse: she took a tablecloth pattern, removed its wrapper, and held it all afternoon without sewing a stitch.

Mme. Barret's visits to the sewing club are frequent but unsatisfying. "Wherever I try to sit down, someone says the chair is taken," she explains. She is unattractive and gruff, with an aggressive stare probably caused by her very bad eyes. She and one or two other disliked and lonely people usually come to this public group hoping for social contact. The women sit in small clusters at intervals around very large tables and successfully exclude these undesirables from conversations by leaving one or two empty chairs on either side of them.

The president not infrequently makes a reference to the sewing club at committee meetings. He jokes about the free cookies, and especially mentions that "we" don't know what goes on there. Since two of the committee members are regular participants in the group, the "we" seems to refer to men rather than to the committee or his faction. Shortly after the club began cutting dress patterns, M. Beliveau arrived at a committee meeting seriously upset about hearing from one of the women that the residence was going to pay for fabric and yarn for individuals who would sew or knit their own dresses. He hoped this was a rumor, and was disbelieving when the director assured him it was true. M. Guerillon exlained that it would certainly be cheaper than buying the clothing in a store. The president hooked his thumbs in his vest pockets and gave an excited speech about the people who would take advantage of a system like this, and how dangerous it would be for the community. Reassurances from the director that those who didn't make clothes would be compensated some other way had no effect. After the meeting M. Beliveau explained to me, not for the first time, that the director had a very good heart, but was young and naïve, and had to be protected from clever and unscrupulous residents both for his own good and for the good of the community.

The establishment of the pottery class gives a close-up view of the development of some basic patterns of social participation at Les Floralies. When an announcement was made in the dining room that anyone who wanted to learn how to do ceramics should come to the workshop in the basement, over twenty people straggled down the stairs and through the maze of corridors during the afternoon. They were a cross-section of the residence community: men and women, both political factions, committee members, and social isolates. By the third meeting, three weeks later, the sorting process had been accomplished; there were seven regular participants, all women, all non-Communists, one committee member, and none of the isolates.

There are several reasons why this group is now female and non-Communist. The class is taught by a woman, the doctor's wife, and the wife of the director also comes every week, usually with her little girl. I was also a regular attender during our stay. On the first day, the teacher made many references to similarities between pottery and cooking, and that day the only volunteers to try molding the clay were women. M. Beliveau came, but made very clear that he was there to inspect and not to participate. He walked around observing all the potters' efforts and all the equipment, making many comments about the difficulty of the work and the fact that only professionals could really ever do it well. As supporting evidence he displayed two elaborate ceramic medallions made by a friend who is a professional potter. At all committee meetings where the pottery class was discussed, M. Beliveau was very dubious about the expense involved when there were many things he considered necessities to be paid for at the residence, such as clothing for its members. He felt that once again the director was being idealistic rather than practical, and was unwilling to give any presidential support to the launching of the pottery project.

M. Clere also arrived at the beginning of the class but spent his time bustling around the workshop showing that he was already familiar with it because of his carpentry work. When a few other men looked in later, they saw only women sitting around the work table, and either backed out or acted as though they had just come to pick up their wives or friends and waited for them without touching the clay. The first group of participants, as opposed to those who moved around and watched during the first two sessions, were also all non-Communists, including Mme. Thibault, at her most earnest, wrestling with a lump of clay. Members of the Communist group who came to look quickly got the impression that they were in the wrong place.

The fact that the pots would be sold at a show was mentioned to the group for the first time at the fifth weekly meeting. No one objected or seemed particularly interested, and when the show took place, many potters bought back their own creations for a few francs.

Every Wednesday afternoon an uneven line of residents walks from the dining hall, downstairs and through a lounge, along a narrow hallway, across the lobby of the research wing, and up a treacherous free-standing stairway into the auditorium to see a movie. The audience varies from about thirty to sixty people, depending on the film. Movies are a social occasion, rather similar to a Saturday night showing on an American college campus: comments are called out during sexy or sentimental scenes; couples hold hands in the dark; and there is a great deal of chatting and walking around to visit between reels. On the other hand, people do not go to the films just for the social contact. For example, one week, when the day was changed, the audience was cut in half because of a time conflict with a favorite circus show on television.

Christmas Eve, Christmas Day, New Year's Eve, New Year's Day, the oldest resident's ninetieth birthday, and several holidays on the Catholic calendar were celebrated at the residence. For Christmas and the New Year, there were special, elaborate meals, including traditional dishes such as oysters and white wine. Christmas Eve celebration was moved to December 22 at Les Floralies, so that there would be no conflict between residence and family parties. That night, only two or three residents were missing. This kind of participation is usual at the residence parties, which always follow a meal. After a special seasonal dessert, the record player is brought out, and people dance for hours. More than once we went upstairs at one o'clock, or even four o'clock, in the morning, while a last group of residents was still whirling around the floor. The only party which was not well attended was the Mardi Gras, which by a complex series of redefinitions became identified as a Communist celebration, so that the president and his followers would not take part. Even on Christmas Day there were only about fifteen residents missing from the dining room, since many people, instead of going to eat with their families, invited them to come to the residence.

These celebrations are not spectator sports. Residents drink and dance. Those who don't dance join in the winey singing of favorite songs; they flirt; they produce and share rare filter-tipped, pre-rolled cigarettes; they relish the special meal. Memories of these evenings become important landmarks in the repertory of experiences shared by residents. One of these parties is often the point from which a new person remembers feeling really part of the community, and others often mention the same occasion as the first time they remember really knowing who that particular person was.

Television watching is both a public, group activity and a basis for private, informal contacts. About a dozen residents watch the set in the fourth-floor lounge every night: men and women, couples and single people, members of both factions, ranging in age from sixty-one (the youngest person in the residence) to over eighty. Many of these people have their own sets at home but enjoy the sociability of watching with others. "It's a change," is the way Mme. Denis explained to me why she and her husband go down to watch every night. She is one of the people who enjoy work in the laundry because they can do it in peace without too close contact with other residents. In a similar way, watching television with the same group every night meets their desire for some social contact without arousing their very strong fears of getting too involved with other people "who might tell stories about you and start trouble."

The same clear distinction between work and leisure activities which appeared from the point of view of jobs in the residence shows up again from the perspective of activities which people take part in purely as recreation. The reactions against attempts to obscure this distinction are quite strong, as the head nurse and her embroidery project demonstrate.

"Staff members don't always get what they want," might be another moral to draw from this same episode. Most residents are capable of resisting considerable pressure from staff members, including the director and the head nurse. The protective and patronizing attitude which the president often expresses toward the director is not unusual among community members. Residents talking about a staff person this way often stress his or her youth and inexperience: the women in the kitchen discussing the business manager; M. Beliveau or Mme. Thibault worrying about the director. Politics comes into these analyses too. Militants in each faction often agonize about the susceptibility of the director to being swayed and misled by members of the other group.

Factional allegiance also predicts to general patterns of participation in organized activities.[5] Thirty-two percent of the residents regularly take part in this kind of activity; however, followers of Mme. Dupont are less likely to join in formal groups of any kind than are supporters of M. Beliveau ($r = .23$, $N = 121$). The committee is dominated by members of his faction, who because of their inside information and influence over expenditure of social funds, in turn tend to dominate organized activities. As we will see in the chapter on socialization, new arrivals who learn to participate in the community through the Communist faction usually experiment with formal groups but then drop out as they simultaneously acquire the faction's point of view and the alternative of informal ties.

Informal Activities

Ties of friendship and mutual help weave the community together in many informal ways; and residents' social lives also extend outside Les Floralies.

Most residents do their housework in the morning. The hallways become more lively then, as people open their doors while they sweep and dust, and everyone makes a trip down the corridor to the garbage chute. The mailman also comes in the morning, and people often stand in their doorways for a minute to chat with him and their neighbors. Morning routine for many men means a trip to the shopping center to buy a newspaper, almost a euphemism for stopping at the cafe for a glass of wine. On Sunday morning the cafe stop includes placing a bet on the afternoon horse race. Although men usually go out on these errands alone, they not only meet each other at the cafe, but also have regular, if not profound, contacts with the same newspaper vendor and bartender everyday. Probably because of these daily expeditions, when men and women are compared in terms of how often they leave the residence, the men go significantly more often ($r = .65$, $N = 120$). Younger residents also go out more often than older ($r = .29$, $N = 119$).[6]

Since everyone in the residence eats lunch in the dining hall, no one passes a day completely alone. Since residents consider their seats permanent, and since they have chosen where to sit, places at table are an excellent source of information about friendship.[7] Once I realized this, I made a weekly map of the dining hall to record any changes in seating arrangements. Not only was this interesting information in its own right; it also led me to other discoveries. Whenever I noticed a change, I made sure to spend time with the people involved to find out the story behind it.

Spatial arrangement in the dining room is another marker of the border between political factions. When I began keeping my chart at the beginning of October, eleven out of twenty-five tables (44 percent) had people from both factions; by the end of March, eight out of twenty-nine tables (28 percent) crossed factional lines. Eight moves in the direction of more factional consistency had taken place. In addition, three of the "mixed" tables were divided two and two, so that one person was not alone with three members of the other faction.

Some residents make ritual rounds of certain tables everyday. Mme. Charriere, proudly the oldest person in the community, greets at least a dozen people every noon, walking from table to table, kissing her women friends on both cheeks, shaking hands with men. Always dressed in black, with her late husband's gold watch chain tucked under a white lace collar, she looks like a frail queen giving her daily blessing. She is the most universally loved person in the residence. People from both factions talk about how good she is, how much she does for others, even at her age, and how refined and elegant she is, particularly in speech, because she was a maid for people who were "very highly placed."

The president receives more visits than he makes, although he and Mme. Beliveau stop at several tables on their way in and out. Their own table is next to the aisle dividing the two sides of the first dining room, and everyone going to the second room walks by them. Before and after every meal other residents stop by to chat, report a problem, or ask a question. A living link among members of the Communist faction is traced by the busy figure of Mme. Dupont, who tours several tables everyday and on Sunday delivers the Communist paper to about a dozen subscribers. She is short, apple-cheeked, and limps severely because of one stiff leg. The speed and force of her cane tapping down our hall was always a reliable indication of the level of political conflict.

An aura of sociability extends out from this meal to an aperitif before or a cup of coffee afterwards. Since coffee is provided every month by the residence, everyone who has a kitchen can offer this kind of hospitality, and almost everyone also has at least one bottle of the vermouth-type drinks which are offered before meals. Especially before lunch on Sunday, residents exchange invitations. The possibility of inviting people to visit seems to be prized as an aspect of living in a private apartment and not in the room or dormitory of an institution. The custom of invitation also discourages the tendency of a few people to take advantage of proximity and knowledge of neighbors' routines by too much dropping in.

In the late afternoon and evening, favorite television programs— serials, game shows, and movies—are a major activity. Friends often watch together, and many invitations or well-established patterns of visiting are focussed on watching some favorite program. Mme. Dupont and a Communist friend and neighbor never miss Zorro, which they interpret as a political show. They cheer on the proletariat, which, defended by the masked champion, always triumphs over evil. Like other residents, they also comment vigorously on the inability of actors to perform tasks which real working people would know how to do: "you can tell *she* never scrubbed clothes in her life!" Although television is often blamed for a decline in social contacts in modern society, at Les Floralies it seems highly compatible with sociability. Watching involves visits before and after the programs, and conversations and commentary continue during the show. Even people who do not watch together often discuss programs at other times. For those who may not actually do many things together, these shows can become a substantial basis for shared experience.

Groups of women or couples also visit each other to play card games or board games. Women also take turns going to one another's apartments to knit or sew together. Visiting is, of course, often just plain visiting; a friend comes by to chat, to share family news, or to gossip about events in the residence.

Some kinds of contacts among residents meet very specific and serious needs. Several people always arrive in the dining room leaning on the same supporting arm. M. Richard, who otherwise spends his time alone reading the worn paperbacks of Zola and de Maupassant stored in his closet library, considers it his personal responsibility to help his frail table partner down to every meal. He doesn't see her for any other reason, and explains that he feels sorry for her, that she is very sweet, but is really just a peasant with nothing interesting to say. When M. Richard went to the hospital with cancer, he made arrangements with another resident to take his place. This man gives his help faithfully, although doing it provokes serious accusations of unfaithfulness from his mistress who lives in Bagnolet, close enough to the residence to hear disturbing rumors that he takes another woman to meals. M. Printemp's steady kindness to this woman is in sharp contrast to his general image in the community. He is very tall and gaunt, constantly wears dark glasses, and speaks very little; other residents call him the undertaker. He is so suspicious of his neighbors that he puts a mark on the vinegar and oil bottles on his table to make sure no one else uses them. Other residents complain about his unpleasant grumbling to the dining room staff. However, careful attention to his daily routine would show a round-trip from the semi-invalid floor to the dining room to help a person he hardly knows, and would even reveal a little gentle teasing about being her "cavalier." According to her, he is the kindest and most proper of gentlemen.

Two residents who are almost totally blind are guided through the day by neighbors and friends who help them eat, dress, walk, and do their housework. One man who is gradually losing his sight in spite of several operations, is cared for by a woman who has become his friend in the residence. These two share a strong feeling of having known better times, of being from a more refined background than other residents. She is the widow of a self-employed builder; he did ornamental plaster work and considers himself a highly skilled craftsman. His proudest job is the plaster friezes in the Paris Opera House, which he sent me to see. They spend a great deal of time together, talking or listening to music on the radio. She reads to him, but never for more than half an hour as she is carefully conserving her own failing eyesight.

The other blind person is a woman who knew Mme. Dupont before they came to Les Floralies. Mme. Dupont eats with Marie Tatu in the dining hall, helping her cut her food, and takes her for a walk every morning, pushing and pulling her blind friend briskly through the underbrush of abandoned gardens in a nearby slum scheduled for redevelopment. They find fruits and potatoes in the gardens, and Mme. Dupont talks politics with the one or two old people and gypsies who are still living on the condemned property. Most of the blind woman's care and entertainment, however, is not in the hands of Mme. Dupont. Another neighbor on the thirteenth floor helps with her housekeeping, does errands for her, and accompanies her to activities in the residence and on trips to Bagnolet. For Mme. Tissot there are no previous ties to Marie; she is a neighbor, a fellow Communist, and a mutual friend of Mme. Dupont.

Since every resident has a minimum of social contact at noon every day, a person's unexplained absence from the dining hall stimulates contact of a different kind. Table partners quickly check up on someone who is missing, going upstairs themselves, talking to someone they know is a closer friend or neighbor, or perhaps mentioning the problem to a staff member. If a sick person does not go to the clinic, he or she usually gets a good deal of attention from other residents, who visit, bring food from the kitchen, run errands, and nag the nurse to send medicine or to come to the apartment. People in the clinic are visited too, although their more material needs are cared for by the nursing staff. In a few cases, I saw residents spend many hours caring for a friend in a kind of plot to keep him or her from going to the clinic, which for some has enough of a hospital connotation to be frightening.

Fears are also sometimes expressed that illness and a stay in the clinic may lead to transfer to the semi-invalid floors. For example, when she returned from the hospital where she was operated on for cataract, Mme. Barret discovered that she was going to make this move. Mme. Dupont found her in tears in her former room, and managed to convince the nurse to let her stay. The rooms on the special floors do lack a kitchen and bathtub, but certainly the stigma of a demotion to being officially invalid is the worst part of the move for people who start out their stay in the community on a different floor. People who move directly into these apartments do not complain about them, and do not share a general perception of themselves as frailer than others in the community. For other members of the community, however, transition to this floor is a spatial dramatization of a change for the worse in health which arouses deep fear about their future physical and social condition.

"Papers" are one of the greatest evils feared by members of this community. When they groan and say that they have to do "papers" they mean some kind of bureaucratic form, usually for taxes, social security, or welfare. A few residents are especially talented at reading and filling out these forms; they are respected as experts, and gratitude for their help is expressed in strong loyalty to them as friends and often as political leaders. At certain times of the year when a deluge of government forms arrives at the residence, two men in particular, the president and M. Rouget, bitter rivals in community politics, make their rounds hour after hour for several days helping their respective, and prospective, supporters. Many residents told me, when the appropriate name came up in conversation, how grateful they are to these men. After a lifetime of looking at forms with confusion and suspicion, sure only that you lose if you fill them out honestly, but you get in trouble if you fill them out wrong, residents are profoundly grateful to someone who is trusted, comprehensible as "one of us," and at the same time capable of unraveling the mysterious "papers."

Friends also exchange various kinds of help based on special skills. A former seamstress sews underwear for a woman who crochets her a blouse. Someone especially skilled at knitting gives advice to another woman, who in return shares her recipes for herbal remedies. Mme. Prevot irons M. Richard's shirts, since they sit at the same table and she noticed the wrinkles. Several women do mending for men friends and neighbors, who in turn help out with household repairs, or heavy chores.

Except in the case of legally married couples and the one pair of kin in the residence (niece/aunt), all of this help—some of it very substantial—is offered and accepted by people who did not know each other before arriving at Les Floralies.

Here, as in any community, people are attracted into friendships for many reasons of style, interests, and circumstances of encounter. However, the informal ties which group residents together and the specific activities which make up informal social life are not random; it is possible to describe consistent patterns. Friendships cross spatial barriers, such as different floors, for instance, but not the social borders of factional loyalty. Different ranks within the construction trades, on the other hand, are no obstacle. Mme. Altman, for example, who feel a strong bond with blind M. Lefevre on the basis of their relatively high past status, has as her closest woman friend someone with absolutely no claim to this kind of distinction.

Factional identification is often a basis for offering assistance, even to individuals who are downright disagreeable. Mme. Dupont's concern for Mme. Barret, for instance, is explicitly based on the fact that her husband was prominent in a Communist-oriented union. Mme. Barret herself is not interested in politics, and participates minimally in residence conflicts. However, because Mme. Barret is "one of us," Mme. Dupont talks to her at the sewing club, tries to persuade others to sit at her table, or intervenes with the staff as in the case of the threatened move to the nonhousekeeping floor.

When "La Mama," a very conspicuous member of the Communist faction, became incontinent and virtually bed-ridden, Beliveau supporters attacked her case as shameful and disgusting, and said she threatened to transform the residence into a nursing home. The Communist ladies in the flowershop talked about the same woman with great sympathy and many references to her courage; faction members visited "La Mama" regularly, bringing her magazines, cigarettes, and gossip.

Women are more likely to visit frequently back and forth in the residence than are men ($r = .24$, $N = 65$).[8] People with a relatively well-recognized political identity also visit more than those whose factional allegiance is less well known ($r = .31$, $N = 65$).[9] The connection between a recognized political affiliation and integration into the community will be discussed in chapter six. The important point here is that it is the strength or clarity of factional identification and not its direction which is linked to visiting.

The reason for this is probably that participation in formal groups, and the informal ties indicated by visits, are not exclusive. Although members of the Communist faction tend not to take part in organized activities, while Beliveau supporters do, there is no tendency for the anti-Communists not to have informal relationships as well.[10] So, knowing a person's factional identity is a basis for assumptions about formal group participation, but it doesn't give any information about amount of visiting. What it does suggest is who the contacts are likely to be with if they do take place.

There is another very small category of people (four residents) who abstain from formal group activities and maintain an active informal social life, although they are anti-Communists. These are individuals whom I think of as "having seen better days." They feel more cultured than other residents and make every effort to emphasize what they see as their differentness. They often complained to me about the vulgarity of many residents, and avoidance of organized activities is their way of minimizing contact with people they find offensive.

A tea party every Wednesday afternoon is such a regular event for Mme. Demougeot, for example, that she calls it her *salon*. She has so little money now that it is almost impossible for her to pay the bus and subway fares to visit friends in Paris. So she extends a permanent invitation to them and to a very few residents for Wednesday afternoon. She then invests all her social funds in cookies or cake to serve with tea. One other woman in the community has become a close friend. They met on a residence trip to an opera in Paris, and soon began to spend time together. Through fastidious mending and ironing, judicious placement of one piece of real gold jewelry, and skillful styling of soft white hair, both of these women manage to appear elegant. They don't swear, and avoid using the argot which peppers the conversation of many residents; and they agree that the others are often unpleasantly vulgar. Organized activities are disagreeable because of the other residents who, these women complain, argue and shout, ask personal questions, retell nasty gossip, and aren't very interesting anyway.

Neither of these women has markedly more education than other residents; they are both poor. Their separateness is self-imposed, and based on the way they see themselves. It is certainly plausible that their attractiveness and charm might have made these women popular and prestigious members of the community. However, they simply do not participate enough in residence social life for this to happen. Mme. Beliveau on the other hand, also feels herself markedly superior to "more vulgar" residents, and tries energetically to assert her status in terms of residence social life. She revels in her role of president's wife, takes part in many organized activities, and once suggested that the administration used stricter selection criteria in admitting the first residents, like herself, than for people who came later.

Contacts Outside the Residence

Sunday is an especially social day at Les Floralies. This fact is appropriately most visible in the dining hall, the major scene for public contacts. The meal itself is more elaborate, with a main course traditionally seen as festive—roast meat or chicken—cake or pie for dessert instead of fruit, and coffee after the meal. The residents dress up, and they linger much longer in the dining room after the meal than on other days. There are also different faces in the room on Sunday. Since many people in France work on Saturdays, and children go to school in the morning, Sunday is the time when most friends and relatives can conveniently come to the residence. Also people in the community like to have guests for the Sunday meal because it is the best of the week. Children, grandchildren, and great-grandchildren are prominent among the Sunday visitors, and the dining room once a week has a noisy miniature population of children, dressed up for admiration, who tour the tables of their grandparents' friends collecting kisses and candy. Other relatives come also; several residents have very close ties to nieces and nephews, for example. Friends appear on Sunday too, often with regularity. Relatives and friends from outside the community get to know friends and neighbors of the resident they visit, and especially on Sunday groups are mingled at aperitif gatherings in many apartments. Guests also appear in the fourth-floor lounges, in the gardens and the lobby, and on the fourteenth floor to look at the view, as residents show them around. Sunday has its sad side too; since it is the day to expect visits, it is the hardest day to accept the fact that nobody comes. A lonely person like Mme. Barret prowls the lobby on Sunday, jumping up each time a car door slams outside, disappointed each time because the people who said they might come are not there.

Some residents see people from outside the community more privately, in their apartments, or outside the residence. Mme. Prevot, the flowermaker, spends one day a week babysitting for her son's children in Bagnolet. M. Boillon goes every weekend to visit a child in Paris. M. Clere hitchhikes several times a year to a village in Champagne to visit his sister. Some visitors, such as the friends who come to Mme. Demougeot's tea party, are rarely seen in public.

Some contacts with people from outside the community are more businesslike. One resident has a prostitute come at least once a week to his apartment on the semi-invalid floor. She is introduced to others in the elevators sometimes as his niece, sometimes as his cousin. The appearance of a priest one day in the residence, on the other hand, demonstrated the close ties which some people maintain with political allies outside the community. Minutes after she saw the priest in a corridor, Mme. Dupont had established that he was there to say a Mass, and a few hours later she was on the phone to a friend in union headquarters to ask him to help her protest this invasion of the secular residence. Leaders in both factions keep in close touch with their unions; and the Communists in particular, probably because they are the minority, often try to bring in outside support during internal conflicts.

Forty-nine percent of the people who responded to the questionnaire said that they had seen a friend from outside the residence within the last week; 30 percent had seen a friend within the last month, and 20 percent within the last year. When asked about contact with relatives, the answers were that 69 percent had seen a relative within the last week; 20 percent within the last month and 11 percent within the last year or more.[11]

Social contacts inside a residence like this one are interpreted by some researchers as substitutes for ties to people outside which can no longer be maintained. If this is so, then the residents who have many outside contacts should be less involved in social life inside. At Les Floralies this is not true. The residents who, according to my observations and to their own reports, have the most contact with people outside the community have no tendency to have more or less social contact of any kind inside the residence than do other individuals. For the purposes of this study, the two aspects of social life are independent of each other, for knowing something about one gives no basis for predictions about the other.[12] The only category of residents which has a pattern of higher contact with people outside the community is the pro-Communist faction, which probably has more to do with their being a minority opposition looking for support, than with their actual political ideology. Age is related not to the frequency of outside contacts, but to the kind. Older residents tend to report more recent visits with relatives than do younger residents ($r = .25$, $N = 44$); younger residents report more recent visits with friends from outside the community than do older residents ($r = .21$, $N = 66$).

Participation in a Gerontological Debate

Activity and disengagement have become cardinal points in many debates among gerontologists since the disengagement concept was introduced in 1960. Although the terms have been redefined many times, the debates continue, and they are still typically focussed on the extent of social participation required to make life satisfying for older people. The notion of disengagement is that a gradual shrinking of the sphere of social contacts is not forced upon older people by other members of society, but results from *mutual* withdrawal. This withdrawal, the argument goes on, does not necessarily make life less satisfying or happiness more difficult for old people: as a prelude to death, disengagement is seen as functional for them as well as for the wider society.[13]

Supporters of the activity position which was formulated in response to the disengagement hypothesis argue that social participation is essential for a satisfying life, and that the older people who maintain higher levels of participation will therefore be the happiest.[14] If the residents of Les Floralies are asked to stand up and be counted on one side or the other of this debate, they remain stubbornly seated. What they do and what they say about themselves could in fact be seen as a vote against the reasonableness of the argument at all.

As far as these old people are concerned, there is no direct relationship between social participation and happiness. Knowing how much or in what ways a person has social contacts gives no basis for predicting how likely he or she is to report being happy or satisfied with life in general, or in comparison with the recent or distant past.[15] The residents of Les Floralies seem to offer support to the gerontologists who have tried to mediate the extreme positions, disengagement vs. activity, by introducing the idea of styles of aging, which has been labeled a "continuity" position in the life satisfaction debate. In short, some people are happy when they are very active, others are happy when they are relatively inactive. From this point of view, life-long patterns of social participation explain the kinds and levels of activity that are satisfying to different individuals.[16]

The Social Map: Categories of Participants

Men play *belote* in this community; women go to the sewing club; Communists are less likely than non-Communists to belong to formal groups; different kinds of people participate in social life here in different ways. To talk specifically about patterns of participation, it is necessary to discover in detail the different kinds of people there are. As people at Les Floralies talk about themselves and each other, the boundaries of several categories emerge. In addition to the primordial distinction of residents from staff members, there are distinctions between people who belong to the CNRO and those from the town of Bagnolet; those who pay their own fees and those who have welfare assistance; men and women; older and younger; more and less healthy; Communists and non-Communists.

However, as we have seen, only a few of these categories have a clear correspondence to patterns of participation: sex, political identification, and, more rarely, health or age. Other bases for shuffling individuals into categories do not have the same kinds of consequences. Occasionally, for instance, a resident is described as being from Bagnolet. "You know he or she is from Bagnolet," is usually pronounced by a critic as a not very subtle euphemism for "he or she is a Communist." Most residents know that there are a few people who came into the community through the town of

Bagnolet rather than the CNRO, but no one could list them all. Residents often make mistakes in this kind of classification; the individuals from Bagnolet never act as a group; and they share no common patterns of participation in community activities. The category edges are additionally fuzzy because there are a few people who lived in Bagnolet before moving into the residence, but who are also members of the CNRO. Residents who pay their own costs form a similar kind of category. Since everyone knows that there are such people but no one knows who all of them are, errors in identification are common; and those who pay or don't pay share no other distinctive ways of living in the community. People who have been in the residence since its early days are also classified together. These "old-timers," like the paying residents, sometimes try to make these characteristics meaningful in the social life of the residence by claiming privileges. As the chapter on social status will show, however, they are not successful. Married couples form a category whose members are almost universally recognized; they all live in distinctive double rooms at the end of each hall. However, they do not ever act as a group, and married people do not share specific ways of participating in community life. Work roles are widely recognized in the residence, although no one could identify everyone in this category. Workers have developed certain attitudes in common and have acquired higher status than people who do not have jobs. However, they never act as a group, almost certainly because this would require crossing factional borders.

Health condition is another characteristic which residents often talk about. "Those of us who are still well," or, "I hope they're not going to turn this into a nursing home," are common kinds of comment on the sight of a person in a wheelchair arriving at the front door. In addition, the separation by floors of those who can do housekeeping from the "semi-invalids" who cannot might further emphasize a category based on health. Of course, appearances are not a reliable basis for judgments of health, and this category, like several others, exists in an abstract way but is not fully "filled in" with recognized individuals. People who consider themselves in relatively poor health typically do not work ($r = .27$, $N = 68$), and are less likely to take part in organized activities ($r = .21$, $N = 68$).[17] However, they do not tend to associate with each other more than with residents who feel healthier; and they are just as apt to have informal ties as anyone else. Given the patterns of mutual help I observed in the residence, it is likely that people who are less well have more contact with those who feel stronger than among themselves.

The patterns of social activity related to age are those that extend outside the community to family and friends. Age is not linked to people's evaluation of their health, and it does not provide a basis for styles of participation inside the community.[18]

Sex and political identification are the social cues which consistently serve as a basis for recruitment into groups and for shared styles of social life in this community. Basic roles, as opposed to those which are more general or independent, are defined by one anthropologist as those which allow the broadest prediction to others.[19] The more basic a role, the more it permits predictions to other roles in the individual's repertory. In these terms, sex and political identification are the most basic roles at Les Floralies. A resident's sex is a strong basis for predicting participation in groups and activities, the likelihood of having many friend and neighbor roles inside the community, and whether or not daily routines are likely to include leaving the residence. If a resident is a Communist, it is predictable that other roles will include participation in relatively few formal groups, either for work or leisure. Participation in the community is more likely to be through more informal roles of friendship and mutual help. Role partners will also tend to include more people from outside the residence.

Both sex and political identification are important principles of social organization in this community. However, they are not related to each other. There is no pattern of women being Communist or men being pro-Beliveau.[20]

Distinctions between *ascribed* social characteristics which are acquired at birth, such as sex or kinship affiliation, and *achieved* characteristics which are acquired through later activities, such as marital status or political allegiance, are central to most studies of social organization. An unusual quality of a community such as Les Floralies is that people are "born into" it as adults. Characteristics which are normally considered achieved may, in the context of the residence, look very much like those which are usually seen as ascribed. Individuals arrive in the community with these identities and do not change them throughout their lives inside. Although it may become more salient to a person inside the residence, and although it may acquire meanings distinct to this community, recognition as being pro- or anti-Communist has the unavoidable and immutable qualities of ascription.

Ascribed characteristics typically classify all members of a community. Everyone can be assigned to a sexual or kinship category; unclear or unidentified cases are rare and are usually considered serious social problems. The case of basic roles is similar. Because these are by definition roles which permeate an individual's participation in a community, it is unusual to find many "unclassified" people. Those which exist should have difficulty taking part in social life. Sex clearly fulfills the requirements of ascription and basic role at Les Floralies. If it is appropriate to extend these terms to political identity, it should also be a basis for categorization of a large majority of the residents, and should be correlated with social participation.

Three-fourths of the residents (72.5 percent) have a clearly recognized political identity. The clarity or strength of this identity is positively related to many measures of social participation: work, visiting with other residents,[21] and general level of social activity inside the residence, as well as to social status (see table 3).

Table 3   Strength of Political Identification, by
                 Possession of a Work Role, Visiting with
                 Residents, Internal Interaction, and
                 Social Status

	Strength of political identification
Possession of a work role	.17* (121)
Visiting with residents	.32** (65)
Internal interaction	.50*** (126)
Social status	.66*** (126)

Sample sizes in parentheses
*Significant at the .05 level
**Significant at the .01 level
***Significant at the .001 level
NOTE: The variables are measured in the following way:
   Strength of political identification is a score based on my observations of the extent to which an individual was identified by other residents as being aligned with either the Catholic-Socialist coalition or the Communist opposition. A high score indicates that an individual was clearly identified; medium that he or she was partially or vaguely identified; low that he or she was not identified at all.
   Possession of a work role is defined both by participation in work activities and by identification by other residents as having a work role. High score indicates that, according to

my observations, an individual works regularly and is clearly identified in a work role. Medium indicates that an individual works occasionally when needed, and identification as a worker is not strong. Low indicates that a person never or very rarely works and is not identified with a work role. (Although participation in work and recognition of that participation are conceptually distinct, I observed no cases where that distinction was made, so the two dimensions have been combined.)

Visiting with other residents is an index based on responses to two questionnaire items: a) When was the last time you visited another resident? Within the last week? Within the last month? More than a month ago? b) When was the last time another resident came to see you? Same response categories. General level of *internal interaction* is a score based on my observations of both frequency and intensity of an individual's social interaction with other residents. A high score indicates either a high level of interaction or several close friends or a combination of these. Medium indicates several social contacts or at least one close friend. Low indicates few social contacts and no close friend.

Social status is a scale based on scores on my rankings of individuals according to their leadership roles, popularity, and visibility. A high score on *leadership* indicates that according to my observations an individual was often seen as a task, emotional, or opinion leader by other residents. A medium score indicates that an individual was sometimes seen as a leader; a low score indicates that he or she was rarely or never seen as a leader.

Popularity scores are based on my observations of the numbers of people by whom an individual was liked and the intensity of their expression of this attitude. Individuals were scored separately on numbers and intensity, and then the scores were combined; a high on numbers and a low on intensity would produce a popularity score of medium. Visibility scores are based on my observations of the extent to which an individual is known in the community, either by name or by an outstanding attribute or activity. Sources of social status and its measurement are discussed in detail in chapter 4.

The details of socialization into the residence which are discussed in chapter 6 will show the mechanics of these relationships: in short, new arrivals whose political identity is not recognized, or to whom it has very low salience, become social isolates. For most people, learning to participate in residence social life goes along with an increasingly clear factional affiliation. Strength of political identity is appropriately correlated with the number of months a person has been in the residence ($r = .17$, $N = 125$). Since judgments about political identity included individuals who had not been at Les

Floralies very long, the proportion of people with recognized affiliations should increase as time passes. The conflicts described in chapter 7 will demonstrate one way this happens, as each time the community is polarized by a factional battle, a few more residents are pulled publicly toward one side or the other.

Community creation, as I suggested in the first chapter, can be summarized as a process of border definition, since both internal and external borders are required to define a community. The two most important social borders inside the residence are sex and factional allegiance. Political identity marks a border which is defined more sharply, or at a higher level, because people with this characteristic not only have in common certain patterns of behavior and ideas about their collective identity, but also actually associate more with each other than with members of the other faction. Although men and women have some distinctive ways of participating in residence life, sex is not a basis for the kind of sharp break in social contact which is marked by the factional border. In the dining hall, for instance, more than twice as many tables have partners of both sexes than partners from both factions—19 out of 29 tables with men and women, as compared with 8 out of 29 with pro- and anti-Communists. This distribution is particularly striking since the numbers of men and women are far more uneven than the numbers of pro- and anti-Communists: 46 men, 81 women; 40 pro-Communists, 53 anti-Communists (33 unaligned).

For newcomers to Les Floralies, learning how to use political identity is more complex than learning how to act appropriately as a man or a woman. The social patterns which distinguish men and women inside the residence are very similar to those they have known all their lives: women sew and knit, men play cards; women visit with neighbors, men go to the cafe. Pro- or anti-Communist sympathies must be channeled into localized meanings, specific to the residence. Formal groups develop factional identities which newcomers must learn, attitudes toward work are transmitted to the new arrivals according to faction, and a continuing ebb and flow of factional conflicts provides a set of internally based landmarks which newcomers must incorporate into their definition of these political distinctions.

The existence of regular patterns of social organization, of which these internal borders are a part, is one basis for the definition of an external border between the community and a wider society. The two kinds of borders mutually reinforce each other as individuals enter the community and learn to be members. As they cross the external border, bringing with them social characteristics and experiences from their lives outside, they begin translating these into markers of the borders which organize social life inside. The definition of these borders, and the new meanings which some of them acquire, in turn reinforce the distinctiveness of the community from the outside world.

Conclusion

Social organization is not only present at Les Floralies, but also, even in this first general look, its development can be observed; social life in the residence has become both more patterned and more distinct from the world outside or the influence of the staff. The functions of the Residents' Committee have broadened and become more visible and well-defined. Work roles and participation in them have increased; and the work/leisure distinction has been sharpened as a result of confrontations such as that between the nurse and the sewing club. A central aspect of informal socializing—the significance of permanent seats in the dining room—has become explicitly recognized and is defended by residents against staff efforts at "mixing." Most basic to social life in the residence, factional borders are progressively being more sharply defined in terms of activities, personalities, and attitudes which have meaning only inside the residence.

The forces for community formation observed in utopias, among squatters, and within and across nations, are already visible here. The general level of participation is high, and residents share a very wide range of kinds of social contacts with each other. Participation in daily meals and in community-wide events, such as celebrations, is very high. Many of the informal relationships include interdependence, and those who work are acquiring attitudes of loyalty and protectiveness toward the residence. Different individuals follow different paths of participation in residence social life These paths cumulate in patterns—and in the shared experience and understanding of patterns which define the social organization aspect of community.

4 Social Status and Community Borders

Introduction

M. Beliveau, president of the committee, leader of the anti-Communist faction, well-known, widely liked, and always regarded with respect by friends and enemies, is a more important member of the Les Floralies community than shy, awkward Mme. Arnaud, who rarely leaves her room except to come to meals on the arm of her "cavalier." Mme. Dupont, who inspires the Communist faction, Mme. Thibault, and Mme. Beliveau are others widely recognized as prominent or powerful, sometimes with approval, sometimes with bitter resentment against "big wheels" or "people who think they're important."

There are differences in social status in the residence. A status system is one aspect of the social organization which is defined during the development of a new community. The relationship of the emerging internal status system to the ranking principles current outside the new community gives a particularly revealing view of its distinctiveness and autonomy. The problems for this chapter are to define the differences in social status at Les Floralies; to discover the ways individuals acquire higher or lower standing; and to compare sources of status inside the residence and outside. The third problem is derived from one of the first questions which occurred to me about residences for older people, the possibility that a community of the old might offer insulation from negative stereotypes of age current in the outside society. If old age is a source of low status outside the residence, it might be the same inside, it might be reversed to a source of high status, or simply made irrelevant. Put in more general terms, this question can be asked about other sources of status such as sex, health, occupation, or income, to give another perspective on the border between the residence community and the society outside.

Ranking is central to the concept of status. The problem for research in any particular community is the basis of this ranking:

in terms of what characteristics are members of the community ranked? A standard answer for the question is now widely used in studies of western, industrial societies. In these settings, social status is usually measured by some combination of income, education, and occupation. At Les Floralies these distinctions are to a great extent eliminated by the homogeneity of its population in terms of all three.

There are virtually no differences in educational background among retired CNRO members and, consequently, none at Les Floralies.[1] However, there is a range of specific occupations within the building trades, and, especially to those closely involved, ditchdiggers certainly might be considered inferior to master masons. There are also people with enough money to pay their own way at the residence, and others who had to turn their pensions over to a public assistance agency in order to come in. In the first months we lived in the community, as it became clear that there were differences in ranking at Les Floralies, I paid close attention to possible correspondences between social position in the residence and former job or present income. They seemed to be minimal. The most dramatic cases are very prominent people whose occupation and income would have suggested a lower status, and the reverse, those whose work and income should produce a higher position than the one they have. Mme. Dupont worked all her life as a maid and cleaning woman. She claims that she learned about politics by scrubbing floors at Paris city hall. M. Rigoulot, on the other hand, was a skilled worker, has an unusually high income, and pays his own costs in the residence, but is among the lesser known and unimportant members of the community. These examples are chosen for their contrast, but they are not at all unique. Several months of encountering many others like them began to persuade me that occupation and income are not the crucial signals for different statuses in the community.

Listening to residents talk about each other and watching them obtain information about newcomers added more evidence. Income and occupation are not essential categories for people's perceptions of each other. Residents rarely know each other's incomes, and except for the vague notion that there are a few rich people, mostly unidentified, who pay for themselves, the shared assumption about finances is that everyone is poor. In this domain, the emphasis is more on common problems than on fine distinctions. Residents are much more likely to know about a person's previous job. Questions about this are common conversation starters, especially with new residents. However, unless it leads to discovery of mutual acquaintances, this information does not seem to have any consequences for social contacts, much less for ranking. The information which the conversation really hopes to uncover, in most cases, is political identification as revealed by union membership. Education is very rarely discussed, and information about other residents' educational experiences is almost nonexistent. Most people assume that another thing they have in common is the fact that they do not have much schooling.

Measuring Social Status at Les Floralies

The next step was to try to induce the qualities shared by residents who are prominent. What is it about M. Beliveau, for instance, that makes him stand out? What does he have in common with Mme. Dupont, who in so many other respects is not only his opposite but his persistent enemy? People know who they are, to begin with, which is already a distinction in this community. Others also have strong feelings about them and for each there are many residents who feel affection, gratitude, and loyalty. One reason for this is another of their common attributes. Residents with a problem, or a question, often stop by Beliveau's or Dupont's tables at noon, or if privacy is required, go to their apartments for comfort or consultation. Broken radiators, a noisy neighbor, the threat of being moved to the semi-invalid floor, all send residents to them. Any situation seen as an emergency, from an earthquake to a priest in the laundryroom, brings people to look for direction from these two. They are both also widely regarded as interpreters of residents' needs and protectors of their rights vis a vis the administration. "He really stands up to them," is the almost universal compliment for M. Beliveau.

Visibility, popularity, and leadership summarize the characteristics shared by Beliveau and Dupont and, used to describe all the other less extreme social differentiations in the residence, these three attributes provide an appropriate measure of social status for this community. Visibility refers to being known and recognized, either by name or by some outstanding characteristic. Most residents have trouble remembering names, but refer to certain individuals consistently by such labels as "white cap" or "the sailor." Visibility can have many sources: the community drunk is as well-known as the president. Being recognized is not sufficient to produce high status, but no one has high status without it. Popularity means being liked, either by a large number of residents, or very intensely by a few. Mme. Charriere, who makes her rounds of greeting every noon, is always talked about with affection. She is outstanding in the community because she is so much loved, but she is not relied on as a leader. Leadership is both formal and informal here: M. Beliveau has a formal leadership role on the committee, for instance, while Mme. Dupont has no formal position of any kind, although a large number of residents come to her for advice and follow her into conflict with other residents or with the director. While the individuals who have the very highest status in this community are visible, popular, and leaders, others reach relatively high levels by different combinations of these three qualities.

In addition to widely used measures of social status, certain methods of determining the ranks of various individuals according to these measures are commonly used by social researchers who work in industrial societies. These methods seemed no more appropriate than the measures for use at Les Floralies. In order to elicit people's judgments of the relative social positions of different individuals, it is obviously necessary to ask them to talk specifically about these people, either in response to their names or to their photographs. Several months of living in the residence left me ominously certain that asking people here to make this kind of comment, particularly as I wrote it down, would lead, first, to bad information and, second, to catastrophe for the rest of the research.

For example, asked to rank photographs of other residents, most people would first of all have wanted to know why I wanted this information. Since they assumed I knew who was important and who wasn't, as I had lived in the community for so long, they could only conclude that I really wanted to know something about *them*, rather than about the people in the photographs. The next question would be, who is she going to tell? For the more fearful, this would be a general concern that if they said something negative about the wrong people they might fall into that vague but dangerous state called "getting into trouble." For most people in this factionalized community, the assumption would be that I was working for "the others," making some kind of political scorecard. Many people also have ambivalent feelings about the existence of ranking in the residence. In theory they talk about it as unjustified and inappropriate, and a threat to the harmony of the community, although in practice they obviously find it useful or even pleasant. In a formal interview these people would most likely refuse to admit the existence of status differences.[2]

Although information about ranking at Les Floralies seemed unobtainable through formal interviews, it was not unavailable. In casual conversations, in daily social encounters, and in reactions to crisis, residents gave abundant evidence for observation of their visibility, popularity, and leadership. These three characteristics were among those on which I rated every resident, and each individual's social status was then defined as his or her total score on these three dimensions.[3] I gave each person a score of high, medium, or low on visibility, popularity, and leadership in the following way. A high score on leadership meant that an individual was often seen as a task, emotional, or opinion leader by other residents. A medium score indicates that the person was sometimes seen as a leader; and low meant that he or she was rarely or never seen as a leader. Mme. Thibault, for example, has a high score as a leader. Not only has she been elected twice to the committee, she also directs the "gerontology" workers, and is sought out by many residents when they need help or information. M. Gillet, the "husband" of Mme. Joly, who has never had a formal authority role, is sometimes seen as a leader. He has a medium score because in several crises people turned to him: the other residents on his floor when the heating failed and when a CNRO party on the fourteenth floor kept them awake; a wider group of residents, when the election conflict broke out. However, after each of these events, he withdrew from leadership, and has never been identified this way on a community-wide basis.

Popularity scores reflect the numbers of people who like an individual and the intensity of their expression of this attitude. I rated everyone separately on numbers and intensity and then combined the scores. A high on numbers and a low on intensity, for instance, would produce a total of medium. The mailman has a high score on popularity because many people talk about him as someone who is nice and kind and helpful. He is also part of a couple, and in addition has a permanent place with his male friends at the afternoon *belote* game. A person who does not "go out" much to residence public events, but who is very much liked by a few friends who visit in her apartment to knit or watch television has a score of medium. M. Richard gets the same rating because of the affection of two people: the woman he helps to the dining room and the other table partner, who irons his shirts. People can have a low score on popularity either because they are disliked by many people, like the explosive Picards, or because they are not known, like Mme. Arnaud, whose one regular social contact is with M. Richard, who helps her as a good deed, and not because he likes to be with her.

Visibility means standing out from the crowd in the residence, being known and recognized by many people. People are highly visible for various reasons: as community leaders, such as Mme. Thibault; as enemies from the point of view of one faction, such as Mme. Dupont from the Beliveau perspective; because of a physical handicap, such as the deaf-mute or the blind woman; because of ethnic background, such as the one Cuban; or because of bizarre behavior, such as "the sailor" asleep in the flower bed after a hard night's drinking. The lowest scores on visibility identify residents who are recognized only by neighbors on their hall, table partners, and a few others with whom they have direct contact in formal or informal activities. On a community-wide scale, someone like M. Richard, for instance, is invisible. In a conversation with other residents it would be extremely difficult to describe him, physically, by name, or in terms of his behavior, so that they could place him as an individual. People with medium scores are known outside the sphere of their immediate friends and neighbors, but not by everyone in the community. Residents who work often have this level of visibility, because repairing electricity or weeding the garden brings them into occasional contact with, or at least into the line of vision of, many other residents.

These ratings on visibility, popularity, and leadership add up to total social status scores for each resident. Counting three points for a high rating, two for medium, and one for low, the highest possible score is nine. Twenty-eight residents whom I identify as having high status have scores between six and nine, which means they have at least a medium rating on all three characteristics. Most of these (twenty-one out of twenty-eight) have at least one high score. Forty-eight people have low scores on visibility, popularity, and leadership; they have the lowest status in the residence, with total scores of three. The medium category includes fifty residents who have total scores of four or five; they all have at least one low rating, balanced by at least one medium or high (see table 4).

People have high status at Les Floralies as community leaders, and as the followers most closely associated with them or as heroes

Table 4 Distribution of Social Status Scores

Status scores			Number of cases	Status style
High (6–9 points)				
Leadership	*Visibility*	*Popularity*		
high	high	high	5	Leaders
high	medium	high	1	
high	medium	medium	3	Satellites
medium	medium	medium	6	
medium	high	medium	4	Heros
medium	medium	high	4	
low	high	high	1	
medium	high	high	3	
medium	high	low	1	
Total high status			28	
Medium (4–5 points)				
Leadership	*Visibility*	*Popularity*		
low	medium	medium	13	Affection
low	low	medium	12	
low	high	low	9	Notoriety
low	medium	low	14	
medium	medium	low	2	
Total medium status			50	
Low (3 points)				
Leadership	*Visibility*	*Popularity*		
low	low	low	25	Independence
low	low	low	12	Withdrawal or Rejection
low	low	low	11	New Residents
Total low status			48	

This table is based on 126 residents because no score was assigned to the one person who died during the study

who are known and loved but not regularly turned to for leadership. Although residents have different status scores for various reasons, the routes into each category are not unlimited. Not all the possible permutations of visibility, popularity, and leadership scores appear; there are a few distinct patterns which produce each

level of social status. The five residents with the very highest score
(9) are all political leaders: the two Beliveaus, Mme. Thibault,
Mme. Dupont, and another militant Communist woman. The
people who are their "satellites," deriving their status by association, typically have moderate scores on all three characteristics,
which also adds up to high status. M. Lapierre, for example, is a
neighbor of M. Beliveau and also eats at his table in the dining
room. He became a member of the committee in the second election
through the influence of Beliveau. Most residents in fact do not
know his name, but refer to him as "the man who eats with
Beliveau." The heroes are people like the mailman or Mme.
Charriere, who are well-known and popular but not leaders. They
have high scores on visibility or popularity or both, and, typically,
medium scores on leadership, as some people turn to them occasionally but not with the consistency or in sufficient numbers to
give them a high rating.

Gracious Mme. Demougeot, who presides with pride over her
Tuesday *salon*, and Mme. Barret, who is so gruff she can't keep any
other residents at her table in the dining room, both have a medium
level of social status. They represent the two patterns of scores
which produce a medium level, which might be labeled notoriety
and affection. Almost half the people in this category (twenty-three
out of fifty), like Mme. Barret, are there because they are visible,
although not necessarily liked and not seen as leaders. The sailor,
M. Fortin with his prostitute, the deaf-mute, and the Cuban do not
have high status; visibility alone is not enough. None of them,
however, are nobodies in this community, and it is this kind of
importance as someone distinctive or as someone whose behavior,
although often disapproved of, makes broad waves in the community, which is reflected in the notoriety pattern of medium
status.

Mme. Demougeot, on the other hand, is joined by half (twenty-
five out of fifty) the residents with medium status in a pattern of
popularity accompanied by either low or medium visibility, depending on the person's range of contacts. Mme. Tissot, who bustles in
and out of many work activities, and who, although not a leader, is
unusually active in the Communist political faction, is better
known, for instance, than Mme. Demougeot. What they share is
the fact that they are very much liked by the people with whom
they come into contact.

The only two exceptions to notoriety and affection as types of medium status are two individuals who have more than a low score on leadership. They are recognized as leaders, since they both have been elected to the committee. However, they have low ratings on popularity because they are considered unreliable and unsuccessful leaders, have very bad tempers, and chase women; one of them also cheats at cards. They can be included, without distortion, in the notoriety pattern.

Low status is a negative category: individuals are in it because they are not visible, are not leaders, or are not popular. However, people are in this position for different reasons, and their reactions to it differ sharply. Some have low status in the community basically as a result of positive choices. Because of satisfaction with a long-time pattern of very little social involvement, or to protect their strong desire for independence, over half of these people (twenty-five out of forty-eight) do not participate actively in residence social life, either formal or informal, and are consequently not as well known as others. In short, they are not important in community social life because community social life is not of high importance to them.

One very unhappy resident, widowed just a few months before entering the community, represents another pattern of low status, one with more negative roots. M. Gernot cannot sleep at night for thinking about his wife's death. He finds the luxury of the residence incongruous to his emotional suffering. He does not like to be alone, but he feels alienated to the point of bitterly criticizing other residents who seem too happy. He often sits in the corner of the lobby or the fourth-floor lounge, flipping pages in a magazine and watching other people. If anyone speaks to him, his responses are startled and abrupt. Most people do not know his story and think he is simply a rather mean and unpredictable little man, very difficult to talk to.

There are twelve individuals who have low status because they are withdrawn through unhappiness, illness, or severe fear and suspicion of others. Mme. Denis, for instance, who was afraid to answer the questionnaire because it might cause trouble for her children, explains that it is much better to stick to yourself because other people gossip and start trouble. "You just can't trust anyone; it's better to stay in your room and keep out of trouble." She works in the laundry because she can do that alone; and the laundress says that if someone else arrives while Mme. Denis is there, she runs away. Four of the residents with this pattern of low status are very frail and chronically sick. Three of these are married and spend a great deal of time in their rooms where their husbands take care of them.

Finally, eleven residents with low status scores had been in the community five months or less; several of them much less. They certainly may acquire higher status as they become more well-known.

Sources of Social Status at Les Floralies

With a language for talking about social status in this community established, and with every resident ranked in these terms, it is possible to ask questions about sources of status at Les Floralies. Once the important people have been identified, the next question is why they are important. What else do they have in common which might explain their position? Are they older, are they men, are they Communists, etc.? A community like Les Floralies, embedded in the context of a wider society, poses questions about the sources of social status in a way which focuses on the border between it and its external setting. As sources of status are identified, those which are internal to the residence can be distinguished from those which are derived from the outside.

The possible relationships between the internal social organization of a new community and the social organization of its external context can be expressed as three patterns: (1) The inside social organization may be as far as possible a reflection of the external. Inmates of a women's prison in West Virginia, for instance, recreated a detailed version of the American kinship system—including spouses, children, brothers and sisters, cousins, aunts, and uncles.[4] The internal social organization of this kind of community may also represent (2) a reaction against some aspect of the outside world, in particular the significance given by outsiders to the characteristic in terms of which the embedded community is homogeneous. Its significance would then be reversed into a "first shall be last and last shall be first" pattern. For example, Hutterites have organized independent communities called *Brüderhof*, where members of the sect live in a communal, pacifist way. The social organization of a *Brüderhof* is explicitly dedicated to overcoming the individualistic, materialistic, and violent values which Hutterites feel dominate the wider American society.[5] (3) The outside significance of a social characteristic may also be simply refused in a pattern which makes the characteristic relatively irrelevant to internal social life. For example, in a condominium residence for retired people in northern California, community members exerted strong pressure against attempts to make external social status relevant to life in the residence. One man insisted on calling attention to his wealth by combining two housing units into one. He also demanded respect on the basis of his previous occupation as a stockbroker. Other residents deposed him from a position on the elected governing committee, and explained their action by saying that he "tried to live in the past" and threatened the harmony of the community in the present.[6] At Les Floralies, looking at such plausible external sources of status as age, seniority, health, contacts with family and friends outside the residence, and former roles such as occupation and political identification, leads to the conclusion that in this community pattern 3 predominates: external sources of status are for the most part irrelevant inside the residence.[7]

Age

Mme. Charriere is often called *"la doyenne,"* which means that she is the oldest person in the residence, and when people talk about her they usually mention that she is ninety. Since she has very high status in the residence, her position suggests that old age may be given the opposite of its external valuation here, so that in a kind of gerontological millennium the oldest become the most important (support for hypothesis 2). However, the table of correlations (table 5) shows that this is not true; advanced age is not related to high status. Of course, Mme. Charriere is living evidence that the reverse is not the case either, since youth certainly is not a prerequisite of status. What the table indicates is that these old people have escaped one aspect of aging in the wider society by making it irrelevant to social status in a community where everyone is old. Mme. Charriere's age probably is related to her status not directly, but as a vehicle to visibility. Since she was the first resident to turn ninety, the director organized a birthday party for her, complete with champagne, a cake assembled out of enough cream puffs to serve the entire community, and dancing after lunch.

Health

One eighty-year-old woman shuffles her painful way every morning to a chair near the dining room door, her worn flannel robe always contradicted by the beret that shows she is "dressed." Although she shouts insults at everyone who sits in the chair she claims as hers, or who puts her in a draft by leaving open the door into the hall, "La Mama" is surrounded by an attentive group of residents before and after every meal. Rather than being a source of isolation or low status, her frailty may help explain her prominence. Since she cannot wash or dress herself or clean her own apartment, she needs a great deal of care from the staff, and the subject of many conversations in the group gathered around her every day is the latest gossip she has pried out of the nurse who

Table 5   Sources of Social Status

	Social status	Sample size
Age	.03	126
Self evaluation of health	.14	73
Contact with family	.07	45
Contact with friends outside residence	.11	67
Leaving residence	.11	120
Possession of work role	.34***	121
Months in residence (as of July 1970)	.13	126
Strength of political identification	.66***	126
Factional allegience	−.03	126
Visiting with residents	.34**	65
Formal group participation	.25**	121

*Significant at the .05 level
**Significant at the .01 level
***Significant at the .001 level
NOTE: The measures for the categories given in this table can be found in chapter 3, notes 1, 3, 5, 6, 7, 8 and 11.

dressed her that morning. Hours spent at her station in the lobby also add to her store of information. Residents often use "La Mama" to transmit messages to each other; and those who do not volunteer information are closely observed or cleverly interrogated.

Excellent health has been proposed as a plausible attribute of status among retired people and could also be derived logically from the hypothesis of external sources for internal social organization.[8] At Les Floralies this relationship between health condition and social status does not appear. Residents' evaluations of their own health in comparison with that of others in their age group are not correlated with social status (table 4), which suggests that external values about health are neither reflected nor reversed inside the residence; again, they seem irrelevant.

This is not explained by lack of knowledge about health. Differences in physical condition are often visible; they are also emphasized by the spatial separation of the nonhousekeeping floors. People's attitudes about their own health are also usually well known, as this is a frequent topic for conversation. "How are you?" "I'm fine," is often used by sociolinguists as a classic example of phatic communion, communication which expresses solidarity but does not convey information; the inappropriateness of a serious response to the inquiry is blatant in most communities. Les Floralies is the first place I had ever lived where "How are you?" is not a ritual question. Here the answer is more likely to be the basis for a detailed conversation about a subject which is of deep and shared concern to residents.

One reason that good health is not a basis of high status may be similar to the reason that youth is not. Most people here assume that various physical problems are part of the difficulties of aging. Taking this as the norm, the individuals who enjoy excellent health are seen as lucky, but not better. People who are disapproved for reasons connected with health are in two categories: the super spry and the unrealistic. The busy vice-president is an example of someone who takes every opportunity to show that he is vigorous and active. In a discussion of aging after lunch one day he stood on his hands on a chair to demonstrate his spryness. This kind of over-concern with demonstrating good health is considered by many other residents to be silly, and a little embarrassing when it takes place in front of strangers. It most emphatically is not a source of high status.

On the other hand, people who are unwilling to accept physical limitations, and who try to do things which are beyond them, are sometimes criticized for being a burden to others. The arrival of a new person with an extreme physical handicap is sometimes a source of fear that the residence will get an institutional image. The extent of mutual help among residents points up the ambivalence of these feelings. Not surprisingly, they vary according to relationships with these individuals. If they are friends or political allies, they are helped. Less well-known residents, seen from a distance, may be severely criticized, so harshly that it occurred to me they may embody deep-rooted fears about physical decline. Of the two ways of responding to these fears, support is offered to friends and allies and rejection aimed at strangers and enemies.

"La Mama" also suggests that access to information through unusually frequent contact with staff members or constant observation of other residents may balance or cancel out some of the disadvantages of physical disability and promote both popularity and a role of informal leadership.[9]

Contact with the Outside

People from the outside coming in and people from the inside going out are two tangible measures of external influences on internal social status. These kinds of direct contact with the outside world, either through leaving the residence or through guests coming in, were observed as a source of social status, for example, in an American retirement community.[10] At Les Floralies people leave the residence to visit friends and family, to go shopping, to get a drink, or to enjoy a walk. Guests come into the residence to see relatives and friends, especially on Sundays and holidays. However, being in touch with people outside the residence does not provide social status inside it. Reports of contact with family or friends, as well as my observations of the physical fact of leaving the residence, are all unrelated to social status (table 5).

Previous Roles

A common stereotype of residents in retirement communities is that they are waiting out leftover lives. They are seen as frozen into the roles they had before entering the new residence, and they are consequently expected to struggle to maintain these social identities inside it. In terms of the hypothesis that the major sources of internal social organization in an embedded community are external, roles which individuals acquired before moving in should be important sources of internal status. Since wide class differences do not exist at Les Floralies, the only occupational identifications available are specific jobs within the construction trades. No former jobs consistently provide higher prestige inside the residence than others. The individuals with formal leadership roles have not had more skilled occupations; and previous jobs do not predict to the other attributes of high status—popularity and visibility.[11] A more general application of the relationship between occupation and status does appear at Les Floralies, but in the present tense rather than in the past. Taking work roles inside the community gives higher status than the more complete "retirement" of participation in only social and recreational activities (table 5).

Seniority

The first residents moved into Les Floralies before construction was completed. Since the residence was opened in December, the first thirty arrivals spent an intimate Christmas, including a much-recounted meal for which the head nurse herself peeled the potatoes. The difficulties and the solidarities of these shared early days in the community make some of the people think of themselves as pioneers. When it was time to choose participants for a trip to Berlin offered by a West German minister who had visited Les Floralies, these "old-timers" protested loudly against the idea of a lottery. They claimed that they deserved to go more than newcomers to the residence. Seniority in an organization is often used as a source of prestige and power in the society outside the retirement community. It has also been observed, combined with age, as a source of popularity in an American home for Episcopalian women.[12] Appeals to seniority as a basis for priority are consequently a plausible strategy but are almost totally unsuccessful at Les Floralies. Only the very newest residents seem to be influenced by these demands. One recently arrived couple, for instance, felt obliged to buy drinks for the more senior residents during the trip to Berlin in order to show their appreciation for being chosen to go in spite of their newness in the community. In general, however, length of time in the residence has no significant relationship to social status (table 5).

Factional Identification

The highest status in this community is reserved for the most militant members of the two political factions, and some of this importance rubs off on other people who are in closest association with them. People like Mme. Thibault and Mme. Dupont bring to life the statistic which shows that the social characteristic with the strongest correlation to social status is political identification (table 5). Forty-four percent of the variance in social status is explained by this one social fact. Mme. Thibault and Mme. Dupont are most vehemently not members of the same faction, which is a reminder that the correlation with social status is of the strength or clarity of political identification, not its direction. People whose pro- or anti-Communist or pro- or anti-Beliveau allegiance is well-known are likely to have higher status than those whose loyalties are apparent only to a few other residents or only in times of extreme conflict.

Conclusion

The sources of social status at Les Floralies are inside the community and in the present. In terms of the three hypotheses about embedded communities, most of the possible external sources of status, including youth and physical vigor, become irrelevant here, rather than reflected or reversed. When the community is looked at from the inside, in its own terms, the residents who are most visible, popular, and most likely to be seen as leaders have in common more frequent visits with other residents, more participation in organized activity, and a greater tendency to have jobs in the residence (table 5). Another characteristic shared by residents with high status, clearly recognized political identification, is derived from past life outside the residence, but acquires distinctly internal meanings and functions.

Correlations between two variables, such as social status and work, or social status and visiting, are always vulnerable to misinterpretation precisely because they only concern two variables at a time. The influence of a third factor on both might be responsible for the apparent relationship between them. In a setting such as Les Floralies where one characteristic—political identification—is so strongly correlated with status, it is important to make sure that other factors which seem to be linked to status actually vary with it independently and not because they are also related to political identification.

The correlations between formal group participation and status and between work roles and status are still significant when the possible influence of political identification is controlled. Visiting and social status, however, do not vary together independently of the clarity of factional allegiance. People who have stronger political identifications are likely to report more frequent visiting with other residents ($r = .31$, $N = 65$), and they are also likely to have higher scores for social status ($r = .66$, $N = 126$). The apparent tendency of people who visit frequently to have higher status is due to the influence of the political variable on both. When this influence is removed, through partialling, the correlation between status and informal participation disappears into insignificance. Although both work roles and participation in formal groups are related to political identification, they also contribute independently to variation in social status.[13]

Understanding why people are important at Les Floralies requires an understanding of how a recognized factional affiliation, participation in organized activities, and a job in the residence are related both independently and in combination to the visibility, popularity, and leadership which indicate social status. The relationship between a strong political identity and high social status is rooted in the factional character of social life in the community. People whom a resident likes and trusts are usually those who share his or her pro- or anti-Communist feelings. Popularity is consequently typically acquired within a faction. Leadership is both gained and exercised in a factional context. Elections are explicitly and energetically fought in terms of factional allegiance, and the residents with high scores as either formal or informal leaders are all factional militants. Faction activity is also associated with visibility. Organized groups acquire factional identities; major events, from dances to decorating for Christmas, are a focus for factional battles; factional conflicts involve many residents, attract wide attention, and place heroes and villains in the community spotlight. If someone is widely seen and well known in the residence, one of his or her most visible attributes will be political identity.

The correlation between clarity of political identity and social status, like any correlation, indicates co-variance, not causality. It does not tell us if a clear political allegiance is a source of high status, or if high status is a basis for strengthening political identity.

Both patterns are plausible. An individual with a strong and widely recognized factional allegiance would be more likely to become a leader, to be visible, and to be liked than someone whose loyalties are unclear. On the other hand, given the polarized nature of the community, someone who acquires the attributes of high status is under great pressure to choose sides and make his or her political sympathies unambiguous.

The data which have been presented here are cross-sectional, that is taken from one moment in time. Additional information about the relationships between political identification and social participation is available from observation of thirty new arrivals in the residence over a period of several months (see chapter 6). The combination of these two kinds of evidence shows that the causal arrows between political identity and social status can be drawn in both directions. The essential fact derived from the correlations and from the case studies of socialization is that there is a strong tendency for these two characteristics to be in congruity.

Political Identity as a Source of Status, and Status as a Source of Political Identity

Most new arrivals are at least tentatively recognized as potential recruits to a faction. On the basis of cues about their political sympathies, members of the appropriate faction become their guides into formal and informal social contacts. As they associate with faction members and become known both by them and, from a distance, by other residents, their political allegiance becomes progressively more distinct. If eventually they become liked, well known, and respected or suspected as leaders, it will be as widely recognized members of this faction.

More rarely, a new resident is not recognized as pro- or anti-Communist until he or she has become active enough in a job or in organized groups such as the sewing club or the pottery class to acquire relatively high status on this basis. When this happens, the persistence of factional conflict will make it extremely difficult for such a person to maintain both prominence and neutrality or ambiguity. The former vice-president is an unhappy witness to the consequences of prolonged attempts to perform this balancing act. He was elected to the first Residents Committee a few weeks after the residence opened. He became well known in the community for that reason and also because he always went along with the chauffeur to pick up new residents and inevitably appeared at their doors with his tool kit to help them move in. When we arrived in the residence, his status scores would have been consistently high. However, after he was defeated in the elections which took place during our stay, he rapidly withdrew from almost all residence activities, with many bitter mutterings about ingratitude and injustice. The reason for his nosedive in prestige is his lack of factional identity. He was a persistent rival of the president and never belonged to his faction. On the other hand, even in the depths of resentment or the heights of competition, he never aligned with Mme. Dupont and the Communists. As factional identities became progressively crucial to the organization of social life in the community, he was simply squeezed out to the sidelines.

The people who are important at Les Floralies show by their behavior that the residence is important to them. They participate in residence activities, work at residence jobs, and are clearly identified with the factions which organize residence social life. The residents with highest status scores are also most likely to reveal the importance of the community to them by making judgments about individuals or ideas in terms relevant to the community rather than the world outside, to express strong emotion in their attitudes toward the residence, to be extremely loyal or extremely critical $(r = .61, N = 122)$.[14]

Social status offers another perspective on the mutual reinforcement of internal and external borders which define the emerging residence community. Factional allegiance, derived from the most important social border inside the residence, is in turn the most important factor in a system of social ranking whose essentially internal sources are another basis for definition of an external border between the community and the society outside.

5 Development of Community Norms

Introduction

"After all, we are here for the rest of our lives." This kind of remark is frequent at Les Floralies, more often as a battle cry than as a sigh of despair. It usually precedes an expression of fierce concern about some community issue. Most residents are here for the same reasons; they are old, retired, working class, poor, and feel that they have virtually no place else to go. Their stage in life as well as their social and financial situations give them many specific problems and experiences in common, as well as a general sense of final commitment to life in this residence. Shared symbols and experiences from the past provide a basis for the we-feelings which are the affective aspect of community. These feelings of distinctiveness and shared fate are reinforced and developed by both the satisfactions and the frustrations of living together in the residence.

A community is defined not only by what its members do, but also by the ways they think and talk about it. Their efforts to maintain the image of it which they prefer may also unite them in efforts to defend it. The people who live there see Les Floralies as a residence, not as an institution or as a nursing home. They see residential separation, age, and retirement as appropriate markers of the border around their community and make great efforts to defend this image from being redefined into border markers of sickness and institutionalization.

The members of any community must cope with certain essential human problems: shelter, food-getting, sexual relations, death, to name a few. At Les Floralies, shared ideas about how these matters should be handled are being distilled into norms which are often distinct from those of the society outside and often different from the patterns the administration would like to impose. Sanctions have also developed to protect the community against threats to its approved definition, its financial well-being, or its physical and social order.

We-feeling and Sense of Shared Fate

"We" is often used to refer to old people, working people, and residents at Les Floralies. The old, people of our age, we old people, are common phrases. Several residents who had just referred to themselves this way, stopped as if remembering that I could not be included in the reference, and explained in an aside that it is much better to call things by their real names than to disguise them with euphemisms. "After all, we *are* old," they say, as if I might not believe it. Common age is the background for shared experience in several senses: physical age, with its pains and techniques for coping with them; social age, or stage in the social life cycle, with the emotional and financial problems of retirement and the problematic pleasures of relations with adult children; and historical age, with a common past branded by two world wars and a depression. Many conversations occur which are difficult to imagine between individuals of different generations. People sometimes roar with laughter at exchanged anecdotes about incontinence or constipation, and these discussions often conclude with a further exchange of favorite home remedies. Mme. Corneille is acquiring a reputation for her herbal recipes. Pungent analyses of certain spoiled and long-haired tendencies of the young also take place. A sigh of relief at return from a visit with the children is shared, and the distinction between profound desire for close contact with a family and the difficulties of sharing a household is immediately understood.

People of this age in France are called the generation of '14 because they were young during the first World War. Their survival of this war in which over one million French men were killed, is one of the life-marking experiences which residents share. Many of the men fought in the war, many women lost husbands to it; everyone had brothers and cousins who were killed. In the 1930s came the material hardships of the depression, which most residents lived through as heads of households struggling to feed and clothe a family. World War II and the German occupation of France took sons from some residents. For all them, it provided a pair of symbols, Vichy and the Resistance, in terms of which they still orient their lives. Although few people fought in the Resistance, and few people gave active support to Petain, almost everyone who lived through the occupation now feels that he or she made a choice between the two. This choice is used as a summary and a justification for current politics, and consequently, in this residence, for recruitment into the factions which are central to social life.

Residents at Les Floralies share above all the fact that they are survivors. They have lived through a gamut of emotional and material hardships which are rarely strung together over one lifetime. Although their political differences assign different heroes and villains to the dramas they have experienced, their griefs and their fears have the same roots, and when they celebrate they sing the same songs.

Most residents also call themselves workers, or "little people," and agree that they worked too hard, for too little money, and for the profit of others. They disagree about who is the enemy and how to fight him, but they generally agree that little people have to fight, or they end up with nothing and, often worse, they have to pay something marked on a form in triplicate in language they don't understand. The combination of being little people and being old adds up for almost everyone here to a persistent worry about money.

Concern about the financial future of the residence both promotes and expresses a sense of shared fate. When the director and the committee bought a pottery kiln, for example, many residents were very upset because the expense seemed frivolous compared to the need for essentials such as clothing. Since almost all residents have very little money, they are acutely aware of their dependence on the residence and, consequently, of the extent to which their well-being is tied to the behavior of others. They express this awareness in concern that a director who is too young and impractical may spend too much on leisure and too little on clothing, or in criticism of other residents who waste food or leave their lights on.

Given the factional division of social life here, it is not surprising that although these financial fears are widely shared, the resolutions proposed for the problem differ with political sympathies. Communists are more likely to say that the retirement fund is wealthy and should give the residence more money, since residents have worked hard all their lives and deserve to be taken care of now. Members of the other faction usually look at the situation in terms of gratitude for all that has been done for them. Instead of asking for more money, they feel that the existing budget should be spent in a sensible way and the residents should avoid wasting anything.

The general notion that the community as a whole must be

protected from certain residents who try to take advantage of being there has acquired a factional flavor. In response to a direct question about whether residents will try to take advantage, members of the Beliveau faction are more likely to say yes than followers of Mme. Dupont ($r = .25$, $N = 62$). The majority of residents agree that people who criticize are ungrateful (82 percent) and that everyone who can ought to work (66 percent). The president's supporters are more likely to agree with these statements than members of the Communist faction, showing again the tendency of the Beliveau group to express positive feelings toward the residence while excluding some of its occupants, as well as the effects of the Communist "work is exploitation" attitude.

These differences will be discussed in more detail in the chapter on community formation, where I will argue that the attitudes reflect different ways in which faction members participate in residence life. Because the committee, as well as most organized activities, is dominated by the Beliveau faction, its members feel more associated with decisions and events which have shaped the most formal, visible aspects of the status quo. The factional filter through which they view social relations makes it perfectly logical for them to feel identified with the residence community as a whole, while separating themselves from some residents who criticize and take advantage although they do not do their share of the work. Members of Mme. Dupont's faction are more likely to think of themselves as an opposition; they show no sense of personal identification with the status quo. Criticism seems to them an appropriate way to try to change things for the better, and they do not seem to make the distinction between the community as an abstract whole and some of its members, which leads to the notion that some residents will try to take advantage.

Definitions of the Residence

"I hate being called Granny; I have a name," is the way Mme. Dupont talks about the insult of being denied individuality and addresssed as a generalized old person. Although people here share many common experiences, past and present, because of their age, one of the values on which they place highest priority is individual privacy. Being at home in their own apartments is the most important protection for this privacy. They reject the notion that they live in an institution, and they emphasize the separateness of their apartments. They all lock doors, even when going to meals, and everyone carries the very large keys at all times. Many residents are unwilling to consider exchanges with other retirement communities in Europe or even the U. S. if a prerequisite for participation is allowing the foreign visitors to stay in their apartments while they are visiting another residence abroad.

M. Richard told me that he was surprised not to find more solidarity among residents—"after all, we are all workers." The evidence he gave for this lack was the fact that so few people address each other with the familiar "tu" form of the second person singular. He is correct that most people call each other "vous," which may be less an indication of no solidarity than another kind of defense against submersion of individuality into a kind of instant intimacy. People distinguish among their social relationships, and generally reserve the "tu" for those they feel are good friends. "Tu" goes with use of the first name, and most residents call each other Monsieur or Madame. Before and after every meal the dining hall is filled with choruses of Bonjour, Monsieur, Bonjour, Madame. (I was called "vous" and Mme. Jennie, a not unusual in-between form, more intimate and informal than the title and last name, but less so than the first name alone.)

Les Floralies is also seen by the people who live there as a residence, and not as a nursing home. People who do not live in the residence occasionally enter the clinic as patients in convalesence. Twice I saw the arrival of an ambulance with one of these patients greeted with hostile anxiety by residents who were in the lobby. Once a meeting of the committee was in session and M. Beliveau, watching the unloading process through the windows, and assuming that the invalid was a new resident, said they ought to just take her directly down to the basement and keep her out of sight. The other occasion produced the same kind of concern from others who said they were afraid of what the residence would turn into if people like that were let in.

"Sick people should stay in their place" is a rule which residents seem to apply in the same spirit of not allowing their community to be redefined as a place for the ill. Two women who have trouble walking, for instance, wanted to go on a trip to Amsterdam organized by the residence. Other people were extremely critical of them because they should have known their own limitations, and would place a great burden on others if they went. The underlying fear, I think, is that trips such as this might be eliminated if too many problems occurred en route. The participation of these women might threaten future outings for the others. As I suggested in the discussion of social status, the ambivalence expressed in these fears on the one hand and the strong support often given to people with physical problems on the other is probably an accurate reflection of the ambivalence these older people do feel about physical aging: between its denial whenever possible and the need to organize a response to it when it attacks you yourself or someone close. Being close to someone at Les Floralies means at minimum being in the same faction. Mme. Tatu and "La Mama" have shown the importance of factional loyalties as a source of help for ill or handicapped residents. The attacks on "La Mama" also are a reminder that the distance from which critiques of these people are launched is typically the other side of a faction border.

The anxiety which residents showed about consequences for other people if handicapped individuals were unable to keep up on a trip, also reflects their developing sense of shared fate: that the impression which certain residents give of themselves may have consequences for everyone.

Community Norms

Conflict, food, sex, and death are universal problems for which members of any community must discover resolutions in their own specific context. At Les Floralies, norms for appropriate behavior in all of these domains are being distilled out of the first few months of living together.

Conflict

They're starting trouble again is an inevitable mutual accusation during conflicts in the residence. Conflict is widely and loudly disapproved, and just as widely and loudly engaged in. Dissonance between what people say and what they do seems to be resolved by the consistent perception that it is the others who started it, and that for the good of the residence they must be opposed. Strong and ambivalent feelings about conflict are condensed into a myth that discussion of religion and politics is forbidden by the director. I never saw any evidence that this was true, but as Kluckhohn has pointed out, a basic characteristic of myth is that its truth value is irrelevant.[1] The significant fact is that this belief is widespread in the community. Like myths in other settings, this one is put to different uses by members of different categories of the population—in this case, the factions. Anti-Communists point to this rule as justification for opposition to Communist attempts to take part in formal activities in the residence: Communists are trying to play politics in the community and therefore threaten its harmony. That is why they must be excluded from authority for the good of the residence. Communists believe in the existence of the same rule, but declare that it is unjust. It denies them their rights of self-expression and must be opposed. They also occasionally simply refute accusation with accusation by saying that it is the Beliveau group that always tries to give a political interpretation to any opposition to their control of the committee and social activities. Both sides refer to the same rule, which they believe exists to prevent conflict, which they agree is a worthy goal, precisely in order to justify why conflicts must continue.

Food

It is no accident that the dining room is a central stage for social activity in this community; food is a major focus of interest for the people who live there. The great moments of their lives are associated with meals. In response to a question about how many years he or she has been married, a resident gives a menu as well as a number, listing the main events of a wedding meal which took place fifty years ago. Whenever we traveled to another region of France, residents told us before we left what we ought to eat there and catechised us when we came back to see if it was as good as they had remembered. A trip to England provoked serious concern, many stories about the horrors of sugared mayonnaise and jam with roast meat, and an offer from our next-door neighbor to pack us a lunch. Many women gave us recipes and came to our apartment to lean over our shoulders while we tried them. The importance of food in French culture, combined with experience of its extreme scarcity during wars and depressions, would be enough to explain the significance of food at Les Floralies. Cross-cultural psychological research also suggests that increased concern about food may be a universal consequence of aging, at least among men.[2]

Not everyone in this community complains, but those who do all complain about the food. Having eaten there daily for a year, I am convinced that this does not simply reflect the actual quality of the food. Surely the importance of food to these old people makes the loss of control over this aspect of their lives a painful reminder of their powerlessness and dependence in general. Their will to redress this situation inside the residence is expressed in agreement that "we have a right to demand what we want." The majority of residents agree with this statement (66 percent), and the majority of their demands focus on food.

The vehemence of many complaints about seemingly minor issues could be explained by this interpretation. In order to prevent residents from marching in to state their protest and display their overcooked or undersalted evidence directly to the chef, the committee and the director, for example, announced a rule that only committee members could go into the kitchen during meals. Angry residents now storm over to the president's table, plate in hand, to state their cases; the committee receives reports about plates not being changed after a fish course; in a general residents' meeting questions are raised about daily calorie intake.

Complaints about eating seem to provide a means of expression for more general fears about being old and about living in an institutional setting at the same time as they create a sense of solidarity among residents and an atmosphere of active resistance which helps relieve some of these fears. Although there is disagreement about who is to blame or what the solution should be, almost everyone can enjoy a good gripe session by agreeing that the rice is watery or the roast underdone.

A menu system and a buffet for hors d'oeuvres were introduced during our stay at Les Floralies. Both of these offer residents a possibility of choice which they seem to enjoy greatly. The tremendous emphasis placed on food gives a sense of choice and control in this area has more influence on general attitudes toward life here than would a similar change in other domains, such as entertainment, room decoration, or clothing. The menu system is based on previously prepared and frozen foods, so that in addition to a freshly prepared *plat du jour,* there are always at least three other main courses to choose from. Residents order the day before so that the chef knows what meals he will need on the following day. Choosing a meal, including vegetables, salad and cheese or desert, from a printed menu, while a waitress writes down the order, created a definite restaurant atmosphere in the dining room.

The buffet is set up on a round table in each section of the dining room where cold cuts, sliced tomatoes, grapefruits, artichokes, and various vegetable salads are arranged on platters. Residents serve themselves and eat this course before the main dish is brought to their tables. The major problem with this innovation is the feeling of some people that others are rushing into the dining room early to get more than their share of the best hors d'oeuvres, such as the grapefruits. The platters are now put out at the very last minute to make this strategy more difficult, and M. Beliveau stands beside the table watching people serve themselves, hoping to shame those he thinks take advantage of the system.

Fears about scarcity, and mistrust of others, are not limited to lunchtime; they also appear at breakfast and dinner. Almost all residents eat breakfast in their own rooms, so coffee, tea, chicory, chocolate, sugar, powdered milk, melba toast, jam, and butter are distributed once a month to everyone except the people without kitchens. Residents explained to me a specific set of limits for each item: one kilo of sugar, 250 grams of chicory, and so forth. During several committee meetings, the director denied the existence of these limits. Residents believe that they exist, and respect them. The origin of this belief is not clear. I once heard the head nurse mention a few sample amounts to a new resident, and she may have been the initial source, although she could also have learned about them from the residents. The striking fact about this myth is that, whatever its origin, it has been elaborated into great detail, and is extremely resistant to even the director's attempts at denial. It is apparently easy for residents to believe that food is scarce, and new residents find the system reasonable when a neighbor shows them how it works.

If people do not take more food than they think they are allowed, they also do not take less. Many cupboards contain four or five kilos of sugar, and when one woman died there were seven large boxes of melba toast on her shelves. When M. Guerillon announced that he planned to visit residents to ask their opinions about residence activities, rumors spread that he was coming to check closets for illegal hoards of food.

Distribution of breakfast foods was originally done individually. Each resident filled out an order form, and once a month the items were brought to their apartments. During our stay the director decided to change to a system in which all the food would be put in the laundry room on each floor, so that residents could take what they needed as they needed it, signing for what they took instead of ordering it ahead of time. M. Beliveau, Mme. Thibault, and another friend on the committee were horrified at this idea, and at the first meeting when it was discussed gave ominous warnings about people who would take advantage of it. Their explanation to me after the meeting was that this was another example of the director's youthful idealism, based on good intentions but dangerously impractical.

When Guerillon persisted with the idea, the president's wife, who is not on the committee, circulated a petition against the plan. She and the president live on the twelfth floor, and they told me that it was naïve to think that people on the thirteenth floor (where Mme. Dupont and several other Communists live) could be trusted not to come down and take food. At M. Guerillon's insistence, over the dire warnings of Beliveau and Thibault, and in spite of the petition, the committee agreed to try the new system for three months starting in January. The debate took place in November, and concern stayed at a high level for about three weeks. Once the plan was started in January there was very little comment about it, and it was still in operation when we left the next summer. People continued to believe in the amount limits, and M. Guerillon told me that residents did not use more food with the new system than with the old.

Food for dinner is also ordered weekly by about forty people who do not go downstairs in the evenings. Eggs, boiled ham, vegetables, fruits, cheese, and wine are brought to their apartments once a week. Residents also consider various specific amounts of food to be "legal" here. Although people cannot order unlimited amounts of food for dinner, there is in reality no strict system of amounts allowed. The business manager does the shopping at the wholesale market, and buys according to current prices and the chef's plans for the communal meals. However, residents instruct newcomers, as they instructed me, that it is permissable to have six eggs, one kilo of beans, four slices of ham, etc. They also often mention the number of francs that may be spent on each resident per week, although they do not agree on the number. Neighbors were very upset if I did not order everything to which they felt I had a right. Residents order as much as they believe they can have, and either give away or trade what they do not use, since the dinner food is too perishable to store for very long.

The mythical rules about food supplies surely have their roots in past experiences of scarcity. Their elaboration and transmission to new residents, however, are examples of the translation process

through which general shared experiences from the past are redefined into specific norms for present behavior in the new social
context of this community. The fears about abuse of an honor
system for food distribution also give another demonstration of
shared fate or all-in-the-same-boat feelings. Although factional
allegiance is the basis for distrust of specific individuals, the general
fear about waste or hoarding of food comes from awareness of
interdependence. Most residents think it is good to have rules
restricting food supply to protect the community from individuals
who might take more than their share.

Sexual Companionship and Domestic Arrangements

"I couldn't go down to the dining room for a week. I was
afraid it would show. And I was so tired." Mme. Joly is talking about the beginning of her affair with M. Gillet. They
came to visit the residence by chance on the same day, so that later
when they both moved in and took apartments on the same floor,
they felt they had already met. At first they shared the floor with
just one other person, until the other apartments gradually filled.
For a while he was the only man on the floor, so M. Gillet helped
the other residents move furniture, attach extension cords, and
generally get settled. He also invited his neighbors to come
whenever they wanted to watch his television, since at first he had
the only one. Several times, Mme. Joly asked him to sit down for a
minute after he had helped her move with something, and one day
he told her the story of his life. With tears in his eyes, he talked
about the wife he loved who died slowly of cancer. Mme. Joly
revealed her own miserable marriage to a gambler. The closeness
they were beginning to feel was first expressed the night she came
back from a visit with some pastry to share with him. He asked if
he could thank her with the traditional kisses on both cheeks. Why
don't we always do that? she replied. Little by little the kisses
moved over, until they were on the mouth; and then "all that"
began, she sighs, "and after so many years, I was overwhelmed,
and so tired, and I was afraid it would show, so I couldn't go
downstairs." M. Gillet told the same story another day. "You see,
it's a second life for us. After all, I'm 76 and Sophie is 71. We never
expected to find this kind of a relationship, which makes it very
precious."

    M. Gillet and Mme. Joly are M. and Mme Gillet to many other

residents, including the people who share their table at noon. Even residents who do not address them this way recognize them as a couple. This recognition is based on several aspects of their relationship: public companionship, shared domestic arrangements, and sexual partnership. Arm-in-arm, they appear at public events in the residence, including, of course, lunch everyday. They have also taken vacations together, for example, in a CNRO vacation center. Since they moved into Les Floralies separately, they have two apartments. As these two individuals have become a couple, however, their apartments have been transformed into one household. The doors face each other across the hallway, and they share all the rooms as it they were part of one large apartment. The kitchen is Mme. Joly's kitchen where she prepares their breakfast and dinner; the living room is his apartment; the bedroom is hers. Although they are not ostentatious, their sexual relationship is not hidden from the neighbors who know that they spend nights in the same apartment. They also sometimes tease each other about it in front of others. In a discussion of a much-read newspaper article about sex and older people, he says, snuggling her at his side, that Sophie is certainly very sensual and needs a lot of attention. As he tells us how they met, he says, "Of course we don't have the relationship you have when you're twenty." "Don't be so modest," she whispers.

"After all, the Beliveaus live together too," Mme. Joly said a little defensively, the first time we talked about her relationship to M. Gillet. The president and his "wife" are the other pair in the residence whose recognition is also based on sexual partnership as well as public companionship and a shared household. M. Beliveau and Mme. Belpois moved into the residence together and took a couple's apartment, although they had not lived together before. The double bed in the room almost made Mme. Belpois change her mind, but after a few days she asked the director to change the door plate to M. and Mme. Beliveau, which everyone in the residence now calls them. Other recognized couples at Les Floralies are known to share a household and public companionship, or only companionship, but they are never addressed as Monsieur and Madame. The assumption that there is a sexual relationship seems to be the prerequisite for this kind of recognition.

The couple which takes care of the fourth-floor garden has also created a household out of two facing apartments. The first time I visited them, the two sides of the dim corridor were linked by a band of sunlight which came in the windows of his apartment and crossed from his open door to hers. They were both in the kitchen of her apartment, sitting knee to knee peeling potatoes for the evening soup, absolutely at home. They are always seen together in public. She, however, makes a point of telling other residents, and me, that their relationship is platonic.

The mailman and his friend Mme. Viatte do not live on the same floor, and until she became so ill that they began eating dinner together in her apartment, they never went into each other's rooms. M. Clere also has a girlfriend, with whom he goes on trips and appears at meals. He delivers her newspaper to her room every day, but at least in the view of other residents this is the extent of their domestic arrangements. In all, there were six unmarried couples who had stable relationships, including, at minimum, public companionship, and in some cases domestic and sexual ties as well.

M. Gillet and Mme. Joly told us about two close brushes that they had with unhappiness because of cruel or jealous gossip. Each of them had been away visiting family at different times, and each was greeted on return by neighbors or acquaintances who told about visits the other had had from someone of the opposite sex. Luckily, they said, they had already told each other about these visits, or there might have been a moment of doubt and painful suspicions to erase. All of the couples in the community—those which formed here as well as those who were married before—feel that they are in a favored position among people their age, and they are prepared for jealousy and even attempts at homewrecking in the residence. Jealousy is always expressed in terms of present relationships, however. New couples talk very casually about their former spouses, with no hint of jealousy of each other's expression of often very fond memories. Attractive neighbors or notorious flirts in the residence, however, are a source of conflict and concern.

At the Christmas party, M. Rouget, one of the most well-known woman-chasers in the community, got very drunk and pawed his various partners like a dancing bear while his invalid wife watched from the sidelines. Several women told me about his advances to them when they first arrived in the residence. He came to their apartments to offer to help them with something, then invited them to come to his room since his wife was in the clinic. He always uses the same line, portraying himself as dedicated to his frail wife, who cannot satisfy his "natural male desires." Other residents have watched the routine long enough to recognize it. The only people who believe him, and usually briefly, are the women with whom he is currently involved. The other resident well-known for running after women is also married, so that although both of these men are widely and strongly disapproved of, it is not easy to separate disapproval for unfaithfulness from disapproval for promiscuity. Disapproval is expressed in gossip or by avoidance, but, probably because neither has triggered a community-wide conflict, it has never become the basis for stronger condemnation. Both these men, for instance, have been elected to the committee.

Less extreme flirtations are never criticized in the same way. At parties a popular event is always the rug dance, a spin-the-bottle type of game in the person who is "it" is put in the middle of a circle with a rug to put down in front of a chosen partner when the music stops. They kneel on the rug to exchange kisses on the cheek and then dance until the music stops, and the chosen person becomes the new chooser. A usually shy person suddenly sitting on someone's lap produces laughter and morning-after teasing, but not disapproval. The most extreme example of a purely sexual relationship, M. Fortin and his prostitute, is condemned not because it is sexual but because Mme. Thibault and other righteous ladies feel that this woman's presence in the residence lowers its tone. She is a threat to the well-being of the community, and it is this, rather than the fact that the danger happens to involve sex, which elicits disapproval.

Norms have developed at Les Floralies for the recognition of couples in terms of their behavior inside the residence. New arrivals learn these rules as they become acquainted with the couples, or hear others talk about them. Many residents explicitly discuss the reasons for using different rules inside the residence and outside, in particular with reference to marriage. A legal marriage is seen as undesirable because "what would the children think?" and also because the woman, if she is a widow, would lose her pension payments by marrying again. The sexual activities which are disapproved of seem to be those, such as blatant promiscuity or hiring a prostitute, which could create serious conflict in the residence or threaten its definition as a nice place to live.

Death

The first death in the residence occurred at night, and the director tried to minimize what he thought would be its depressing effect on other residents by giving it no formal recognition. No announcement was made in the dining hall; no plans were made for residents to participate in a funeral service; no one was informed of the time the hearse would arrive. Word spread in the dining hall that someone had died; versions of who and how varied by the table. In the afternoon a confused assembly took place in the lobby as residents gathered in various interpretations of formality and mourning, some in black suits or dresses, others in ordinary clothes with a hat added to mark the extraordinary occasion. Since the dead woman's family appeared, bearing a large sheaf of flowers, the general feeling that something was going to happen was confirmed, but it was completely unclear what or where. Several small expeditions set off to follow up various hypotheses of where a body might be put, and small, anxious groups of residents wandered through the halls of the clinic, and down the concrete labyrinth of the basement and heating plant, cautiously opening doors, and peeking around corners. A triumphant although properly solemn Mme. Beliveau hurried back up the basement stairs to announce that she had found "it" in a tiny room across from the laundry. A few women who heard her report first hurried down in time to see the body. Other people stationed themselves at different entrances to the residence, watching for the hearse, which appeared at the service entrance next to the laundry just after Mme. Beliveau had discovered the morgue. Several attempts to get the car up a steep ramp without losing the coffin out of the back added the final flourish of uncertainty and confusion.

The dining room, the hallways, and the lobby were agitated that evening. "I don't want that to happen to me," several people told me—"that" not being death, they specified, but a bungled, undignified funeral. The anxiety tinged with disappointment which permeated that day brings to light two basic facts about rituals. First, in a very profound sense, they give people something to do; and second, they are also, quite simply, important events. The worried people who looked for a ritual in the lobby at Les Floralies—and who later demanded it from the director—wanted the reassurance and the distraction which a ritual can provide for those who, faced with situations such as death, would otherwise have to make the terrifying admission that they are confronted by something totally beyond their control. Those who are left behind need something to do precisely because in a deeper sense there is nothing they can do. In the complaints which circulated in the days following the non-funeral, there was also a sense of having missed something. People had, after all, been cheated out of a major event because something as important as a death had gone unmarked. The fact that the desire for ritual was based on more than religious habit is made clear by the many vociferously anticlerical individuals, including the president, who expressed these feelings.

The following day, members of the community, through the committee, presented a formal request to the director for a clear procedure to be followed for announcing future deaths and for providing information about funeral services and transportation for those who want it. Later deaths were announced by President Beliveau, who went from table to table in the dining room to avoid the impersonality of the microphone. Notices were also posted on each floor, and residents who wanted to go were taken to funerals in the residence mini-bus.

The powerful reaction of residents to this first death, of course, underlines the contradictions in attitudes of younger and older people towards death. It also demonstrates how, in a new community, response to one event can become the basis for definition of a new rule for approved behavior. Given their sense of a shared fate (if her death is handled in this way, mine will be too) and their confrontation with a common problem (the close possibility of death), one death was a sufficient stimulus for demanding a norm of ritual response.[3]

Sanctions

Everyone calls M. Colette "the sailor" and he lives up to his name, wearing a yachting cap and antique blue jacket and roaring out his conversations in what he considers nautical style. He also drinks a great deal, and the morning after one party when he was discovered face down next to the fish pond in the dining room is well-remembered. Most residents know about his drinking, and although it is not approved by many people, they usually either say it's sad because he is really very nice, or they laugh at his misfortunes when under the influence. One night, however, he got very drunk and banged on the doors of two women neighbors, cursing and threatening. They told everyone how terrified they were, and the next day at noon M. Colette was put in social quarantine in the dining hall. The women who had been at his table simply left, and no one stopped to speak to him on the way in or out. After a few days, he began coming late to lunch, so that he could slip in the door and sit down without having to endure the others' walking by without a greeting. His isolation lasted about three weeks. It was ended as a few people, some particular cronies, some just soft-hearted, began to stop to chat with him. Then the two offended women sat down for a few minutes at his table and later reported to their friends that he was forgiven. Finally, after another week, Mme. Dupont and Marie moved permanently to his table. M. Colette's crime and punishment are evidence that people at Les Floralies, like members of all communities, not only make judgments about behavior they consider right or wrong, desirable or not, but they also share ideas about ways these judgments should be enforced.

"You must have eaten like animals at home if you can eat this shit," was the shouted exit line for the only people who left Les Floralies during our stay there. They worked up to this final scene through several table changes and increasingly loud complaints to neighbors and waitresses. With her crumpled, toothless witch's face, Mme. Picard and her silent husband, trailing behind to carry the napkin bag, were quickly recognized by everyone in the residence. Reactions were varied, although unanimously negative; some people were angry, some resentful, many afraid. After their grand departure from the dining room, the Picards were forbidden by the director to eat there, and although they announced loudly that they would leave the residence as soon as they could get out, it was not clear whether they decided to leave or were asked to leave. In any case, to general relief, they left. Before their departure, this couple experienced every degree of sanction available in the residence. First, they were unable to find a permanent place in the dining room. Then, residents complained to the committee, which asked the director to speak to the Picards. Finally, he expelled them from the dining room, and after this exclusion from the center stage for social interaction, they appropriately left the community altogether. The Picards were the only residents I ever saw experience this complete range of sanctions.

Public sanctions against undesirable behavior naturally involve the dining room, where the entire community comes into public contact everyday. Since table places are chosen, rejection can be expressed by leaving someone's table. Mme. Faivre, for example, is a shrill, disagreeable woman whose dark glasses and paisley turban give her the appearance of a cross, exotic bat. She sat with Mme.

Thibault and two other residents in the first dining room, and consistently ate their share of the food. Since she was on a salt-free diet, Mme. Faivre's serving was brought separately, while the others helped themselves from a platter for three. Complaining in a continuous whine about having to be on a diet, she cheated by eating from the platter as well as her special portion. Mme. Thibault spoke to her about it several times, and then one day she and the two other women left the table for good. Their reaction to Mme. Faivre's behavior was public, although it did not include, except as spectators, anyone but themselves.

The isolation of M. Colette was actively carried out by a much larger proportion of the community, since he was not only left alone, but also many people refrained from greeting him before or after the meal. The explanation for the different degree of treatment is surely the seriousness of the offense as a menace to the community. His threat of physical aggression raised the possibility for the first time of violence in the residence. Reaction against him therefore was reaction against the danger which this possibility posed for everyone in the community. Mme. Faivre on the other hand was disturbing only three people, who were able to avoid her and punish her at one blow by abandoning her table in front of everyone.

Mme. Faivre and the sailor were both punished for specific acts, and eventually were reintegrated into dining room sociability. Other residents joined M. Colette at his table; Mme. Faivre was allowed to move to a new table group. Both these sanctions were successful. Mme. Faivre was noticeably chastened, quieter and eating only her own share of food; and there were no more attacks from M. Colette, although he continued to drink heavily. Other residents are more permanently antisocial and almost continuously isolated. Mme. Barret is rude and unpleasant all the time, and although staff members "invite" various docile or new residents to her table, they always leave. The only relief to her isolation comes from Mme. Dupont, who talks to her at such social gatherings as the sewing club and helps her when she has a serious problem, such as the threat of being moved to the semi-invalid floor.

These spatial demonstrations of rejection are not always possible. They require at minimum the cooperation of the guilty person's table partners, which, since seating is based on choice, is not always available. For the more extreme reactions such as the Colette case, they must evoke concern and consensus across factional lines, unless everyone involved happens to be on the same side.

For the women who wanted to stop M. Fortin from bringing a prostitute into places, such as elevators, where they were forced into distressingly close contact with her, the dining room technique was not a possible strategy. The three other men at his table were unconcerned about his behavior, and certainly felt stronger ties to him than to the women who might have put pressure on them to move. When public isolation is not available, or when, as in the Picard case, it does not work, residents try more official channels. The complaint about Fortin was brought to the committee, which finally asked M. Guerillon to speak to him on their behalf.

When Mme. Tournier went into the kitchen to shout at the chef about her undercooked veal and then said she would slap Beliveau if he interfered, the committee asked Guerillon to write her a letter. They agreed to ask him to forbid her to go into the kitchen, with the further threat that if she did she would be excluded from the dining room altogether. The fact that her attack was on a staff member is probably the reason that an official reaction seemed appropriate. Also, the committee, by deferring to the director for the administration of these sanctions, avoided direct confrontations with other residents which might have aroused serious resentment of their putting themselves above the others.

In both cases, when M. Guerillon wrote letters the reaction was very successful. The people who received them gave up their undesirable behavior, did not express resentment at the correction, and continued their other patterns of social involvement in the community. Mme. Tournier in fact was more active in organized social life after this incident than before, as she took charge of the newly opened bar.

The Picards, the sailor, M. Fortin, and Mme. Tournier are not random examples of public sanctions; these are the only cases of this kind which I observed in a year. In private, residents express their dislike or disapproval in ways which appear in many communities: they shut their doors, turn their backs, ignore an outstretched hand, refuse invitations or never return them, place unkind remarks in a gossip channel that will be sure to deliver them to the right victim.[4] M. Rouget or the handicapped women who wanted to go on the trip got these kinds of treatment. If private means are not successful, their impact can be increased by performing them on a public stage in the dining hall, as Mme. Thibault did with Mme. Faivre. However, public sanctions, such as a "quarantine" or official letters from the director are much more rare. The cases which occurred all involved severe threat to the well-being of the community: to the physical safety of its members, to the relationship between staff and residents, to the quality of life. The rarity of these sanctions reflects the rarity of behavior anti-social enough to require them. Residents are so rarely seriously antisocial, I think, because their participation in social life depends so entirely on membership in this community. The commitment which comes from lack of alternative makes the threat of being forced to leave extremely frightening. Most residents are vague about their rights, and feel that they could be sent away from the residence. The departure of the Picards strongly reinforced this feeling, since regardless of the facts, most people perceived that the director had made them leave.

Conclusion

The community which is developing inside this residence represents a cautious alliance among individuals who find themselves in a lifeboat situation. Individually they have already survived a great deal; future survival depends on their cooperation. Their shared physical, social, and historical age is the basis both for shared symbols which make communication possible and for the shared needs which make it necessary. As members of a community they can mutually provide responses to the greatest pains of aging: physical decline, loneliness, and the loss of social roles.

The regularities of their shared social lives are already being distilled into norms distinct from rules imposed by the staff—such as those about food, death, or seating in the dining room—and from the world outside the residence—such as those about the recognition of couples. Both private and public sanctions are used to protect the community from various threats. Through gossip, avoidance, and other relatively private signs of rejection, residents try to protect the community from people they think menace it with becoming a de-individualized institution or a nursing home. Extreme conflict between residents or between residents and staff members, as well as threats to the quality or "niceness" of the residence, are sanctioned publicly.

As the factional differences in certain attitudes remind us, there are bases for persistent conflict among residents. When they do join into political combat, residents reconcile what they are doing with their feeling that conflict is dangerous for the community in much the same paradoxical way that national leaders talk about war: in order to preserve the community, that is, our image of what is good for it, we have to threaten it, that is, fight with those who have a different idea of what it should be. Conflict at Les Floralies is, in short, a further indication of the value placed on this community: it is worth fighting about.

The external border between the residence and the society outside acquires another dimension from the feelings and beliefs which residents share about living there. They view the community as a distinct way of life, they value it as a means of social and physical survival, and they try to protect it from inside and outside threats. Within this context of widely shared attitudes and beliefs, there are differences which often follow factional lines. These differences retrace the internal borders which channel feelings about the community and ways of thinking about it, as well as social participation.

6   Socialization into the Community

The first day at the residence is remembered by some as terrifying, by some with waves of sadness, by others in tired anger over expropriation from a life-time home, by some with the disbelief of sudden transplantation into a world of luxury. Although it is remembered in many ways, this first day is never forgotten. In the following months, it is reminisced over again and again in all the flashbulb detail of high emotional experience: who was in the car, what did we eat for lunch, where the driver missed a turn, first faces seen in the residence, first hours alone in the new room, what was left behind.

Several people usually arrive at the residence together. The chauffeur drives a Volkswagen mini-bus to pick up about four new arrivals at once. These early morning trips were a regular part of my year at Les Floralies. The driver, the head nurse, M. Clere (while he was vice-president), and I left the residence with a list of names and headed for the working class neighborhoods of Paris or the country villages, spread out into suburbs, which surround the city. Whether we climbed four or five flights to a tiny apartment or zig-zagged from one landmark to another trying to locate a cottage "across from the monument" or "behind the old mill," we arrived in a similar scene: an old person wearing most of his or her good clothes at once, armored against the unknown with a best suit or dress, an overcoat, gloves, hat, umbrella and an assortment of shopping bags and ancient suitcases. Most people had been waiting since dawn because they were told we were coming in the morning. They waited without knowing exactly what they were waiting for and were a little dazed when we actually appeared. There was considerable fluster and confusion as we all hurried around the suddenly empty space. Some people seemed to be trying to slow down the leave-taking, anxiously asking the nurse, item-by-item, if they would need a long list of utensils or furniture, or inviting me on a tour of their rooms. M. Richard insisted on taking us around the corner of his street so we could see how close he lived to the Elysee Palace. Others rushed down the stairs or through the courtyard and never looked back. Neighbors and children were often there for embraces and promises that things would be fine, and "you'll see, we'll come to visit."

We were usually late; either there were more people to get or we had to hurry back for lunch. So the nurse hustled people into the car as the chauffeur stowed their things, and, rather bewildered, the new residents began their first contacts with each other and with us as "representatives" of the community. Some tried to give themselves an identity as fast as possible by presenting an avalanche of details from the past: job, family, crises, vacations, moves, all jumbled together at high speed. Others focused intensely on the future with excited comments about the residence, how beautiful it was, how comfortable, how they could hardly wait to get there. Others seemed numbed into total silence by the enormity of the transition embodied in this short ride.

Arrival at the residence is planned in time for a cocktail with the committee. The director introduces the newcomers and committee members, and then the president gives a short welcoming speech. Beliveau, solid and dignified, solemnly points out the responsibilities the new residents will share for keeping Les Floralies as beautiful as it is, for example by sweeping the corridor in front of their apartments. He usually mentions the proper use of the elevators, and warns the new people about shutting the doors firmly so the cars won't be stuck on their floor. M. Clere, anxious to share the spotlight, manages to interrupt at about this point to say that they should also be very careful not to confuse the laundry chute with the garbage dump.

After a toast to the new arrivals, the committee guides them to the dining hall for their first public appearance in the community. For the first meal, the new group eats at a separate table in the second dining room, usually with the head nurse, occasionally with the director. Information provided by them is as overly general as that from the committee is overly specific: pleasant words of welcome and reassurance, "you'll be fine here," "if you have any trouble, come to see me." The nurse sometimes adds a reference about how to get medicine and, rarely, a comment about an activity, such as the sewing club or the possibility of working in the residence.

New people either say nothing or fill in the silences with their own soothing litany of comments about the beauty and comfort of the residence, the kindness of the staff members they have just met, the quality of the food. They almost never ask questions; they haven't learned what to ask. An all-in-the-same-boat feeling is always expressed when someone mentions the problems of getting the welfare agency to agree to pay the residence fees. Almost everyone immediately joins in with complaints about the wait, fears about demands on children, and occasionally with a success story of speedy response.

Rooms are assigned either after lunch or, if there is time, just before the cocktail. People typically have very little choice of room. The nurse asks them only if they want to be up high, or if they prefer the garden side or the Paris side of the building. Sometimes she shows them one or two apartments, and they choose, often on the basis of the predominant color in the curtains and upholstery. The apartments are completely furnished, and when the new resident finally shuts the door to be alone for the first time, the shiny aura of chrome and linoleum and the unfamiliar luxury of a private toilet and bath emphasize the strangeness of the new situation.

Most people describe the first few days as very painful, and a common reaction is an intense attempt to assert themselves in the physical environment of their room, as if in preparation for the prospect of entering the new social world outside its doors. They move furniture, scrub floors and windows, add shelves, partition the closet, and install photographs, cushions, doilies, knick-knacks, and often one symbolically major piece of furniture, such as a chair, cabinet, or sewing machine.

As the new residents venture out of their rooms to begin learning to be members of this community, their experiences cluster into distinct patterns. The single piece of information which best predicts which pattern a new person will follow is pro- or anti-Communist political sympathies. In any community there are certain key characteristics which people look for in newcomers as cues to their proper place in the choreography of social life. When I first saw this process at Les Floralies, it reminded me of Arizona—not of retirement villages there, but of Navajo Indian camps. When I traveled in Arizona with a Navajo friend, each time we came to a new household, questions were immediately exchanged to identify the clans of the people present. The initial fishing for signals, plus the tremendous amount of guidance for future behavior carried by the one crucial piece of information, parallels the search for political identity at Les Floralies. The process at the residence is simply more one-sided. Since most new arrivals do not know ahead of time the significance of political recognition, it is the established residents who start to probe for pro- or anti-Communist leanings.

In a new community such as Les Floralies, the way newcomers learn to be members is a central factor in the definition of its borders, both internal and external. A characteristic from past life outside the residence—in this case, political identification—is the key signal for their integration into social life inside. Its use in the socialization process leads to internal meanings and functions for this characteristic, which are transmitted in turn, as learners become guides, to later arrivals. Political identification has become the basis of internal factions and the most important social border inside the residence. The distinctive meanings and uses of this border in social organization inside the residence reinforce its distinctiveness and consequently the external border between it and the wider society.

Socialization into Les Floralies: A Place in the Dining Hall

Entrance into the dining hall is an accurate metaphor for entrance into social life at the residence. The first day the new arrivals are clearly on display at their separate table. If someone in the community has seen one of them before, on a CNRO-sponsored vacation, or on a job, this is often the moment of recognition. Several new people told me how relieved and excited they were to see a familiar face and to hear someone say "didn't I meet you in the mountains," or "weren't you a mason for Girard & Co.?" New names also begin to circulate as the committee members talk over the morning's experience at their own tables. Sometimes a name is recognized when a face has changed or been forgotten. This kind of instant recognition triggers a move, often the next day, to a regular table with other established residents, either the person who knew the newcomer, or with someone else chosen by that person.

Incorporation into a permanent place in the dining hall, with its indication of social incorporation into the community, takes longer for most new arrivals. Some move as a group in the next one or two days from their isolated place at the new table to a more centrally located empty table. This may be gradually recognized as their place, or they may move on individually to tables with other residents whom they meet as hall neighbors or through some formal activity. This process takes about a month. Of the thirty people who arrived in this period, seventeen had settled after one month into a place from which they did not move during the rest of our stay. Four more moved only once, three moved twice. These twenty-four are indicated on table 6 as having found a permanent place in the dining hall.

The six newcomers who did not find a stable place follow a sharply different pattern. Four of them changed table partners, either moving or being left by others, an average of 5.5 times in the same period. The other two are the Picards, whose violent exit from the dining room followed their third table change and preceded their final departure from the residence. The lack of attachment to a place in the dining hall is paralleled for all six of these people by a lack of other kinds of social ties. Five of them remained isolates in the community, never acquiring either a formal or informal pattern of participation.

Entrance into Organized Activity

Faced with very little concrete information about appropriate behavior in an abruptly new social setting, most new residents grasp at any mention of an organized activity as a blessed cue about what they are supposed to do. Twenty out of thirty newcomers tried some organizing activity within their first three weeks. Of the six dining room nomads who never found permanent table partners, three never tried a formal activity and three migrated from one to another, but never continued any. The parallel between lack of spatial and social stability points out not only the significance of a stable place in the dining room as a symbol of social attachment, but also its concrete consequences as a location in the network through which information is passed, for instance, about the existence, time, and place of organized activities. As established residents talk about what they're doing, a new person may hear about a card game, the sewing club, or the possibility of working in the laundry. More rarely, the nurse announces a club meeting or a pottery class over the microphone in the dining room.

Discovery of Informal Ties

Although most new residents try some organized activity soon
after arrival, only some maintain these activities after they develop
more informal ties to other residents. Others drop out of organized
activities when they no longer need them as a way of sharing
regular contact with other residents. Organized activity which is
tried and dropped represents for most people not a failure to
participate but a shift in style of participation. Eight of the ten
residents who experimented with some formal activity and then
dropped it kept up a high level of informal social contact, often
with people they met through the organized activity. Those who
acquire the informal style of community participation stay in the
organized group just long enough to meet other residents with
whom they can share the more informal contacts of visiting,
invitations to aperitif or tea, or going for a walk. The two women
whose withdrawal from organized groups was not compensated by
informal ties have already demonstrated their difficulty in creating
attachments by being the most frequent movers in the dining room.

The choices made by new residents, or about them, in terms of a
place in the dining hall, entrance into organized activities, and
continuation or withdrawal from formal groups as informal ties are
developed, cluster into three dominant patterns of socialization
into the Les Floralies community. One pattern is defined by the
people who find a permanent place in the dining room, enter
organized activity, and continue it as they discover informal ties.
The second pattern describes the individuals who also find a
permanent place at a table and experiment with organized activities, but drop them as they develop more informal contacts with
other residents. The newcomers who follow neither of these
patterns and participate only at the most minimal level in the
community are most likely not to find a permanent place in the
dining room, not to try any organized activity, or to try and drop
several without developing any compensatory informal ties.

Not surprisingly, at Les Floralies the key to the puzzle of who
follows which pattern, the crucial cue which established residents
look for before they launch a newcomer on a particular path
toward participation, is political identity. Recognition of a pro-
Communist or anti-Communist political identity and the salience
of this identity for the new person are excellent predictors of his or
her socialization experience and eventual pattern of participation in
the community. Although a pro- or anti-Communist orientation

Table 6   Patterns of Socialization

Permanence of table	Participates in formal activity	Continuation in formal activity	Informal ties
PERMANENT TABLE—24 6(3)* no contact 18(7) contact	TRY FORMAL ACTIVITY—17 2(1) no contact 4(2) contact, low salience 11(4) contact, high salience	CONTINUE—9 (2)	HIGH INFORMAL TIES—7 (1) LOW INFORMAL TIES—2 (1)
		DO NOT CONTINUE—8 (5)	HIGH INFORMAL TIES—8 (5) LOW INFORMAL TIES—0 (0)
	DID NOT TRY FORMAL ACTIVITY—7 4(2) no contact 2(0) contact, low salience 1(1) contact, high salience		HIGH INFORMAL TIES—2 (1) LOW INFORMAL TIES—5 (2)

NON-PERMANENT
TABLE—6
3(2) no contact
2(2) contact, low salience
1(1) contact, high salience

TRY FORMAL
ACTIVITY—3
2(2) contact, low salience
1(1) contact, high salience

CONTINUE—0
(0)

HIGH INFORMAL TIES—0
(0)

LOW INFORMAL TIES—0
(0)

DO NOT
CONTINUE—3
(3)

HIGH INFORMAL TIES—1
(1)

LOW INFORMAL TIES—2
(2)

DID NOT TRY FORMAL
ACTIVITY—3
3(2) no contact

HIGH INFORMAL TIES—0
(0)

LOW INFORMAL TIES—3
(2)

SOURCE: "Learning to Be Retired: Socialization into a French Retirement Residence," *Journal of Gerontology* 29 (1974):211–23.

N = 30

*Numbers in parentheses represent individuals identified as pro-Communist can be discovered for almost everyone who comes to Les Floralies, political identity is more central to the self-image of some people than others. For Mme. Dupont, M. Beliveau, or M. Lapierre, political loyalty is seen as the central focus of both past and present social involvement of almost every kind. Others, like M. Richard for instance, acknowledge a general political orientation, but it has relatively low priority as a guide to everyday life.

Recognition requires both that a political identification exist and that it be visible. The instant recognition of a new person which sometimes takes place in the dining room can be based on knowledge of political tendencies revealed, for instance, by union affiliation. A few new arrivals have names so well known that recognition depended only on verification that the person was *the* Gardet whose husband was a Resistance hero and edited the Communist Party newspaper. For most people, a more elaborate exchange of cues is necessary: newspaper subscription, attitudes about the Resistance and the Vichy regime, mention of a union official who facilitated the red-tape of entrance into the residence, attitudes toward the Communist suburb in which the residence is located, or comments about current national political issues. M. Beliveau and Mme. Dupont explicitly look for this kind of information about newcomers, and often get it by exposing their own identity very clearly and then interpreting the reaction. Litmus paper–style comments such as (from the president), "The residence is great, but it's in a funny place—the whole town is run by the Reds," usually get quick and clear results.

Political Identity and Socialization
A Permanent Place in the Dining Hall

The first public appearance for a new arrival is in the dining hall. Successful or unsuccessful efforts to settle at a table also make public his or her progress toward attachment to a social network. The newcomers who found a permanent table and the social nomads who demonstrated their lack of attachment by frequent table changes differ sharply in terms of both political recognition and salience of political identity. Of the six people who did not find a place, three had not been identified politically by other residents, and two had a recognized political affiliation which had very low salience for them (table 6). In both cases, a political identity was assigned to them on the basis of their relationships to other people for whom politics is or was highly salient: to Mme. Barret as the widow of a prominent union official, to Mme. Defaux because she came from Bagnolet, well known for its pro-Communist voting patterns.

Entrance into Organized Activity

The first public step beyond the dining room for most new residents is participation in some organized activity. Half of the newcomers who were never attached to a place in the dining room never took this step—that is, never tried any formal activity; half tried one, but let it drop. Those who never tried were those who had no recognized political identity; those who tried but dropped were those whose identity was recognized but of very low salience to them (table 6). Nine of the newcomers had no recognized political identity, seven of these nine never tried any formal activity. Information and persuasion are probably the keys to this relationship. Since there are only rare and erratic official channels of communication to inform new residents about organized activities, they are dependent on informal sources. The established residents who make an explicit effort to make contact with new arrivals are leaders and activists of the two political factions. Their interest in newcomers is naturally in their potential as recruits to the faction. Once the potential is recognized, the individual is introduced to other faction members, who provide information about formal activities as well as about the everyday needs of ordering food, changing sheets, getting light bulbs and toilet paper, catching the bus, or finding the church. This kind of information is very precious to the new arrival, who is shown vividly the advantages of association with a group of people who "know their way around." In addition, he or she learns such norms as the existence of permanent places at tables in the dining hall, use of isolation at meals as a sanction of antisocial behavior, belief in shortages of supplies for breakfast and the consequent need to stockpile sugar and biscuits, the acceptance as couples of unmarried residents who share households.

The individuals whose political identity is not recognized or who are not seen as possible or desirable recruits to a faction, are consequently cut off from easy access to the information needed for participation in organized activity. A deaf-mute, for example, was clearly seen as an unlikely recruit, and neither faction pursued the awkward process of communication through gestures and notes, which was not only difficult, but also unsuitable for the subtleties of exchanging initial political cues. The most obvious case of undesirable recruits were the Picards, who quickly became notorious for shouting insults, loud and vulgar enough to shock retired construction workers, in the dining hall, the corridors, and the lobby. Although they were early identified as Communists, since they subscribed to the appropriate newspaper, the Communist faction made every effort not to claim them—while the others took every opportunity to point out their identity, from a distance.

Substitution of Informal for Formal Participation

Recognition of any political identity is the usual catalyst for first contact with an organized activity. However, it is the direction of this pro- or anti-Communist identity which is related to continued participation in formal activity versus a shift toward informal contacts. New residents who try formal activity but who gradually drop out and direct their participation into informal channels are likely to be oriented toward the Communist faction. The Communist group does not control the Residents Committee; they had one member or none during the year of this study. Most formal activities, since they come under the jurisdiction of the committee, are dominated by the anti-Communists; and, as we have seen, Communists tend to participate less in organized activities than their political opponents. Although information about the existence of these activities is part of the general information about the residence offered by faction members, a new resident who is guided into the community by Communists is not likely to stay in formal activities for long.

By not giving information about formal activities or by immediately talking about their domination by the opposing faction, the Communists would risk discouraging potential recruits either by suggesting less access to information or less access to participation than the other side. A newcomer who found out later, from a neighbor or a table mate, about activities which his would-be guides had not mentioned might begin to wonder if they really knew their way around the residence after all. In addition, rejection of formal activities is two-sided. Not only do the anti-Communists not welcome members of the other faction, but the Communists also criticize the activities for being dominated by the committee.

As we have seen, Mme. Dupont also rejects work activities because they exploit old people and "take bread out of the mouths" of young workers who might otherwise get jobs in the residence.

This kind of rejection of organized activity or work is very difficult to express to newcomers. They are noticeably resistant to any criticism of the residence during their first few weeks there. In fact, their first complaints seem to be a good indication of a threshold of confidence and security in the new setting.[1] The new resident who is guided into Les Floralies by Communists is consequently just as likely as the others to learn about organized activities and to experiment with several. Continuing contact with his or her new Communist acquaintances, however, usually leads to adoption of their version of social facts of life in the residence— that is, rejection of most organized activity as personally and ideologically undesirable, and withdrawal from formal participation.

Most newcomers who experiment with an organized activity and then drop it replace it with a high level of informal contact inside the residence, which explains the possibility of Communists acquiring high status even though they tend not to participate in formal activities.

Three major routes into the social world of the residence are open to the new arrival. Two lead to a high level of participation in the new setting, one does not. The three factors which almost entirely determine which path an individual will follow are the recognition by other residents of his or her political identity, the direction of this identity as pro- or anti-Communist, and the salience of the identity to the newcomer. A new arrival who is clearly identified as anti-Communist and who gives this identification considerable priority in making social choices will move from a stable place in the dining room to regular participation in formal activity, which will continue both as a vehicle and an accompaniment to a high level of informal contacts. The newcomer who is clearly identified as a potential recruit to the Communist faction and for whom political identity has high salience will follow the same path from a stable place in the dining room to participation in organized activity, but this formal participation will be replaced by a high level of informal contacts. Recognition of political identity leads to socialization into high participation in residence life; the direction of the political orientation points toward participation which does or does not include organized activities. The new-

comers who do not signal a political identity, or who don't
respond to the cues of the faction members who make contact with
them, typically don't try any formal activity and never develop a
high level of informal participation, but become the social isolates
of the residence community.

M. and Mme. Myotte, for example, began their first day at Les
Floralies in company which personified the choices to be made in
the following weeks: their first meal was shared with the president
on one side and another newcomer, the unmistakably pro-Communist "Mama" Magnin on the other. This unlikely combination
occurred because both the head nurse and the director were unable
to have lunch with the new arrivals, and since Mme. Beliveau was
also away, the president decided to invite them to his table. Mlle.
Magnin always makes clear her Communist sympathies in short
order and with sledgehammer efficiency: she roars out gratitude to
the mayor of Bagnolet, who, rather than the CNRO, sponsored her
entrance into the residence. This alone is enough to identify her as a
Communist, and the ensuing accounts of pistol-packing participation in the strikes of '36 would erase any momentary doubts. Since
it was immediately obvious where "La Mama" stood, reactions to
her were sufficient first indications of the opposite sympathies
shared by Beliveau and the Myottes. Less than two weeks later,
Mme. Myotte was having tea with Mme. Beliveau while the
president and his wife explained how to fill out the form requesting
breakfast supplies, and other, more abstract, facts of life in the
residence.

This encounter is a good example of how initial cues about
political sympathy are used. That morning M. Beliveau arrived in
the office with a stack of order forms, and met Mme. Myotte who
was saying to the secretary that she didn't know what to do about
getting food for breakfast. Given his judgment about her anti-
Communist—or, at least, non-Communist—leanings, based on
their first meal, the president was quick to invite her upstairs so his
wife could explain the forms. If the first indications had been of
pro-Communist sympathies, this invitation would not have been
extended.

Since they had all arrived together, the Myottes and Mlle.
Magnin, as well as M. Printemps (the "undertaker" and Mme.
Arnaud's "cavalier"), continued to eat at the same table until the
Myottes could find another place and a gracious excuse to move.
The always helpful mailman provided the answer ten days after

their arrival. He stopped at their apartment to help M. Myotte repair the lock on their door. When the Myottes stopped by his table that evening to say thank you, Mme. Viatte asked them where they ate, and said why didn't they join her and M. Deffontaines since there were two places? The Myottes were delighted, and Mme. Myotte described at great length how unhappy they had been with the others, who were very "vulgar." The couple the Myottes joined are very popular; many people stop by their table to chat, and of course the new table partners are introduced to everyone who comes by. M. Myotte has some difficulty talking clearly because of an operation which left his mouth twisted. He participates in conversations by composing poems and limericks about the topics under discussion or the people talking, which he writes on pages torn from a little notebook and distributes on the spot.

The first two weeks were more painful for M. Myotte than for his wife, they said. After he finished building shelves in their two closets, he sat in the apartment with nothing to do. She said this bothered her less because she was more used to being at home, and after all had lots of unpacking and arranging to keep her busy. M. Myotte's public role in the residence began when a neighbor mentioned that her sink was leaking. M. Myotte, a retired plumber, fixed the leak, and his reputation spread quickly enough to keep him complaining about too much work to do in the following months.

When, four months after the Myottes' arrival, the committee was looking for women to meet with the chef to discuss menus, Mme. Thibault and the other women on the committee asked Mme. Myotte, who accepted. Two weeks later, both she and her husband also began to work in the laundry several days a week.

Both of the Myottes also discovered people with whom they enjoyed sharing more informal social contact. He was often invited for a drink by the people he helped with his plumbing skills. They were invited as a couple to visit Mme. Viatte; and as Mme. Myotte spread the word that she liked to play *belote*, she was invited to games with several different women.

The Myottes' path from the dining room into organized activities which they kept up in addition to informal ties is characteristic of six of the group of new arrivals which I observed. All recognized as non-Communists, these six were guided into life at the residence by members of the Beliveau faction. Their political identity was important enough to all of them to ensure responses to the kind of initial contact which the Myottes experienced, and although most of them were not militants, they were all available for mobilization behind the president in times of crisis.

Mme. Prevot began her entry into the Les Floralies community in the same way as the Myottes, by quickly settling into a permanent place in the dining hall. However, since her guides were members of the pro-Communist faction, she joined organized activities only to drop them as both her informal contacts and her political militance increased. Her experiences are representative of those of another six newcomers, whose recognized pro-Communist sympathies were the basis for their temporary participation in organized activities and eventual substitution of more informal ties.

Mme. Prevot's first four months in the residence spanned a transition from the frightened first days when she cried in her room and told other residents she understood why old people killed themselves, to the Christmas party where she danced a *quadrille* in Jeannette MacDonald frills, and spent an exhilarating evening surrounded by friends and admirers. The president's wife made her the ultimate left-handed compliment that night by remarking, "isn't it too bad she's one of *them*?"

Mme. Prevot's adjustment to the residence most definitely involved becoming one of "them." Her first response to my question about getting used to the community was that the most important thing was finding people with the same ideas. She found the key person for her own recruitment into the faction in the car which brought them to the residence. Mme. Gardet, who arrived the same day as Mme. Prevot, is the widow of a Resistance hero who edited the major Communist newspaper until he was shot by a German firing squad. The two women were attracted to each other right away, during the ride to the residence; and the name Gardet is so well known that establishing political sympathies was a simple matter of verifying that this was *the* Gardet. In the weeks that followed, Mme. Gardet guided her new friend into contacts with prominent members of the Communist faction at Les Floralies, who in turn took charge of Mme. Prevot.

All of her energies were turned to keeping busy during the first few weeks at the residence. She scrubbed everything possible in her apartment. For a month, she went to the kitchen to work every morning, since Beliveau had mentioned this job during the welcoming cocktail. She made frequent visits to a son who lives in

Bagnolet. All this activity was not enough to make her forget her worries. She told everyone near her of her fears that she would not receive public assistance and would have to leave the residence, or that if she did get the money, terrible demands would be made on another son to share the costs.

Her stable place in the dining room was a sign of the social incorporation to come. Since there was no room at the table to which Mme. Gardet was immediately invited, Mme. Prevot stayed with the other newcomers who ate together the first day. They are both non-Communists; however, a new resident from Bagnolet who eventually joined the table balanced the factions, and also put Mme. Prevot in her turn in the role of welcomer and guide.

Since the age of thirteen Mme. Prevot had worked making artificial flowers out of silk and organdy. During lunch the first day, she described this work with pride as "a métier d'art." She wished she could keep making flowers in the residence. The director was eating with the new arrivals that day, and suggested setting up a workshop to make flowers for Christmas decorations. By mid-October, Mme. Prevot had stopped going to the kitchen and had started to work alone making paper flowers; she was quickly joined by Mme. Gardet. This core group, with occasional help from two non-Communist women (one from Gardet's table, one from the committee) worked everyday until Christmas on their project. They all called each other "tu" and used first names. Mme. Prevot felt that it was the flower job that made her a part of the community, because it was through this work that she had found friends. She and Mme. Gardet were together constantly, often working until late at night, and there were also many invitations back and forth to the apartments of the other flower-makers, and to those of other members of the Communist faction. Having been identified as "one of us" through her closeness to Mme. Gardet, Mme. Prevot found sympathetic neighbors on the thirteenth floor, where there were six faction members, including Mme. Dupont.

Conversations during the long hours of twisting wires and paper into roses revealed the progress Mme. Prevot was making into the community via the Communist group. Complaints about the director's demands for decorations imposed on him the role of boss. The "workers" then protested that they had too much to do, and agreed that when there are jobs in the residence, people should be hired to do them: old people should not be exploited and young people should not be deprived of work. Mme. Prevot, by early

December, was the most vocal in stating these positions, typical of the Communist faction—and markedly different from her own eagerness to work in the residence only two months before. A great deal of information was also exchanged about the health, domestic affairs, and activities of other pro-Communist residents during these sessions.

The public assistance decision had been made by this time, and Mme. Prevot's money worries were resolved. Her anguish over dependence on her son was calmed, although never completely dissolved, by his insistence that he was able and willing to pay his share of her fees. The frequent visits to her other son, who lived very near the residence, had also subsided by this time. It was unsettling to hear the "interfering mother-in-law" story inside-out, as she described holding back the tears of resentment and rejection when her son told her she should not come to their apartment so often. By January she was making one visit a week, and, no longer looking for relief from loneliness and boredom, she now felt she was doing a duty by helping out on the day the five children had no school. Her complaints about taking time from her life in the community to help her child and grandchildren were a startling contrast to the earlier pain of rejected emotional dependence on them.

After the highly conflictual elections which the Communists lost dramatically because of what they saw as a plot led by Beliveau, Mme. Prevot's comment was, "there's no one from our side left." One of her neighbors responded, "You're new here; this should be a lesson to you about how things work." By January the flower work was over and Mme. Prevot had only one formal activity left, the three-person committee which planned menus. She was very satisfied with her informal social life, which included both her close relationship to Mme. Gardet, and an extensive network of contacts with other faction members. Mme. Beliveau's regretful recognition that Mme. Prevot was "one of them" sums up both the widespread admiration of Mme. Prevot and also the clarity of her identification with the pro-Communists who had guided her into community life.

No obvious representative appears for the seven people who were not contacted by a faction, never tried a formal activity, and had very little informal social life. They have in common only the fact that neither political group saw them as potential recruits. Some, such as the impossible Picards, were seen as undesirables. Some were not recognized because the signs available to observers were not clear enough. Mme. Arnaud, for example, arrived the same day as Mme. Prevot and Mme. Gardet, and came from Bagnolet. She consequently was probably seen as a pro-Communist. Since she was not, she gave no cues to be picked up by Mme. Gardet, but may not have been approached by the Beliveau group because they made a false birds-of-a-feather assumption. Moreover, politics was not important enough to Mme. Arnaud for her to make any effort to signal her sympathies to the president and his supporters.

Nineteen of the thirty arrivals observed followed one of these routes into the residence: six anti-Communists became active in both formal and informal styles; six pro-Communists experimented with formal participation and then substituted informal activity; seven newcomers were not identified as potential recruits to either faction, never tried a formal activity, and developed ony a very low level of informal contacts.

Of the eleven apparent exceptions to these patterns, nine seem to be the attractive kind of exception which, if it doesn't prove a rule, at least doesn't disprove it. Two newcomers, one pro-, one anti-Communist, made political contact soon after entering the residence, but instead of trying a formal activity, they moved directly into a network of informal contacts. Although there are clearly some unexplored factors of personal preferences for informal versus formal activity, the general rule that contact with a political faction is the key for entrance into social participation is not broken. The relevant comparison is with the seven people who had no political contact, never tried formal activity, and never moved beyond a minimal level of informal participation.

The salience of political identity accounts for four more apparent reversals of the general pattern. Two pro-Communist newcomers dropped out of organized activities, but never developed more than a low level of informal contacts. Two residents contacted by the anti-Communist faction substituted a high level of informal contacts for formal activity. For all of these individuals, political identity had very low salience in everyday life. Both recognized political identity and a high level of salience are necessary to guide an individual into the dominant participation styles. However, people whose identity has been recognized are always available for mobilization in conflicts, even if the salience of this identity is too low to make it relevant for everyday participation in the residence. All four of these "nonconformists," for example, voted with the appropriate faction in residence elections.

Two clearly identified recruits to the Communist faction are unusual because they continued to work. Political identity was not highly salient to either of them, and, in addition, both jobs represented minimum involvement in organized group activity, since they were done either alone or with a maximum of one staff member or one resident. The committee also had a correspondingly minor interest in these individual work activities.

A recognized and highly salient political identity was not sufficient to establish one new resident at a permanent place in the dining room during her first three months, although she eventually did find a table and acquired a high level of informal participation. "La Mama's" interpretation of her own behavior suggests that some new arrivals use temporary stays away from the residence as *rites de passage* to facilitate entrance into the more usual patterns of socialization into the community. Mlle. Magnin had great problems getting used to the residence. Living with strangers was painful after having been a well-known character in Bagnolet, and she was very afraid of losing her independence after a lifetime of living alone. Her expressions of hostility to staff members and other residents were frequent, loud, and vulgar. About two months after moving into the residence, she went to the hospital. Her reaction on returning to Les Floralies she described as a return to a community where she was known, where people were interested in her, where she was well-treated—on every account the contrary of her initial opinions. Everything looked different when she came back; she felt as if she belonged. The appropriate finale for the experience was a party a few days after her return, at which she became the center of attention, growling out "Valentine," and "Le Petit Vin Blanc" along with the band. Her permanent table place was established three weeks later.

The *rite de passage* aspects of this experience—separation (leaving the residence), marginality (stay in hospital), and re-incorporation (return to residence) are clear.[2] Several other residents reported similar feelings about stays in the clinic, in the hospital, participation in a residence trip, or even a week spent visiting a family. The celebration of feeling part of the community by prominent participation in a party also happened to many new residents, such as Mme. Prevot at Christmas, for whom that day became a landmark of really belonging in the residence. It was often also the moment from which other residents could remember recognizing the new person. Since a *rite de passage* is usually interpreted as a ritual map for bridging the no-man's land between social roles, it is not surprising that individuals faced with entrance not only into a new community but also into a new kind of community might invent or discover aspects of this kind of ritual.

Conclusion

Learning to participate in the social world of Les Floralies follows an already documented pattern of adult socialization through which basic orientations are translated into a new vocabulary of behavior appropriate to a new setting.[3] New arrivals are guided into the learning process according to signals of a social identity which summarizes basic attitudes and beliefs acquired in many previous situations. Learning to be an active member of the community requires learning how a Communist should participate or how a non-Communist should participate, an inventory of specific behaviors, such as with whom to associate informally, whether or not to work, in addition to more widely shared norms about food, death, sex, or methods of social sanction.

The demands of a new situation, however, may promote a more complete kind of translation, a more complex kind of learning, for some adults. The centripetal force of daily acts and choices may pull more basic orientations into redefinitions in the present tense. This process seems especially likely for older or retired people entering a new situation where they have dramatically greater opportunities for social participation than in at least the immediate past.[4] Although at Les Floralies identification as pro- or anti-Communist, clearly derived from a person's past social life, is the catalyst for participation in present social life, this basic identification acquires new meanings inside the residence. As people repeatedly line up along the same factional borders to fight about matters relevant only inside the residence, the definition of these opposing sides—in terms of shared experiences inside the residence— becomes part of the shared understandings which are one marker of the border between this community and the society outside.

Although conflict and community are too often used as opposing terms, at Les Floralies the two are intimately intertwined. People learn to participate in the community through factions whose existence implies conflict. The meaning of the factions is progressively redefined in terms relevant to the community they are helping to create.

7   Conflict and
          Community

Introduction

Elections for the six seats on the committee were held in mid-December. The ballot box was set up in the dining room after lunch; voting began at two o'clock. By two-thirty all but thirteen residents had voted, and when the polls closed at half past three only two people had not filled out a ballot. Over fifty residents sat in a ring of chairs watching and waiting for the results. Conspicuously "dressed" for the event, they seemed to be waiting for a photographer to snap the picture entitled "importance of political conflict at Les Floralies."

The factional borders which are guidelines for participation in this community are both maintained and redefined through frequent use in conflicts. The factional borders are sharpened by the conflict process at the same time as the substance of these conflicts shifts the focus of factional identity from outside the community to inside. As conflicts expand, few people can resist the tide of polarized emotions. Even residents who ordinarily do not pay much attention to the political divisions are pushed and pulled to choose sides. Once they have done this, their allegiance is public, they are that much more available for mobilization in the next conflict, and the faction border is one step more sharply defined. Each conflict which expands to include most of the community reiterates the faction boundaries, and provides another landmark for their definition in terms of events and personalities inside the residence. The shift from an initial signal of political identification which summarizes much of residents' past lives to definition of faction borders in primarily internal terms also emphasizes the external border between the community and its context.

Looked at in detail, the conflicts which developed during our year in the residence illustrate these processes. They also show the ways in which conflict in this community is like and not like conflict in other places. The extent of similarity between the way

126

conflict expands in this residence for French old people and reports of the same dynamic in disputes over school-bonds or flouridation in a variety of American towns offers some unexpected additional justification for using the word community to describe Les Floralies. Although conflicts expand here very much as they do in other communities, the factors which contain conflicts in other settings are far less effective. This difference underscores again the importance of the factions to residence social life, as the connecting link between conflict and community participation.

Conflict 1: The Reluctant Candidates

Conflict which focused on the December 1969 elections to the committee began around the first of the month, when four of the six incumbents did not sign up to run again. The only two who volunteered to be candidates were the vice-president and Mme. Cassard, the one Communist on the committee. Two other names appeared on a printed announcement of the elections. Mme. Clignet agreed to run because the director encouraged her to do so. She is a warm-hearted, energetic person, with pleasantly ample breasts and belly, which often bounce together under her apron with laughter or indignation. A little scatter-brained, she does not always grasp a joke or a political situation immediately, but when she sees the punch line or the principle, amusement or anger is voluble and usually accompanied by a little dance step with the nearest partner, or a vigorously brandished finger, jabbed in fencing style toward an invisible enemy. By co-opting her onto the committee, the director wanted to channel her into what he considered positive directions and away from a tendency to criticize. She was flattered by his insistence, and her assumption that Mme. Cassard, a friend and neighbor, would be reelected, was the final persuasion. Although M. Beliveau adamantly refused to run, a good friend added his own name to the list, explaining that "since no one on our side is running, I'll be a candidate to stop the Communists." This list of four official candidates was circulated by the mailman, along with a ballot marked with three blanks for women and three for men. Since there were only four volunteers for six positions, a list of all residents was also included so that other names could easily be written in.

Appearance of the printed notice one week before the election suddenly made visible in black and white that there was only one candidate clearly aligned with the anti-Communist faction. M. Beliveau began to get anxious visits from his friends and supporters, and he finally took the stance, made famous by General de Gaulle, that he was being drafted back into public life by a call for help in time of crisis. He and his friend M. Lapierre, who had already signed up to run, along with the two women incumbents, Mme. Thibault and Mme. Petit, began an active but secret search for another man and another woman to fill a non-Communist slate. At a series of meetings in the Beliveau apartment, faction members closest to the president proposed and discussed names and sent envoys to the selected candidates until two appropriate people had accepted. This list began to circulate, sometimes verbally, often in writing, through the social networks available to faction members. News reverberated out from the Beliveaus and Mme. Thibault as they made conspicuously casual visits to other residents known not to be Communists. Public conversations with table partners, at card games, or in the television room were cryptic, according to the strategy that if the other side didn't know there was a campaign going on, they wouldn't organize an opposition.

Too many interrupted conversations, suddenly closed doors, an obvious atmosphere of suppressed excitement in certain corners of the dining room, and the inevitable information leaks finally raised the suspicions of Mme. Dupont and other members of the pro-Communist faction. Someone at the same table as a friend of Mme. Clignet's casually mentioned that she knew the same committee would be re-elected. Mme. Clignet's friend protested that this wasn't possible, and the other woman obligingly reported a visit from Mme. Thibault. Some Beliveau supporters had also carried their campaign to the second floor, where one woman who, as the other residents said "sometimes got confused," heard the story, and later chattered about a list to someone outside the faction. Two days before the elections, people began to gather in Mme. Dupont's apartment to decide what to do. They made up a list of their own, interrupting themselves continually to shout their anger at the underhanded, dirty tactics of the other side. In the little time they had left, they passed the word to sympathetic ears.

The day of the elections, ballots were read aloud and the committee tallied votes in front of the residents assembled in the dining room. Continuous whispering and shushing accompanied the reading, as the voting patterns quickly made clear that people were choosing slates rather than individuals. As the entire Beliveau list piled up votes, members of the Communist group began to show tension, some stiff and silent, some making audible comments about "the conspiracy." Beliveau walked ceremoniously out of the room when his fiftieth vote virtually guaranteed victory. Mme. Cassard's face became redder and redder as it became obvious she had been rejected, but she sat it out until all the votes were counted. M. Clere, as vice-president, was asked by the director to read the results. He started off as fast as possible, but Mme. Beliveau and M. Lapierre interrupted several times with righteous requests to slow down. Two separate swarms of people left the dining room as soon as the totals were announced.

Celebration in the Beliveaus' apartment centered on satisfaction that people do appreciate all we've done for them, and that we showed those Communists up as a trouble-making minority who don't have a chance to take over the residence. The Communist losers gathered in the hall outside Mme. Clignet's room, where their loud analysis of the plot gradually attracted an audience: "They're all buddies of Beliveau. Nobody ever heard of Demaison, but she eats at the same table with Beliveau so she got elected. Bonnetage drinks, and stands under the stairs to look up women's skirts—but he plays cards with Beliveau. They're all *Force Ouvrière* (Socialist-oriented union). They went arm in arm to Mass and lit a big candle to be sure to win. Now there's no one from our side left on the committee."

M. Clere's lack of identification with either faction was made visible by his absence from both these groups. His position on the original committee is, I think, explained by two things. First, M. Clere could be described as "a young person's old person," who personifies the word *spry*. He is the resident who stood on his hands in the dining room. He paints watercolors and hitch-hikes all over France to find new subjects. When visitors come to the residence, they are almost inevitably taken to Clere's apartment to see his work. According to residents' reports, when the first elections were held, shortly after the residence opened, the director asked certain people to run, and then the residents chose among them. At that time, it seems likely that the director saw Clere as a potential leader, and also that with his energetic curiosity and bustling helpfulness he was highly visible to other residents. His defeat in the second year's elections emphasizes the fact that he never developed a clear political identity. He was not seen as a Communist; however, because of his persistent rivalry with Beliveau, he was not perceived as a member of that faction either. Most of his support came, predictably enough, from the newest residents, whom he had helped move in. They were astounded that others could be so ungrateful as not to vote for him. Clere was furious. He immediately decided to leave the residence and for several weeks talked to the director and to people at his table about plans to transfer to another community run by the same retirement fund. He refused on several occasions when the head nurse asked him to do the kind of minor repairs which he used to perform frequently and with obvious pleasure in the gratitude and special access to information about other residents which they provided. He became more than ever anxious to spend time with staff members, visitors, new arrivals, and the anthropologist rather than with other residents whom he bitterly and frequently accused of ingratitude.

Two days after the election, Mme. Clignet and one of her friends decided that maybe the vote was illegal because of the secret slate. They planned to take a copy of the Beliveau list to ask advice from a union lawyer. Organized activities which had included members of both factions became settings for continuation of the conflict. Mme. Demaison, the "unknown" from Beliveau's table who was elected with him, had worked with Mme. Prevot on the flower project since its beginning. After the elections, Mme. Prevot, Mme. Gardet, and their Communist friends barely spoke to her. Mme. Prevot stopped showing her how to make the flowers, and talked around her to the others until Mme. Demaison finally stopped coming. The gerontology workers split into two groups, as Mme. Clignet, Mme. Cassard, and their friend and neighbor Mme. Tissot refused to work with Mme. Thibault. The three agreed among themselves on a time and place to meet and do their part of the work without telling Mme. Thibault.

For Mme. Clignet, the elections marked the end of a friendship and the beginning of clear-cut affiliation with the pro-Communist faction. Since she came from Bagnolet, and had belonged to a Communist-oriented union, Mme. Clignet had never been seen as a possible recruit to the Beliveau side. On the other hand, she is Catholic, and when I first met her, saw herself as quite distinct from such militant Communists as Mme. Dupont, whom she criticized for dragging politics into everything. Mme. Clignet and Mme. Thibault had worked at sewing machines in the same garment factory and recognized each other when they arrived at the residence. They ate at the same table, played board games in each other's apartments, and worked together for the gerontology. They introduced themselves to me, arm in arm, as best friends. Despite Mme. Thibault's strong allegiance to the Beliveau faction, the friendship was possible because of Mme. Clignet's lack of interest in politics. She was initially as critical of Beliveau as of Dupont for being too political. Once Mme. Clignet's potential sympathy for the Dupont side was stimulated and made public by the elections, the friendship snapped under the strain of conflicting loyalties. When Mme. Clignet discovered her friend's participation in the election plot, she considered it a betrayal. With the encouragement of Mme. Dupont and Mme. Cassard, this betrayal was explained by Mme. Thibault's enjoyment of being a boss, and her allegiance to Beliveau and his "clan." Mme. Clignet broke off relations with Mme. Thibault, first refusing to speak to her at meals, and finally making the ultimate public gesture of rejection by moving away from the table. The best friends are now Clignet and Cassard, a personal tie consistent with Clignet's new active role in the pro-Communist faction.

I was not exempted from the currents of conflict which polarized the community during the elections. The logical conclusion for many residents was that if I was studying them, I must be doing it for the benefit of one side or the other. Choices to be made from a list of all the residents seemed to offer a rare opportunity for observing natural preferences and rejections, outside the artificial situation of an interview. I was uneasy about asking people directly whom they had voted for, but the desirability of knowing finally tempted me to try. In a sensitive situation, a few warm-up questions about how people had decided to vote, whether they had asked for or given advice, seemed like a good idea. In one of those unforgettable shifts of perception which occur during field work, I realized after the first few conversations that I had the problem upside-down. People rushed through handshakes and almost pushed me into a chair in their eagerness to tell me whom they had voted for, and why, but became uneasy to the point of icy denial when I asked about how they had decided. The controversy for them was about the existence of a plot, and even a hint that they had discussed choices with other people seemed to be an accusation that they had participated in the conspiracy of secret slates. Whom they had voted for, on the other hand, was so self-evident that it was nothing to hide.

The "which side are you on" question finally exploded to the surface three days after the elections. As I came out of an apartment on her hall, Mme. Thibault loomed out of her door to demand "I suppose you're asking them who they voted for? We should have just signed our ballots!" When she backed into her room far enough to let me inside, we sat down to talk it out. She said I must be asking questions to report back to Clignet and Cassard, since their friend Tissot had accused her of sneaking around underhandedly to get elected. Mme. Thibault decided that since I lived on the thirteenth floor with her accusers, I must be working for them. She didn't sleep all night thinking about it, she said, and went to see Beliveau and the director first thing in the morning.

Facing Mme. Thibault, who was wrapped in a long, black coat which to me looked appropriately judicial, I was convinced that my research in the residence depended on an explanation of why information which had such painful and personal meaning for her was useful to me in a different and distant universe of general questions about community formation and social organization in age-homogeneous residences. To my profound relief, she seemed very reassured, especially when I explained that in particular for new residents, knowing how they voted could help me understand their experiences of integration into the community. She said she would try to help me by talking to other people who had been upset, "in fact, everyone *ought* to help you." It was too late, however, for Mme. Thibault to stop the buzz of anxiety and suspicion which she had started. Two other women went to see the director saying they had talked to me, and was that going to get Mme. Thibault into trouble? After a long lunchtime consultation with the mailman, one of the most widely known and liked individuals in the community, I decided to stop any formal questions about the elections. They had already taught me my first lesson about the force of factional conflict at Les Floralies.

Conflict 2: The Leisure Satellite

Mardi Gras is the Catholic holiday which provides a last celebration before the sobriety of Lent; it occurs in early February and, consequently, about two months after the elections. Several residents invited friends to their apartments to eat the crepes which are traditional at this season, and the chef planned to serve them after dinner that night. Mme. Clignet, Mme. Prevot, and another Communist, Mme. Tournier, decided to follow another old custom by dressing up in men's clothes. They invited everyone on the thirteenth floor, plus a few other friends, to come to one of the lounges for the party. The three "men" were irrepressible, flirting with women, asking them to dance, making obscene jokes and gestures. Mme. Clignet discovered that by opening her fly and sticking out a piece of shirt-tail, she had a "penis" which sent women squealing and giggling around the room. My husband was a great success in a mini-skirt and a tennis-ball bust. The group grew when several people came over from the sewing club meeting next door, and the party went on all afternoon. Mme. Tournier went downstairs to invite the director to come, and when he saw the costumes, he urged the women to wear them downstairs to dinner.

There was applause when the people in costume entered the dining room, but when the women and their friends started to sing, no one joined in. Although the handyman brought out the record-player, only about thirty people stayed after the crepes were served, and the party was over by 11 P.M. Members of the committee were conspicuously absent, and several told me pointedly the next morning that they had gone upstairs at nine o'clock. The political interpretation of Mardi Gras had been assigned well before anyone came downstairs for dinner. When one of the guests at Mme. Beliveau's crepe party mentioned that she heard there would be some people dressed up in the fourteenth-floor lounge, the president's wife replied firmly that she hadn't heard about it, and didn't want to know what *they* were doing.

The organizers of the costume party were angry at the snub from the committee, and discussed at length that evening how absurd it was for a social committee to be against social events. Two days later Clignet, Prevot, Cassard, and Tournier got several other residents to come to a meeting to discuss forming a leisure committee to organize more parties. When representatives of the group went that night to see the director, he was enthusiastic about the idea, said there was money available for these activities, and asked them to put their proposal in writing. The next day they gave him a petition signed by fifteen residents, nine of them identified with the Communist faction, plus M. Gillet and Mme. Joly, who are neighbors of several Communists, and one woman who ate at the same table as someone who signed. The petition proposed the creation of a leisure committee with fifteen members which would meet once a week to plan social activities.

The leader of the delegation to deliver the petition was M.

Rouget, a member of the pro-Communist faction notorious for his temper and his personal dislike of Beliveau. Many people did not want him on the list of candidates for the committee, for instance, because he was seen as too likely to start fights, and might lose votes from residents otherwise sympathetic to their side but who did not like Rouget's tactics. On the other hand, he was also regarded as a forceful and clever spokesman; and several of the women involved in writing the petition thought it was appropriate to have a man confront Beliveau and the male director. In M. Guerillon's office, Rouget made a violent verbal attack on Beliveau and the committee, saying they did not really represent the residents, simply wanted power and enjoyed being important, and never made any report of their activities to the others. "They're a phantom committee; we never know what they do. They don't do what we want, so we're organizing something for ourselves."

The director told the leisure group that he would take their petition to the committee at its next meeting. The petition was not brought up at the next meeting five days later; a long list of other agenda items took too much time and the group adjourned for lunch. Immediately after the meal Mme. Clignet and several supporters ambushed me in the hallway to ask what had happened at the meeting. When I said nothing had happened, they went to see M. Guerillon again to find out why their question had not been discussed. He encouraged them again, mentioning the possibility of hiring a staff member specialized in entertainment to work with the new committee. The group was still worried, and agreed that it didn't seem necessary to go through the committee at all if the director approved their project.

Beliveau, on the other hand, sharply criticized Guerillon for having accepted the petition at all. He warned the director that it was very dangerous to deal with those people as a group, that they would think he was giving them support, and that he should have sent them directly to the committee, which was, after all, in charge of social activities. As the two men guided a group of visitors around the residence, Beliveau used the audience as a chance to expand on the leisure proposal as just one more example of Communist trouble-making. "It's always the same little clan. They can't possibly say honestly that we don't have enough leisure activities. That's a pretext to get power away from the committee."

A special meeting of the committee was held two days later to catch up on unfinished business, including the leisure petition. The director read the letter out loud and then passed it around. He then read his own proposed answer which approved the new idea; head-shaking and worried looks were the response. Beliveau insisted that his own letter be read also, and its sharp refusal was accompanied by murmurs and nods of agreement. The petitioned request was criticized by Mme. Thibault and Mme. Demaison because it came from a very small group of residents "and always the same ones"; it wasn't for everyone since it suggested a committee of fifteen and would divide the residence community. Beliveau said they had no right to use residence rooms for secret meetings. He, Thibault, and Lapierre said repeatedly that if the proposal was accepted, the committee would only be a phantom, with no power, simce there would be another group called a committee which could hold meetings, and have access to the social funds. The director tried to refute all of these arguments saying the new committee would be open to everyone, that it couldn't spend money without the old committee's approval, and that everyone had the right to use rooms in the residence. Several luncheon guests were hovering in the lobby, waiting for Guerillon, and since the committee showed no signs of yielding, they could only agree to meet again before dinner.

The atmosphere of tension and determination in which the Committee assembled that evening melted into satisfaction as the director read his compromise letter. Although it essentially approved the idea of a group of residents interested in organizing leisure activities, it included a new sentence stating that all activities and meetings had to be approved by the committee. The committee also agreed with Beliveau's request that his letter, now similar in all major points to Guerillon's, be included in the response to the petition. The discussion ended in a chorus of agreement that this was the only way to handle the "opposition" which was once again trying to cause dissension.

The director delivered the letter to Mme. Clignet in her apartment the next morning, and asked her to go to the committee to discuss new leisure projects. "The last time I did something for you [ran for office], I got it in the neck," was her refusal. Organizers of the petition gathered around her in the dining hall at noon to analyze the situation. Disbelief that the director could be overruled by the committee led to bitter jokes about needing committee permission for all residence activities: "Do you have a permit to visit Mme. Clignet? I'm going to the bathroom without a permit. Do you have permission to empty your garbage?"

Everyone agreed that it was impossible to accept the new rules:

"How can we go to them for permission for anything when they were elected illegally anyway?" That afternoon, Mme. Tournier and M. Lagrange, who had been at the residence just over four months, decided to beard the president in his lair. They appeared at the *belote* game and demanded an explanation for the committee's refusal of the petition. Beliveau told them, they claimed, that they had to have the committee's permission, in writing, before they could hold meetings. He also accused the group of trying to hide politics behind the proposal for leisure, they said. Relishing his story and oblivious of any contradiction, M. Lagrange reported that he told the president that politics should not be involved in life at the residence, that people should have a right to their opinions, but should not go around attacking others. "Then I said, 'I was arrested as a Resistance fighter, and what did you do in the war anyway?' "

Post-mortems and planning of new strategies continued into the night in various apartments and hallways. Whenever Rouget was not present, the others debated the possibility that they had made a serious mistake in letting him lead the original delegation to the director. Without his temper and his personal attacks on Beliveau, some thought, the president might have been less opposed to their idea. On the other hand, since they had lost anyway, many of them were glad that at least Rouget had really told off the director and let him know what they thought of Beliveau and his committee. When Rouget was with the others, he tried to persuade them to go on meeting until the committee made them stop. The others refused to push things this far, agreeing with Mme. Tournier who said that after all they did not want to divide the whole residence into two camps.

The group generally agreed that if all activities had to be approved by the committee then they would not participate, but would organize separate parties for themselves. The women were especially insistent that they would not do any more work for the community. Also, if the money was controlled by the committee, there was no point in being careful not to waste it, since nobody had anything to say about what the savings were spent for. There was intense speculation about why the director let the committee overrule him. Prevot thought he was just inexperienced and needed to learn to be more firm; Tissot and Tournier insisted that Beliveau had some kind of connections in the union which put Guerillon at his mercy.

Conflict 3: Union of French Women

A stack of newsletters from the Union des Femmes Françaises became a subtheme to the conflict over the leisure committee. The papers arrived in the residence office almost simultaneously with the leisure petition. The mailman said he did not see any names on them, so he brought them to Beliveau to ask him what to do. The president's perception of the UFF as a pro-Communist organization was reinforced by his finding the name of a well-known member of the Dupont faction on the packet. He told the mailman to give one paper to her and kept the rest. He also made a scene in front of the secretary by shouting that the Communists had no right to send their propaganda into the residence and that they were all a bunch of slippery eels. When the woman who was expecting the papers discovered what had happened, the Communists were furious. Mme. Clignet gave an eloquent description of the heroic war-work the UFF had done, and all agreed that the president had gone too far when he prevented people from getting their own mail.

In the days after the leisure conflict and the fight over the UFF newspapers, members of both factions gave me gloomy descriptions of how badly things were going at the residence: the other side was dividing the community into two hostile camps.

Conflict 4: The Priest in the Laundry

The priest who appeared in the fifth-floor laundry room was the catalyst for another conflict which, however, never spread to as many residents as the first three disputes. Mme. Beliveau sent the committee a written request for an Easter Sunday Mass in the residence. The letter stimulated a committee discussion of weekly Masses in the community. The group was divided three against three on the issue. The president was under painful cross-pressure between his own aggressively anticlerical principles as a Socialist, and his Catholic "wife's" public and private insistence on the Mass. She followed him to the door of the meeting room, whispering last minute arguments and instructions. Beliveau and the other two committee members opposed to the Masses phrased their position in terms of inevitable political repercussions. The Communists would demand equal time and place for meetings, they argued. The others responded with the principle of religious freedom. Many residents had trouble getting to the church, they said, especially in winter, and were consequently deprived of their right to worship. The final compromise decision gave permission for one Mass on Easter Sunday and for private visits by the priest to individual apartments on request.

When word spread through the Communist faction that a priest had celebrated Mass on the fifth floor, one man (an anarchist) wrote a letter of protest and posted it on the bulletin board in the dining hall. Mme. Dupont wrote her letter to an acquaintance in the union, asking him to make a formal complaint to the directors of the retirement fund. The most militant faction members spent many hours discussing the fact that religious services did not belong in a secular residence, and that it was unjust to let the Catholics have a room for the Mass when the leisure committee was not allowed to meet. "There's nothing more political than the Church after all, so why should they have a meeting when we can't?"

Conflict 5: M. Fortin's Niece/Cousin

The young woman who came to visit M. Fortin several times a week was easily recognizable by her bleached blond hair and high-heeled sandals. She usually arrived with a man whose scarred face and leather jacket made him look almost costumed for the part of a tough. The three locked themselves in Fortin's apartment for several hours at a time, supplied with a string bag full of wine bottles. Occasionally the young woman spent the night.

As we saw in chapter 5, the fact that she was introduced as a niece or a cousin did not soften the blow of sharing an elevator with a prostitute for Mme. Thibault and her friends. Other residents thought the situation was exciting and even admirable; hypotheses were exchanged about the possible combinations of activities, actors, and spectators in the little apartment. Mme. Thibault and the others, however, finally sent a formal letter to the committee and the director asking them to do something. Discussion in the committee opposed Fortin's individual rights and the "open" character of the residence to the rights of the offended women and the principle of not allowing nonpaying guests to stay overnight. They finally concluded with a request to the director to speak to M. Fortin, reminding him that guests who spent the night had to be paid for and should stay in one of the residence guest rooms, and generally asking him to be more discreet. He recruited no supporters to his side to protest this reprimand, and apparently complied with it.

Conflict 6: The Drunken Sailor

M. Colette's "attack" and subsequent mealtime quarantine (chapter 5) is another dispute which was not redefined into factional terms but was relatively quickly and calmly resolved, this time by informal means instead of a formal appeal to the authorities.

Conflict 7: The Bar

A small bar was set up in a corner of the lobby in June 1970. Residents and their guests could buy beer, wine, or soft drinks here before lunch and dinner. Members of the committee and the director spread the word that volunteers were needed to tend bar. Mme. Tournier told M. Guerillon that she would like the job. Her quick, gold-toothed smile and bouncy good humor made the committee think she would be perfect behind the counter. She had been involved in the leisure conflict, but was not generally known as a central member of the Communist faction. However, after she accepted the job, she asked several friends to work with her, and the committee was confronted, after the fact, with Mmes. Clignet, Cassard, and Tissot as the other bartenders. The president was angry, and the committee spent most of a meeting deploring the plot of the same old clan to take over leisure activities.

When the bar was officially inaugurated, everyone in the residence was invited for a free drink, and the work of the sewing club and the pottery class was on display. Afterwards the record player was brought out and a group of residents began a traditional line dance. No committee members and no strong Beliveau supporters participated, at least not willingly. Mme. Thibault was at one point dragged into the line and spent several uncomfortable minutes trying to look uninvolved as she was whirled around the floor. During our remaining month in the community, the most militant anti-Communists never were regulars at the bar, and most committee members went there only on the official occasions when they welcomed new residents or visitors.

Conflict in Other Communities

Comparison of the patterns which emerge from conflicts at Les Floralies with generalizations based on many studies of community conflict emphasizes on the one hand the appropriateness of calling this residence a community, and on the other the centrality of the factions to its social life.

Conflict Expansion

Community conflict is described by most of its scholarly spectators as dynamic and expansive. Once a conflict starts, it tends to expand in a predictable pattern to include more people and new issues unless specific blocking conditions constrain it. Engagement of new people in the conflict often requires expansion of the original issues. New issues are introduced and old issues redefined as the initial participants, especially those in the weaker position, appeal to potential allies inside and outside the community. Specific issues tend to become more general as a community polarizes into a "we-they" alignment.[1]

The shift to more abstract, general issues does not necessarily correspond to a weakening of emotional involvement in a conflict, since less specific issues allow people to translate the conflict into terms with the greatest emotional significance for them. Redefinition and expansion of original issues characteristically includes their translation from symbols which are essentially referential, such as prices or salaries, to symbols which evoke an emotional response, such as "the American way of life" or the threat of enemy subversion. This change in the language of conflict is related to the tendency for conflicts to move from disagreement to antagonism, from issues to personalities.[2] Disagreement with an individual or group about some specific question develops into hostility against a generalized enemy who is feared and hated for whatever reasons are the most salient to various individuals on the other side.

Direct contacts between people on different sides of the conflict become increasingly rare as each participant's need for cognitive consistency pushes him toward total rejection of those with whom he disagrees and increasing contact with those who share his opinions. Formal organizations in a community also tend to line up on one side or the other; and often new partisan organizations are formed specifically to carry on the business of the conflict. According to Gresham's Law of Conflict, the culmination of the tendency for conflict to expand toward emotional hostility and social polarization is the emergence of new leaders, typically extremists who have little sense of identification with the community.[3]

Containment of Conflict

This avalanche view of community conflict is modified by a series of barriers or detours which may stop or slow the expansion process. Presence of many individuals who feel a high sense of identification with a community should keep conflict in legitimate channels, preventing expansion from disagreement to antagonism. These people are likely to be involved in conflicts, and consequently conflict may be frequent, but it should stay within legitimate channels so that Gresham's Law does not apply.[4]

If many people have conflicting loyalties to groups or individuals likely to take opposite sides of a conflict, there should also be less conflict at the community level, as these people will be paralyzed out of participation by the cross-pressuring demands of their various affiliations. Co-optation of opposition leaders into an established power structure under attack is a strategy for weakening the solidarity of an opposition which, if successful, may also cut off expansion of a conflict. Appeal to goals or values which transcend a specific conflict is another strategy of containment. If opponents can be referred to some greater good to which they all aspire and which might be threatened by their conflict, they may be motivated to resolve their differences quickly and within legitimate channels.[5]

Agreement on the initial issues of a conflict is also proposed as a constraint to expansion, as attempts at redefinition will be less frequent. The general snowballing tendency of community conflict also suggests that any factor which tends to constrain expansion will be most effective early in the history of the conflict. Therefore, the longer its history of past expansion, the more difficult a conflict should be to contain at any given time.[6]

On the other hand, conflict may be defused, according to some observers, as it becomes a habit. If the same sides face each other in a conflict over a long period of time, the opponents will come to agree on the definition of what they disagree about and on the procedures for resolving their differences. Conflict is therefore kept within legitimate channels which are created in the course of the conflict itself.[7]

Generalizations about Community Conflict Applied to Les Floralies

Expansion of conflict in Les Floralies follows the dynamics described for conflict in many other kinds of communities; however, factors which constrain conflict in other communities seem to be less effective here.

Conflict Expansion—Redefinition

The initial issues in all the expanded conflicts were redefined as original participants tried to mobilize supporters. Most attempts at redefinition were initiated by the side in the weakest position to begin with: it was the pro-Communist faction which tried to redefine the election issue into a question of procedural illegality by protesting the secret slate. It was also the pro-Communist faction which tried to expand the election, the leisure committee, and the Mass conflicts to include support from outside the residence. Redefinition in terms of political affiliation came most prominently from the anti-Communists, as shown for instance in the leisure committee dispute. Since the majority of residents at the time of this study were not Communist, they could potentially be mobilized into an anti-Communist position. Working from an essentially negative stance, the Beliveau faction has a diverse group of supporters for any issue defined in political terms. Devout Catholics and equally devout anticlerics can be aligned in a conflict defined in terms of a Communist menace. The Communists, on the other hand, have much less to gain from redefinition in terms of political identification, since this makes available to them only the smaller group of residents with the narrower pro-Communist orientation.

Expansion from Specific to General Issues, Referential to Condensation Symbols, and Issues to Personalities

Specific conflicts over amount of leisure activity in the residence, individual candidates for office, delivery of mail, and celebration of a Mass all expanded into confrontations defined by general issues such as political ideologies, freedom of political expression, or religious liberty. Debate over general issues was carried out as an exchange of emotion-arousing symbols such as Communist conspiracy, the Resistance, the Catholic Church. Fools, slippery eels, Reds, and a phantom committee, plus various drunkards and dirty old men, appear on both sides of the expanded conflicts as disagreement boils over into open and personal antagonism. Generalized and distorted images of the other side transform anticlerical Socialists into Catholics or volunteer bartenders into the menace of Communist take-over.

Social Polarization. Mme. Clignet's change of tables in the dining room, the refusal of the committee to participate in the Mardi Gras party, the split of the gerontology workers into two groups, and the Communist domination of the Christmas flower project are examples of social polarization resulting from various episodes of conflict. Especially immediately after one of these disputes, residents were far more likely to eat, work, and relax with others on the same side than with a member of the opposition.

Partisan Organizations. Although formal partisan organizations did not form in the community, informal groups of core faction members met for secret strategy sessions throughout every conflict. Formal groups of residents, such as the sewing club, the afternoon *belote* players, or various work groups either took on a unified political character during conflicts (Christmas flowers were Communist, sewing club and *belote* game were not) or, like the office workers, split into separate groups.

New Leaders. The appearance of M. Rouget in the leisure committee conflict accords with what Coleman calls Gresham's Law of Conflict. Well-known for his extremist views and for his violent personal attacks on Beliveau, Rouget played a minor part in the election events, but appeared in the leisure committee dispute, which might also be seen as an expansion of the election conflict.

Containment of Conflict

Some of the roadblocks to conflict expansion observed in other settings are also effective at Les Floralies; several are far less significant there than in other kinds of community.

Identification with Community. The frequency and rapidity of conflict expansion in the Les Floralies community suggests, according to other studies of community conflict, that few residents have a strong sense of identification with the community. If many of them had this sense of identification there might be many conflicts, but they should remain in legitimate channels, and should not expand into antagonism, personal attacks, or extreme social polarization. At Les Floralies, on the other hand, the residents for whom the residence is most important, who devoted the greatest emotional energy to social lives focused inside the residence, are the faction leaders who provoked the series of redefinitions resulting in extreme expansion of many conflicts. In general, the residents with the strongest political allegiance are those for whom the community is most important ($r = .42$, $N = 122$). The most passionate participants in these conflicts are those who have a clear vision of what they think the residence should be and are willing to fight with all weapons at their disposal to put their ideals into effect. Involvement in the community and identification with it push these people toward expansion rather than containment of conflict.

Since a retirement residence is a new kind of setting for community in general, and since Les Floralies is a new residence with most of its original population, one explanation for the failure of identification with the community to contain conflict in legitimate channels is that it is not yet clear what are legitimate channels in this new community. Residents on both sides of many conflicts contradicted this explanation by their symmetrical critiques of each other for personal attacks, redefinition in political terms, and social polarization. There was wide agreement that expansion of conflict into antagonism and deep social division was undesirable; each side blamed this kind of illegitimate expansion on the other. The distinctive characteristic of this community which makes identification with it a catalyst rather than a constraint to conflict expansion is certainly its factions. Since formal socialization agents are almost nonexistent, individuals who are not channeled into one faction or another soon after arrival remain extremely inactive in the social world of the residence. The individuals who become involved in the community—and therefore in its conflicts—learn the attitudes and behaviors by which they express this involvement through participation in a faction. Logically enough, therefore, involvement does not make them champions of conflict containment. Since their involvement in the community is filtered through factional allegiance, once any conflict is redefined into factional terms, they will expand it as far as necessary in the interests of winning, always feeling that a victory for their side is a victory for the community as a whole.[8] Factional distributions are reinforced by every conflict which does expand into these terms; and, conversely, the deeper these familiar channels of alignment are drawn into the map of social relations in a community, the more likely it becomes that any conflict will be redefined into factional terms. Since redefinition of issues is one measure of conflict expansion, the fact of factionalization promotes it.

Cross-Pressure. The vehemently anticlerical president of the Residence Committee, prodded by his wife to support a Mass in the residence, was trapped in the kind of cross-pressure which in many communities prevents individuals in this position from participation in conflict, and thus may curtail its expansion. The dispute over the Mass did not, in fact, expand very far beyond its original issues and participants. Beliveau was not the only resident caught in contradictory loyalties. Many members of his faction are also Socialists and anticlerical; their own opposition to religious intervention in the residence was at odds with their usual anti-Communist alliance with the Catholics. On the other side, some members of the Communist faction, like Mme. Clignet, were Catholics, although they had belonged to the Communist-oriented union and were consequently socialized into the residence through the Communist group.

Co-optation. Co-optation of opponents into an established power structure is a technique of conflict containment observed in many communities. Although there were opportunities for co-optation in the conflicts at Les Floralies (for example, the leisure committee, the secret slate of candidates, the bar), the Beliveau supporters who dominated the committee were too mistrustful of members of the pro-Communist faction to risk their participation in legitimate authority. The attempts at co-optation which were made— encouragement of Mme. Clignet to run for office, or support of the leisure committee proposal—were made by the director and were strongly rejected by the anti-Communist committee. Although Beliveau and his followers were anxious to reduce the level of conflict in the residence, they felt that inclusion of individuals from the other faction in any decision-making group would be too dangerous; it would be a first step toward take-over.

Superordinate Goals. Although the well-being of the residence itself or the fulfillment of the common needs of the retired workers which it served were both available as goals or values which might have transcended specific disagreements, they were never effectively used to contain conflict. Frequent appeals were made for harmony in the interest of "our home" by both residents and staff members. However, members of the factions often had opposite definitions of what was the good of the residence, so if these exhortations had any effect, it was to convince each side that its struggle to improve life in the community was being obstructed by its contentious opponents.

Initial Agreement on Issues. M. Fortin never argued the fact that he spent many hours locked in his room with a young woman and a sack of wine bottles; the drunken sailor never denied that he was drunk. Each was a case in which the deviant thought his activities were legitimate and other residents did not. The issues were agreed on by both sides in both cases from the beginning, and neither was redefined into terms which might involve a larger proportion of the community.

Timing of Containment Factors. The first effects of cross-pressure appeared very early in the conflict about the Mass, at the meeting when the committee considered Mme. Beliveau's request. The apparent influence of divided loyalties on containment of this conflict is consistent with the hypothesis that constraining factors are more effective the earlier they appear in the evolution of a conflict.

Extended Participation of Same Opposing Groups

The conflicts at Les Floralies, which are consistently redefined into oppositions between the same political factions, contradict the generalization, derived from studies in other settings, that if the same two sides remain in conflict over a long period of time, they are progressively more likely to agree on issues and on norms for the conduct of the conflict. This agreement is then supposed to restrain conflict from expansion to other participants or into highly emotional hostility and social polarization, which is certainly not the case at Les Floralies.

Conclusion: Conflict and Community at Les Floralies

The similarities in the progression of disputes over flouride in the water of an American town and about recreation in a residence for retired French construction workers are as striking as they might seem unexpected. They become totally reasonable if the focus of comparison is shifted from differences in the actors and the substance of conflict, to the fundamental similarity that both settings are small communities. Differences in the effects of many conditions which restrain conflict in other situations, but which remain consistently ineffective at Les Floralies, point up the ways in which the residence is distinct from other communities.

Neither the age of the people at Les Floralies nor the fact that they happen to be French seems a likely explanation for the failure of many constraints on conflict to operate here. In terms of conflict, the critical feature of social organization in the residence is its factionalization. There is no paradox in the discovery that patterns of conflict give evidence both for the existence of community in the residence and for its factionalization. One of the most basic propositions linking the concepts of conflict and community is that involvement in conflict is a kind of participation in a community.[9] At Les Floralies, it is through the factions that people learn to be members of the community. The residents whose factional allegiances are most clear-cut are the most active participants in both organized and informal activities and the residence community is more important to them than to others.

If the political identities which permit recruitment into factions have consequences for participation in this community, their use in the community in turn has consequences for them as factional borders. The kind of disputes described in this chapter reinforce these borders at the same time as they translate the political identification which marked them into terms meaningful only inside the residence.

The terms Communist, anti-Communist, Socialist, or Catholic are seldom used inside the residence to describe the factions, except in private and by the most militant members. Most people use terms which are not so much euphemisms as translations into identities relevant inside the community: the opposition, the gripers, the president and his clan, Mme. Dupont and her friends on the thirteenth floor. The primordial distinction of we versus they is the most common way of talking about the two sides, and each new conflict provides another point of reference for what "they" did and how "we" responded. The shared belief that political conflict is forbidden and dangerous for the harmony of the community, is probably a reason for this verbal smokescreen. It helps to obscure potentially painful awareness of the contradiction between what people say about politics and conflict and what they persistently and vigorously do.

The internal focus of the factions is also apparent in the asymmetry of appeals for help to outside political contacts. Mme. Dupont, for instance, asks a friend in the union for help in defending the residence against a clerical invasion, but the reverse does not occur.

Neither faction is mobilized to participate in politics outside the residence. There is a remarkable lack of attention to external political events by comparison with the intense involvement in even apparently minor internal conflicts. Conversations about political events outside the residence, either national or local, are extremely rare. It is just as rare to hear a conversation about any event inside the residence without a factional interpretation.

That residents for whom outside political identity has relatively low salience—such as many of the people who voted in the elections—can be stimulated to participate in internal conflict also underscores the translation of the original markers of faction borders into terms relevant inside the community. Mme. Clignet, to take an extreme example, was recruited into active participation in the pro-Communist faction on the basis of events inside the residence. Her appearance as a player on a community-wide stage and her movement into the active core of the Dupont faction were almost simultaneous. Her experience is in sharp contrast to that of M. Clere. Both entered the residence in its first two months, when, from what I could induce, socialization experiences were quite different. New residents had a great deal of contact with staff members; factional distinctions had not yet surfaced; most organized activities had not yet been launched; many norms widely agreed upon a year later had not become explicit. At that point neither M. Clere nor Mme. Clignet had a clear political identity. The same comparison a year later, when M. Clere, who still has no clear factional allegiance, is rapidly losing status and withdrawing from social activity and Mme. Clignet, newly recruited into a faction, is just as rapidly gaining on both counts, emphasizes once again how crucial these divisions have become as channels for community participation.

Perceptions of the factions as social borders marked by behaviors and attitudes relevant to life inside the residence provide
shared understandings needed both for definition of a community
and for participation in it. Since at Les Floralies, this participation
follows factional lines, each conflict clarifies the definition of these
channels for participation at the same time as it emphasizes the
importance of the community to its members and its distinctiveness
as a locus for social life.

8 Community Creation at Les Floralies

Les Floralies as a Community

The residents of Les Floralies are members of a community. The reasons for this community's existence do not center around the fact that its members are old people, although their being old gives its existence particular significance for pressing problems of the elderly in modern society. The same factors which account for formation of communities in squatter settlements, utopias, and within or among nation states also explain the emergence of community at Les Floralies. From this point of view, age appears as one of the background factors providing a basis for potential community formation. Like ethnicity or religion, it is a source of present common problems and shared past experiences which may or may not be recognized and translated into the we-feelings of community. The age of the Les Floralies residents, on the other hand, assumes primary importance in questions about the significance of this kind of community for the integration of older people into their societies. Does participation in this kind of community represent segregation, isolation, being "put away"? Or does it offer possibilities for satisfying social life which are often lacking in the wider society?

The characteristics of Les Floralies which make it appropriate to call the residence a community, and the factors which promoted community formation, are reviewed in this chapter. Several types of separate residential settings for older people have been studied by sociologists and anthropologists. Information which they report about public housing, privately sponsored residences, trailer parks, and retirement villages, as well as "natural" concentrations of old people in apartment houses or towns is compared in the final chapter with my conclusions about Les Floralies. Common patterns can be deciphered in this scattering of studies. The fact that they are consistent with observations at Les Floralies leads to broader questions about the significance of residential separation as an aspect of age-grading or age border definition in many modern societies.

Characteristics of Community at Les Floralies.
Territory

Because they live at Les Floralies, residents by definition share the territorial aspect of community. The boundaries of this territory are also clearly marked for both outsiders and insiders: it is a building with a sign over the door and a fence around it. Local neighbors and merchants recognize residents as being from "the home." Residents in turn are protective of their shared space. They worry about outsiders who might intrude, and although they value very highly their freedom to come and go, many would like to have the doors locked at least at night. Whether or not people share a territory is an absolute judgment. They do or they do not; and people at Les Floralies do.

Social Organization

The regular patterns of social living which define a social organization are also present to a high degree at Les Floralies. The flow of everyday contacts can be charted into roles, groups, and factions; attitudes about problems fundamental to continuation of these contacts—conflict, sexual relations, death, food-getting and sharing—can be described as widely shared norms and beliefs. Leaders, heroes, couples, workers and disreputables are all roles which are clearly defined, and in terms derived from life inside the residence. Many friendship groups are recognized by other residents; and the faction borders which order so much of social life not only are evidence of social organization but, because of their redefinition in internal terms, also demonstrate the distinctiveness of this social order from its context. Similarly, a ladder of social statuses is both an indication of orderly, patterned interaction and also, in its internal focus, a further emphasis of the independence of social organization at Les Floralies.

The development of the committee as an institution is an important aspect of the emerging social organization, as well as a good example of the process. Originally defined very vaguely as a social committee concerned with recreation for residents, the committee now is seen not only as a decision-making body concerned with issues well beyond the area of recreation, but also as a mechanism for conflict resolution, and as an intermediary between staff and residents. The election conflict was very important in making the committee more visible and more salient to many residents. The committee's triumph over the petitioners for the "leisure satellite" emphasized perceptions of its possible influence—on the director, and consequently on the lives of other residents. Specific incidents, such as the petition about the Mass, or the requests for public funeral arrangements, were channeled through the committee, and broadened its domain of action beyond that of recreation. Issues such as M. Fortin's "niece" or Mme. Tournier's fight with the chef, which were brought to the committee, set a precedent for its role in conflict resolution. In both these cases the committee asked the Director to take action, which also reinforced the notion that it was appropriate for residents to reach the director via someone on the committee. In a mutually reinforcing spiral of events, the committee is becoming more visible and more important to residents as its functions are expanded and defined.

In answer to the first question, is there social organization here, the response is clearly yes. Both consistent patterns of behavior, and widely shared beliefs and attitudes about this behavior, can be identified. Once again Les Floralies, when contrasted with other residential groupings in modern industrial societies, scores very high on measures of community.

Particularly relevant to the definition of borders around a new community, and particularly important in an institutional setting, is a question which goes beyond presence of social organization to ask about its relationship to the context of the surrounding society. Sources of social status at Les Floralies, for example, are not a reflection of those which are current outside the residence. They also do not directly reject outside patterns, but rather emphasize the distinctiveness of this community by making many external sources of status simply irrelevant. If the staff are looked at as representatives, or at least as members of the wider society, it is also striking that social organization among the old people not only goes beyond patterns imposed by the staff, but often exists in opposition to staff efforts. The possessive permanence of seating in the dining hall, central to informal socializing, persists in spite of staff proddings and invitations to residents to move around. Factional identities for activities organized by the staff not only go beyond their plans but are usually unknown to staff members. The detailed beliefs spun out about the food supply also go far beyond staff intentions or knowledge, although they start from a basic activity—food distribution—which is directed by a staff member. The entire web of informal relationships, friendship, mutual aid, couples, has developed and exists outside of staff influence. The factions which are key strands in this web of sociability are most definitely not approved by the staff; the director made several unsuccessful attempts at reconciliation or co-optation, each of which was duly interpreted by the factions as his susceptibility to manipulation by the other. Demands for a ritual recognition of death resulted from acute disagreement between the old people and a young administrator. The possibility of participation in funerals is now part of social life at Les Floralies because some of the old people recognized a need and asked for a ritual response to it. Residents also express and enforce ideas, quite distinct from official rules, about how people should behave here. M. Colette, for example, was sent to Coventry by other residents for an act which broke no formal rule. In other cases, an official rule may be manipulated by residents as a way of sanctioning disapproved behavior which the rule was in no way intended to cover: M. Fortin's prostitute, a threat to the community's image but not a rule-breaker, became an illegal overnight guest, susceptible to banishment by the director.

The consistently patterned relationships, and the shared beliefs and attitudes about them, representative of social organization, are present at Les Floralies to an extent unusual in residential settings in urban, industrial societies. The order of social life here is also often distinct from that of the wider society, of the past lives of the residents, and of the intentions and control of the staff.

We-feeling

"We old people," "we working people," "we people who lived through the wars"—all these frequent uses of "we" provide the basis for the new one, "we residents." The sense of shared past and present experiences pulls these people together at the same time as it makes them feel distinct from others. Basic assumptions about the world, such as shortage of food or division of the social spectrum according to such symbols as Vichy and the Resistance or Communists and non-Communists, are shared as automatically as the words to "Le Petit Vin Blanc." Physical aches, or the social pains of

retirement or relationships with grown children, stimulate com-
miseration, exchanged remedies, and, at minimum, a feeling of
being understood and not suffering alone or as a deviant.

With a basis for we-feeling in their common historical, social,
and physical age, reinforced (or not fragmented) by their common
social class, residents suddenly found themselves in a situation
where, as they say, "we'll spend the rest of our lives." Their
developing awareness of a shared fate is evidence for the we-feeling
aspect of community at Les Floralies. The acute concern that the
actions of any resident will affect the future of all the others is one
expression of this feeling. Mme. Tournier's fight with the chef, M.
Fortin's prostitute, the handicapped women who wanted to go to
Amsterdam, were all seen as possible threats to all members of the
community: staff members would be very angry with them all; the
residence would be seen as disreputable; trips for everyone might
be curtailed. Worries about the financial status of the residence are
another indication of we-feeling, and also progressively bolstered
it. In this case, an increasing number of residents saw themselves as
more practical and experienced than the young director, who they
were afraid would spend so much money on leisure "luxuries" that
there would be too little left to pay for clothing. The fear that
unwise budget decisions would have painful effects on everyone
reflects a sense of common fate. The interpretation of what were
seen as financial follies in terms of youth and inexperience emphasize age as a source of we-feelings. Even the fierce factional battles
are a quickly dissolving contradiction to we-feeling. People fight
about what is good for the community because they feel tied to it
and to each other. The intensity of the battles is itself evidence for
the force of these feelings.

Both the external and internal borders of community have been
created at Les Floralies. The border between the residence and the
world outside is marked in many ways: spatially, socially, and by
perceptions and attitudes. The residence building is highly visible,
clearly labeled, and the boundaries of its territory are defined by a
fence. Social contacts also trace a border, as both in frequency and
in range they are concentrated inside the residence. People at Les
Floralies spend more time and do more kinds of things with each
other than with anyone from outside. The fact that this shared
social life can be mapped out as the roles, groups, statuses, and
norms of a distinct social organization also indicates a border.
People are workers in the residence, important in the residence,

leaders in the residence, even couples in the residence. Each of these definitions in terms of present life at Les Floralies is another reminder of the border. People here also see themselves as distinct from outsiders. Their "we" derives from common age and social background, but now also refers to their situation as residents, in contrast to staff members, in contrast to other older people, in contrast to others who live in Bagnolet, in contrast to the society outside in general. Residents are also recognized by neighbors and local merchants. The border is also revealed by the experiences of those who cross it. Newcomers to the residence have a lot to learn in order to participate in its social world. The adjustment process is recognized by everyone as a distinct part of their experience. For many it is painful, and often people discover *rites de passage* to ease the transition. In the first year the residence was open, a consistent pattern of informal socialization had developed, through which established residents guided new arrivals into both formal and informal activities.

The factions which channel newcomers into contacts with established residents are the most important internal social border. Their function in the socialization of new residents was the first step toward their redefinition into symbols of opposition derived from life inside Les Floralies. This redefinition in turn makes the internal borders a further marker of distinctiveness from the world outside.

Creation of Community at Les Floralies

Community exists at Les Floralies. Two kinds of factors are involved in answering the question of how this community was created. A variety of background factors, present from the first days of the residence, suggested the potential for community formation. Residents were alike not only in terms of age, but also in terms of social class and experience as participants in French culture, characteristics which were highly salient to most of them. Most residents perceived very little alternative to being at Les Floralies; their decisions to enter were based on that fact. Being "here for the rest of our lives" was an important source of identification with this community. Moving into a situation which combined the worst features of being known and unknown was a frightening and painful transition for almost everyone, the kind of transition which in many studies of initiations or community formation precedes high commitment for those who survive it. The only things which were not ambiguous in anticipations of the new setting were false but detailed images of poor farms and old folks homes. As people turned over all their assets to the welfare system in order to enter Les Floralies, they made a very great investment, which to them seemed irreversible. Material ties of property or social ties of kinship which are sometimes seen as threats to community were minimal in the residence. Talented, energetic leaders were available,[1] and the residence is small enough for social contacts to be face-to-face: two more fundamentals in the community formation process.

Urban squatter settlements, international organizations, and utopian experiments suggested other factors prompting community formation which may or may not take off from this base of background characteristics, and then build beyond it to community. With the details of life at Les Floralies in hand, we can ask how these factors were involved in the formation of a community there. Social participation in community-wide events, decision-making, interdependence, work, and a wide range of kinds of contacts; the presence of threat; and the development of symbols all played their part in the emergence of community at the residence.

Participation

The broadest possible statement of the relationship between participation and feelings about a group or collectivity is that the more they participate, the more its members will value the group or collectivity (possibly to maintain cognitive consistency) and the stronger solidarity will be among them. Observations of community formation in a wide range of settings have also identified more specific relationships between various kinds of participation and different aspects of community.

A general judgment about participation in social life at Les Floralies is that it is both widespread and active: many residents take part regularly in a variety of ways. At minimum, everyone shares a meal once a day. Both elections and parties attract almost universal participation. About 60 percent of the residents have very frequent informal social contacts. Thirty-two percent are regularly involved in organized group activities; 27 percent work. Given this base-line of participation, it makes sense to look more closely at the specific kinds of activity which have promoted community formation in other settings. Do they also have an impact at Les Floralies?

Community-wide Events

Many community meetings, especially when they occur daily, are characteristic of successful utopian experiments—those which create stable communities. Frequent meetings which bring the individual into contact with the collectivity promote we-feeling. "Participation ... makes a member more involved in the group, keeps him more informed of events, gives him a greater sense of belonging."[2] Taking part in community-wide events, in particular political meetings, was also pointed out as one factor in the emergence of a remarkable community among squatters in Nairobi, Kenya.[3]

The time and place to start looking for the effect of this factor at Les Floralies is certainly noon in the dining room. Every resident is guaranteed participation in one group experience everyday, since eating this meal in the dining room is obligatory. The significance of the dining room as a stage where friendship, conflict, leadership, and censure are made public removes any notion that this meal represents spatial but not social togetherness. Even a person who sits and eats in silence is a spectator to the daily dramas of community life. People appear in the residence for the first time in the dining room; their progress toward social incorporation is marked by a permanent table place. Leavings as well as arrivals are learned about here, as the announcement of death is also made in the dining room. As people make their rounds of greeting, as those with problems stop by a leader's table, as conversation continues, the flow of information is both visible and audible. Banishment from social contacts is signaled by sitting at a table alone.

The small, round tables undoubtedly make possible very different social consequences for eating together than the long, institutional tables I have seen in some residences. The table group of four offers a possibility for immediate, primary ties which consistently appear in studies of human groups as essential for linking the individual to a larger community. This possibility in turn depends on the principles developed and insisted upon by the residents themselves, of choice and permanence in seating.

"Dining room" is very often my immediate answer to friends and colleagues who ask about reasons for community in this residence. I am always shocked at the different image of the residence which appears instantly if I imagine it without the shared noon meal.

Put in the perspective of community formation in settings as disparate as urban slums and rural communes, the dining room at Les Floralies appears as a highly important stimulus to daily group experience. A small population offers the potential of face-to-face interaction, but this cannot be realized without a public arena where social contacts can be made and observed. In the dining room residents are reminded daily that they are part of a collectivity, and they are kept up to date on important social information, often as eye witnesses. Every day they share reactions to this information with table partners, whose presence in turn becomes for others additional shared knowledge of a social map.

Meals are not the only community-wide events which take place in the dining room. Parties also go on there, and, except for the one Mardi Gras dance which was defined as a Communist party, there is usually extremely high and enthusiastic participation in these events. It was always far easier to count the few people who were missing, because they were ill or away from the residence, than to list those present. Memories of Christmas or New Years celebrations, with details of who danced with whom, who was drunk, who sang, are one element in a developing repertory of shared experiences which is a basis for feelings of distinctiveness as a community.

The dining room was also the scene of the elections, which offer another example of extremely high participation in a community activity. The elections added another landmark experience, peopled with villains and heroes, to the community repertory. Because they presented the possibility of residents' acting as decision-makers, the elections also raise the question of the "participation hypothesis" and its relevance to the residence. This hypothesis states that when members participate in making decisions which affect a group, they are more likely to value it and to feel solidarity among themselves. Applied to the process of community formation, the hypothesis suggests that participation in decisions affecting the potential community should promote positive feelings toward it and toward other members.

Decision-Making

The clandestine election campaign, the residents assembled to observe victory or defeat, the aftermath of attempts to undermine committee power for the first time focused the attention of many residents on the possibility of serious participation in making decisions affecting the community. For most residents, those not in the militant core of a faction, this had been not so much an impossibility as simply something that had never occurred to them. The residence had a director, so they assumed he made all the important decisions. Since they were welcomed by the committee on arrival, everyone knew it existed, but for most it was seen as vaguely concerned with social events but certainly not as a powerful group of representatives. Residents who received help, advice, and comfort from M. Beliveau or Mme. Thibault usually thought of them as exceptionally kind and knowledgeable individuals, but these attributes were not particularly linked to their being members of the committee. The December elections made this link highly visible and gave it intense emotional significance for many residents. The personal loyalty that many people felt to individuals such as Beliveau or Thibault became political as a result of the election conflict. Many residents told me that they had never taken the committee too seriously, but if, for whatever reason, M. Beliveau (or Mme. Thibault, or M. Clere), who had been so kind and helpful, wanted to be elected, well then he or she should be. The realization that respected people took the committee so seriously was, for many residents, the first step toward looking at it more seriously themselves.

The factional borders which channeled the election battle, as we have seen, also became more sharply defined as a result of the conflict. Although early social contacts are guided by previous political sympathies, for most residents the quality or content of these contacts had little or nothing to do with politics. When the Beliveaus helped Mme. Myotte with her food order forms, she did not perceive there was anything political about the encounter, although from the Beliveau perspective it is clear that she would never have been invited to their apartment if the president's sensitive antennae had detected a pro-Communist potential. The elections translated many personal feelings of affection, loyalty, or gratitude into political terms. When M. Beliveau explained to people like the Myottes that the trouble-makers who were attacking him were Communists, their relationship to him took on a new dimension: they were all anti-Communist. For M. Beliveau, this way of looking at the world was derived from life-long experience; he simply applied it to the residence. For many others like the Myottes, although pro- or anti-Communist were certainly political choices with which they were familiar and in which they had participated at some level of involvement in union membership, it was events and loyalties centered in the residence which gave these identities more intense significance for daily social life. Mme. Clignet's movement into active faction membership is another example of this process.

Factional conflicts which followed the elections all focused on control of different aspects of community life. The struggles were derived from the assumption that residents could have an important influence on their situation, and consequently the intensity and frequency of factional conflict both reinforced this idea and spread it to wider numbers of residents. The leisure committee battle, which immediately followed the elections, made a particularly important contribution to growing interest and belief in resident decision-making. The people who presented the leisure committee petition were stunned to find that the committee had overruled the director's obvious enthusiasm for their proposal. As a participant in all the discussion between M. Guerillon and members of the committee, I am convinced that his enthusiasm was sincere: the director himself was surprised at his inability to convince the committee. Realization of the extent of committee influence on the director was a shock but of course was also the impetus for more attempts by the "opposition" to get into similar positions of potential influence. And the snowball effect continues. This factional conflict over resident control produced further evidence of the possibility of that control, at the same time drawing more residents into factional alignments and consequently making them more aware of their possible participation in making decisions which affect their lives.

Two specific issues demonstrate this awakening concern about decisions, a concern that could only develop after the elections and consequent conflicts posed the possibility of some resident influence. One complaint often expressed by people to whom I talked during the election period was that they never knew what went on in the committee anyway. There were no reports made, and general meetings in which residents could ask questions and bring grievances were rare (two per year). This attack on the committee was started by members of the Dupont faction, but it became a very widespread comment during and after the elections. Beliveau and the committee, incidentally , agreed with the need for reports and for general meetings, and had on their own made these requests to the director for months. The force of factional divisions is neatly demonstrated as essential agreement is redefined into two positions. The Communists demand more information flow to restrain committee dominance; the committee members now say they need more information flow to protect themselves from accusations of being a power elite.

Expression of worry about budget mismanagement also increased after the elections. Again, this was an issue which members of the Communist faction used to attack the committee by saying too much was spent on leisure and not enough for clothes. Committee members had frequently raised this same problem with the director. Although there is wide concern about buying clothes, often discussed in terms of residents' age and experience versus the director's youth and lack of practicality, the issue does not seem likely to blur faction alignments, since proposed solutions to the problem split along faction lines. The president and his supporters tend to think of the budget in zero-sum terms. Since there is only so much money, expenditures for leisure have to be cut back in order to have enough for necessities. Mme. Dupont's position is that the residents have worked hard enough all their lives to be provided for now. Both clothes and recreation are supposed to be supplied, so if more money is needed, the retirement fund should increase the budget.

Resident participation in making decisions about life at Les Floralies is still at a relatively low level. However, awareness of the possibility of this participation, and conflict over which residents should be involved sharply increased, mutually stimulating each other, in the months following the elections. Since neither the conflicts nor the issues of general meetings and money for clothing show any signs of subsiding, it seems likely that concern about participation in decisions, and probably that participation itself, will continue to grow.

According to the "participation hypothesis," taking part in decisions should produce positive feelings about the residence and toward other residents. There is some evidence that this is happening, although, as usual, the effects are filtered through factional divisions. A variable measuring loyalty to the residence was constructed from items on the questionnaire.[4] The residents who score highest on loyalty tend to be members of the Beliveau faction. Since the entire committee was from this faction, and its leader was the president, its members participated more in making decisions than did followers of Mme. Dupont. Even those who were not directly involved in decision-making could think of themselves as associated with this process, while residents in the other faction typically thought of themselves as the opposition, and as excluded from any influence on decisions. The loyalty responses are consequently at least consistent with the hypothesis. Answers to another question point in the same direction. When I asked people if they thought that residents had a tendency to take advantage, supporters of M. Beliveau were more likely to say yes than were members of the other faction. They made a distinction, in other words, between the residence community, to which they feel loyalty, and some other residents, from whom they feel the community needs to be protected. These responses also seem consistent with the participation hypothesis, given the added factor of factional differences.

Vigorous and often widespread participation in factional conflicts, which are all focused more or less directly on attempts to control different aspects of residence life, can also be seen as indications of positive feelings about the community. People care about the residence enough to fight about what happens to it. The time and emotional energy they invest in these battles in turn should give participation in the community even more value. Although stormy demonstrations of concern about the residence cannot be seen as *caused* by participation in decision-making, since they involve both factions, they are derived from growing awareness that participation in decision-making is possible. A weaker version of the hypothesis therefore seems to apply.

Valuing the residence and solidarity with other residents are clearly distinguished from each other, for instance, in the questionnaire responses about loyalty and taking advantage. The simple relationship between participation in decision-making and feelings of solidarity does not apply, because the faction borders are at their most acute when decision-making is involved. Taking part in the factional battles, however, does increase solidarity within the factions. Since individuals are so consistently linked into this community through their ties to factional subgroups, the possibility of resident influence on decisions, via its stimulation of factional conflict, does promote social integration.

The participation hypothesis tells us two things about the consequences of decision-making for community formation. First, the residents who actually make decisions, and their supporters, are more likely to feel loyal to the residence as a community, although they exclude some residents from these positive feelings. Second, the possibility of residents' influence on decisions promotes the conflicts which sharpen the internal borders of social organization and knit individuals into the factional subgroups through which they are attached, both socially and emotionally, to the community. These effects became visible after the elections brought the possibilities of resident decision-making into the spotlight. The residence had then been open one year; concern and conflict about decision-making, with their consequences for community, have continued to increase since that initial explosion.

Work

The natural experiments in community formation provided by utopias show that communal, unpaid work can be a source of success. The experiments which resulted in stable communities were far more likely than the failures to have work systems which involved no wages, little specialization, and frequent communal projects. Working together for the good of the community appears to promote feelings of "connectedness, belonging, participation in a whole, mingling of the self in the group."[5]

At Les Floralies, not all residents work, so we cannot expect the effects to be so universal. However, the residents who do work share certain attitudes toward the community. For those who choose to work, this kind of participation seems to produce feelings of identification with the community as a whole, although not with all residents. People who work, for instance, are more likely to be highly loyal to the residence. The distinction between this feeling and attitudes toward other residents is enunciated in their response to the statement, "We have a right to demand what we want in the residence." People who work tend to disagree ($r = .48$, $N = 64$). Rather than answering only for themselves as workers, I think they are answering in terms of all residents, including the majority who do not work. They do not feel that the proper relationship between residents and the community is one of demanding, because they see themselves as on the receiving end of the demands from other residents. Since they express an identity with the community for which they work, they disapprove the notion of "demands" which sets up a residence/residents opposition.

The career of Mme. Prevot is a reminder of the way in which work can be a road to satisfying social participation and feelings of belonging in the residence. Her first weeks in the kitchen were a desperate attempt to fill the hours she otherwise spent trying not to think about her financial and family troubles. As she moved into the flower-making project, work became a source of daily contact with a group of new friends, whose developing closeness was bolstered by faction membership. Ask Mme. Prevot about her adjustment to life in the residence, and she will immediately tell you about work and the discovery of Communist friends, the intertwined reasons for her current happiness. The fact that increasing involvement in the Communist faction eventually led to withdrawal from work, of course, does not negate the importance of working in her initial adjustment to the residence.

Work at Les Floralies is done initially for many different reasons. People want to pass the time; they want to maintain the status of a skilled role; they want to contribute to the community to which they feel gratitude. As the work roles continue, however, there is a convergence of experiences. Almost every job involves social contact: usually in a work group, sometimes with individuals who ask for specific repairs; even for the most antisocial, like Mme. Denis, there is continuing contact with a staff member seen as a friend. In addition to producing social ties, working seems to stimulate feelings of loyalty and identification with the residence. The strain toward cognitive consistency probably contributes here. People who work tend to value and want to protect the community in which they have invested their time and effort. It also makes sense that they see themselves as part of "the way things are done," since they do many of these things, and consequently resist criticism and demanding which they see as directed at themselves.

Looked at from the point of view of its consequences in utopian experiments, work has contributed to community formation at Les Floralies through its effect on the social participation and attitudes of certain individuals. As was the case with participation in factional conflict, feelings of solidarity developed within a work group (which typically does not cross faction lines) are not extended to all residents. Feelings toward members of the work group, and toward the residence as a community, are distinguished from disapproval of "some residents" who criticize and make demands, although they do not work. Since the essential difference between Les Floralies and these experiments is that the residence is not a planned attempt at communal experience, it is not surprising that the effects of work, like those of the factions, are more similar to the dynamics of "natural" communities. Various individuals are linked to the community through their immediate ties into sub-groups, and their feelings about the community spring from different sources and may not be extended to every individual in it. Since work is not paid, it has also not had the possibly divisive consequence of producing income differences.

From a more general point of view, the presence of more than thirty people with widely recognized work roles, of course, also strengthens the social organization aspect of community. There are many jobs whose definition is relevant only within the context of the residence (menu planner, food basket packer), and those which are carry-overs from outside activities (plumber, electrician) are performed only within the residence community and within the residence system of nonfinancial reciprocity. Shared understandings about these roles are an important element in the distinctive social organization of the residence.

Although some people worked almost from the day the residence opened, the number of work roles, as well as the number of residents who work, has substantially increased. There are several reasons for this increase, with its subsequent consequences for social ties and feelings about the community. The kitchen workers, for example, trace their existence back to the first Christmas meal which was prepared by the small group of first residents and the staff. The president has always been a member of this group, and his presence is a reminder that several of the first workers in the residence were committee members, individuals such as Beliveau and Thibault who subsequently acquired high status. They attracted others into their work groups, and probably contributed to both the factional and status connotations of working in general. Some individuals, M. Clere with his tool kit or Mme. Mueller with her watering can, simply saw a need and started to work. As other residents arrived, they could observe these activities, and some of them volunteered their own new skills, such as M. Myotte the plumber, or Mme. Prevot with her flowers. Factional conflict has also produced some work groups by fission—for instance, the split of the office workers resulted in two groups, each factionally "pure."

Interdependence

Cooperative brewing and selling of illegal beer was one reason for the high level of community achieved in a Nairobi squatter settlement. Awareness of interdependence was intensified by occasional police raids and the need to raise communal funds to bail out those who were arrested. Interdependence, usually economic or military, is also a source of emerging community among nation states.[6] In general, awareness of interdependence promotes feelings of shared fate, and the mechanics of interdependence, the social contacts through which it is played out, promote the definition of social organization. Although exchanging hand-made underwear for a crocheted blouse, giving an arm en route to the dining room, or preparing meals during a neighbor's illness are not as dramatic examples of interdependence as co-operative moonshining, they have great significance for the people involved. Because of this significance, interdependence also has consequences for community at Les Floralies. Residents share three kinds of relationships which involve interdependence: help in sickness or with a handicap; reciprocity of goods and services; and social, emotional ties of friendship.

Help with Illness or Handicap

For Mme. Tatu, who is guided through her days by other residents, dependence on their help is extreme, and she is intensely aware of that fact. For many other people who are ill and then recover, the support they receive from friends and neighbors is also a deep source of reassurance. The actual care represented by housekeeping chores, errands, or meal preparation is greatly appreciated. However, the most important kind of care is often the less tangible fact that someone is aware of the illness, will drop in to check up, and will act as a gadfly to insure staff attention. Residents did not feel secure without this knowledge. Many people told stories about failures of the elaborate system of emergency buttons which were supposed to summon a nurse at any hour of the day or night. Few people had actually tried them, but a few often repeated stories of those who rang and then waited for hours, frightened and alone, until a neighbor found them, were sufficient to weaken the impact of the system on psychological security. The head nurse was also seen by many residents as unreliable. The kindest said she was overworked and harassed; those who disliked her said she was disorganized, incompetent, or even that she really did not care about the residents. Her presence in the building was not sufficient to make many residents feel secure in the face of possible illness. The fear of being ill or injured and lying alone and helpless, possibly even dying, without anyone knowing, is a specter which recurred with frightening regularity in residents' conversations, often when they described their previous living conditions or those of some old person they knew outside the residence. The solace which the concern of friends and neighbors brought to this fear was a profound source of interdependence. It touched not only those who actually experienced illness and care, but also the others, who by observing these incidents could feel vicarious relief for their own possible future need. For both participants and observers, these experiences contribute directly to we-feeling, as they demonstrate a way in which residents' lives are bound together. The content of this particular kind of interdependence also leads to we-feeling in another way by showing these old people the commonality of the illness and injury problem for all of them who live alone.

Exchange of Goods and Services

Other non-emergency kinds of services and various material objects are also exchanged among residents. Products of knitting, crocheting, specialized sewing (for example, of men's pants or women's underclothes), knowledge of herbal recipes, even ironing, are either exchanged against a specific item, or offered in friendship and reciprocated more generally by invitations to coffee or aperitif and small gifts such as cigarettes or candy. For people whose incomes are miniscule, these exchanges often make possible having a new item of clothing, or having an old one refurbished. The significance of this kind of reciprocity becomes clear with the realization that without it, access to the item or the service would simply be impossible. The resident workers also perform many services, which are often seen as very difficult to obtain from the staff repairman. Repair of a leaky sink, a blown fuse, or a stubborn drawer makes life instantly more comfortable. It also provides a pleasant sense of arranging things between friends instead of making bureaucratic requests which emphasize the asker's dependent position vis a vis the staff, and to which responses come slowly if at all.

Participation in these transactions is not as widespread as in care for the ill or support for someone with a handicap. However, for those who do offer and receive things or services, the experience leads to feelings that life is more manageable and more pleasant because of relationships with other residents. Both kinds of interdependence are factors in community formation: the content of the exchanges leads to we-feelings; the social contacts through which they take place promote definition of social organization.

Social and Emotional Ties to Peers

The possibility of having social relationships with peers at all is for most residents greatly broadened because they are at Les Floralies. Interdependence in the most general sense, and perhaps the most important, is promoted by this availability of peers as friends and neighbors, sexual partners, and participants in the mutual process of defining appropriate norms for these and other social relationships in old age. Looking at interdependence in this way leads to the last of the participation factors suggested by other examples of community creation, the proportion of kinds of social contact shared by potential community members.

Range of Shared Contacts

Most residents do more kinds of things with each other than with anyone from outside. In some cases, of course, this is because residents have few active social ties outside Les Floralies. Many do, however, and although their emotional ties with specific individuals outside the residence, such as children, may be very strong, they almost never share the range of activities with these people that they do with other residents. Residents often share certain kinds of relationships with people both inside and outside Les Floralies. Help in an emergency, such as sickness, often comes both from children and from neighbors. The emotional significance of a visit from a child may be very great, but usually more actual assistance comes from neighbors who can attend to daily needs. Strong affective ties which develop inside the residence coexist with close relationships to children. Couples such as Mme. Joly and M. Gillet, or M. Deffontaines and Mme. Viatte, share highly emotional relationships inside the residence, and also maintain very close ties to their children. Both couples entertain the children together at Les Floralies, and also go away on vacation with them.

The one kind of tie which exists between parents and children but almost never occurs among residents is that of financial assistance. The only cases in which I observed money being given or loaned among residents was within couples. The almost universal lack of money makes this distinction hard to evaluate. Residents are certainly involved in exchanges of both objects and services, and they are most punctilious about reciprocity.

Many of the contacts which take place with people outside the residence are shared with other community members. Shopping trips to Paris or Bagnolet, a visit to the local cafe or just going for a walk very frequently involve more than one resident; women in particular usually leave the residence with someone else. The arrival of guests in the residence is also often the occasion to invite friends and neighbors from Les Floralies for an *aperitif* or coffee.

Residents of Les Floralies share a high proportion of kinds of social contacts with each other—perhaps less than the perennial examples of community such as the Bushmen or the Pygmies, but far higher than even the most closely knit urban neighborhood. They do not go outside of the residence to work; they leave rarely for entertainment, and then almost always with someone from Les Floralies. Political involvement pulls people inward, rather than sending them outside the residence. Battles are fought with inside rather than external enemies. Relationships between the sexes develop and are recognized inside the residence. There is no indication that people participate in community life to compensate for lack of outside ties, or that frequent contact with children or friends from outside is contradictory to intense involvement in life inside the residence. Emotional ties to children seem to be part of a distinct aspect of residents' social lives. They are different from, and therefore not in competition with, emotional bonds with other residents. Many contacts with friends and relatives from outside Les Floralies actually take place at the residence, and are often shared with other community members.

It is because residents at Les Floralies share such a high proportion of their social contacts with each other that many of the other factors in community formation can operate here. Generally high levels of participation in community activities, concern with decision-making, interdependence, and the appearance of community symbols would be far less likely if residents engaged in only a restricted range of encounters, while most of their spectrum of social contacts lay outside Les Floralies. It is through sharing many kinds of contact that residents become aware of the commonalities which lead to we-feelings; and a distinct social organization is recognizable as this variety of social ties stabilizes into patterns and evokes shared ideas about what the patterns should be and how they should be maintained.

Threat

Although the residents at Les Floralies do not face the bulldozers or nuclear coalitions which have stimulated feelings of community among squatters or nations under threat, they do feel threatened in certain ways which lead them to awareness of their shared fate. In terms of threat, the residents are more similar to some utopians who wanted to create a better social world precisely because their position, for instance as a religious minority, was precarious in the wider society. Although these old people certainly did not come to the residence with the intention of creating community as a haven, the community which is emerging there does gain some impetus from their feelings of being threatened by the world outside—or its representatives inside—and from the protection which the community offers against this threat.

Because they are old and poor, most residents are frightened by many aspects of living in the wider society. They are afraid of inflation, of being hurt or injured alone, of being attacked in the street. They also feel more diffuse kinds of threat from changing times. Developments in technology and the growing emphasis on education have shifted the value on their manual skills. They do not understand "the youth of today" and are afraid of what they will make of society. As old people and retired people they feel they have little status, and most of them feel helpless to do anything about it.

Many residents talk about the physical safety and security offered by Les Floralies. Although they feel uneasy about having so little cash, they also count on the financial security of living there, where they are promised food, clothing, and medical care as well as shelter regardless of economic ups and downs in French society. Because they are *all* old and retired, as we saw in chapter four, these sources of low status outside the residence become irrelevant, and can in a sense be escaped, inside. Many residents are beginning to believe that they can have some control over their lives in the community, a possibility which is minimal to say the least in the world outside. Les Floralies offers protection from threats to physical and financial security, to status and sense of personal efficacy, all threats which continually faced these old people in the world outside.

The world outside is present in the residence in the persons, and attitudes, of the staff. There are two ways in which residents feel threatened by the staff; and we have already seen what they do to protect themselves. Financial decisions which seem to residents to emphasize luxury items such as a kiln over necessities such as clothing raise fears of the residence running out of money. Residents try to combat this threat by participation in decision-making to bring their own practical experience to bear on what they fear is the youthful impracticality of the director. Residents also feel threatened by the attitudes of a staff member, such as the head nurse, who, they complain, often treats them with minimal respect, ordering them around or not bothering to close a door during a physical examination. She also poses another kind of threat, since residents see her as disorganized and unreliable as a source of medical attention. Residents help each other in illness, not only offering care themselves, but often making sure that a nurse comes to visit and brings medication when it is needed. Protection against loss of dignity is more difficult. Residents do sometimes turn to leaders such as Beliveau, Thibault, or Dupont to complain, and these complaints may then be transmitted to the director. The most common solace which residents offered each other, according to my observation, was the catharsis of a gripe session, in itself a source and reinforcement of we-feelings.

Threat plays a role in the formation of community at Les Floralies as it does in other settings. The precarious position of the poor older person in French society is not as extreme as that of persecuted minorities or illegal squatters. The old people, as in many industrial societies, suffer more from neglect than from organized attack. However, the financial and physical insecurities of old age and poverty are extreme enough to make the residence seem the only alternative available to many people. This kind of "no place else to go" commitment promotes a sense of shared fate among residents as it does among squatters or utopians. Escape from the status consequences of age has resulted in an important aspect of distinctive social organization at Les Floralies, the irrelevance of age in its social status system. Reaction to perceptions of threat from staff actions and attitudes have stimulated participation in decision-making and interdependence, which in turn promote community formation.

Symbols

As people's lives intersect on an increasing number of dimensions, certain aspects of their lives together may be elevated to the status of symbols which represent their common experiences and evoke emotional responses to them. The presence of these symbols, distinctive to members of the emerging community, then further promotes community formation by emphasizing their separateness and uniqueness both in terms of their shared experiences and of their feelings about these experiences. At Les Floralies, certain individuals and events are becoming symbols. The factions are symbolized by political identities whose meanings are drawing more and more substance from conflicts inside the residence.

Mme. Charriere is for many residents a living symbol of successful aging. She is the oldest person at Les Floralies, and this status was made public at a community party. People talk about her with a clear note of pride. They admire her for specific characteristics, and her presence in the residence seems to spread some of these admired qualities to the community as a whole. She is bright and active, residents say, always properly dressed, she speaks nicely, and "at her age!" she is always helping other people. As we saw in the chapter on social status, she is one of the few residents who can be regarded as a universal "hero" in the community; admiration for her, and its frequent expression, cross faction lines. Perhaps the best way to sum up what residents express about her is to say that she symbolizes the ideal community member.

The worst possible community member, representative of everything most residents feared about living in a collectivity, with no control over the choice of other members, is also embodied in a person who has become a symbol as universally feared and disliked as Mme. Charriere is liked and admired: Mme. Picard. Vulgar, violent, slovenly, rude, Mme. Picard was often described as a witch by other residents. Her public performances in the dining room made her known to everyone, and even after she had left the residence her name was enough to evoke fear and distaste.

The president, M. Beliveau, is in many ways a symbol of the community itself. He has been there since it opened. Residents are greeted by him when they arrive, they turn to him for help, and they respect his ability to be taken seriously by the staff, especially the director. Even for Mme. Dupont, the president is a focus for respect because he knows how to be "militant." On her side, Mme. Dupont has become a symbol of the Communist opposition. The reaction evoked is of course positive and affectionate from her followers, negative and fearful from her enemies, but in either direction, the intensity of the response is high. The factions themselves are progressively being identified less by the external political allegiances which trigger membership than by these leaders, and by specific events in the residence, such as the elections or the leisure conflict. The symbolic status of these people and events provides a kind of shorthand for expressing widely shared attitudes and feelings. Because these symbols grow out of the interchanges of daily life in the residence, they are understood only by residents. Newcomers or outsiders have to learn how to interpret statements such as "it's Mme. Dupont and her friends again," "it's just like the elections," or "that horrible Mme. Picard." Both the referential content of these shared symbols and the emotional response which they arouse are further bases for feelings of distinctiveness and give another emphasis to the border between residents and outsiders.

Conclusion

A community has been created at Les Floralies. From the beginning, a series of background factors which have promoted community formation in other settings were present to give a first impetus to the process here. The old people who arrived composed a relatively homogeneous population, not only on the basis of age, but also in terms of social class and experience as participants in French culture. They came to Les Floralies because they saw little alternative, a kind of choice from necessity which has fostered community among urban squatters and utopian experimenters. The transition or initiation required to become a resident was, for most people, painful and preceded by acute apprehension. In many groups and communities the individuals who successfully emerge from this kind of social transition feel commitment to their new membership commensurate with the difficulty of acquiring it. The financial investment required for entering Les Floralies was for most residents total: they gave up income and assets in a way which they perceived as irreversible, the kind of investment which in utopias is associated with the formation of successful communities. The material distinctions considered invidious to community integration in intentional, planned communities are minimal at Les Floralies, as are the exclusive kinship groupings which utopian planners fear will pull individuals away from the community. Because the residence is small, social contacts were destined to be face-to-face, making possible rapid effects of other factors promoting community formation. Talented, vigorous leaders were among the first residents to arrive.

Acting in the context of these "raw materials," many kinds of participation, perceptions of threat, and the development of symbols have brought community at Les Floralies to its present level. Residents share with each other a high proportion of their total range of social contacts. These many kinds of contact lead to awareness of all the things these people have in common which may become bases of we-feelings. The patterning of this variety of social ties, including beliefs and feelings about these patterns, is the basis for social organization. Participation in community-wide events— meals, celebrations, elections—is at a generally high level and, as in squatter villages and utopian experiments, has stimulated both we-feelings and the definition of social organization. Interdependence among residents, an important source of community in all the settings where its creation has been observed, is extensive in cases of illness or handicap, and affects the residents who know about these relationships as well as those who actually engage in them. Exchange of goods and services is less widespread, but represents a highly significant kind of interdependence for the residents concerned. Interdependence is a source of feelings of shared fate: a relationship of interdependence implies that what happens to an individual is bound up with what happens to the friends or neighbors involved in these relationships.

Although resident participation in making decisions at Les Floralies is at a relatively low level, it has increased since the residence opened; and concern about increasing this participation further, and conflict over which residents should influence decisions, have continued to mount since the elections. The participation hypothesis, examined in the context of Les Floralies, suggests that this increased concern about resident decision-making, and the hints that their influence is actually becoming greater, have had consequences for community formation. The residents who see themselves as taking part in making decisions feel more loyal to the community. The possibility of resident influence stimulated factional conflict which expresses feelings that the residence is important and worth fighting over. These conflicts also produce solidarity within the factions, as well as pulling increasing numbers of residents into factional alignments. Since individuals are linked into this community both socially and emotionally through the factions, the conflicts, derived from perceptions of the possibility that residents can participate in decisions, have an important effect on the definition of social organization and the development of we-feelings.[7] Working in the residence also promotes identification with the community for those who have jobs. Although residents participate in different ways and to various degrees, the many strands of participation cumulate in widespread value for the residence as a whole, and increasingly strong interpersonal bonds within the subgroups through which individuals are linked to the community.

Les Floralies, then, offers the same kind of haven from threat often represented by squatter settlements, utopian communities, and international alliances. The threatening nature of the wider society for poor, old people is an important source of their commitment to this community. The escape it represents from status consequences of age outside is one basis for the distinctiveness of its social organization. The community is of survival importance to its members, and they fight to make it into, and maintain it as, the kind of community they want because they are there for the rest of their lives. Feelings of threat from staff incompetence or negative attitudes have influenced not only attempts to participate in decision-making but also development of we-feelings both as old people versus young and as residents versus staff.

Symbols which summarize shared experiences and feelings about them are sources of community distinctiveness here as they are in utopias or in an urban squatter settlement.

The emergence of community at Les Floralies has been explained without great emphasis on the fact that its members are old. The factors which affected the formation of community here are essentially the same ones which have been observed in many other circumstances. The relationship between age and community can, however, be turned around. Instead of "what is the significance of age for the formation of community?" the central question in the final chapter becomes, "what is the significance of this kind of community formation for older people?"

9 Age Borders and Community Creation

Introduction

"So what?" should be the most frequently asked question in social science. Now that we have seen this case study, now that we have the results of that survey, so what? What do we know about human behavior, or at least about some specific domain of human activity, that we didn't know before? A community has developed in this residence for retired French construction workers; so what? What can the case of Les Floralies tell us about old people and community creation?

A major reason that the residents of Les Floralies can tell us something is because they are not speaking to us alone. Their experience is not unique. As I mentioned in the introduction, older people in a wide variety of separate settings—public housing, private apartments, retirement residences—have convinced researchers using an equally broad range of techniques that a residential age border has consequences for social contacts and for morale. With two caveats, their messages are: social interaction is greater, because of increased contact with age-mates, and morale is higher.[1] The first caveat is that the effect of age density on social contacts has been almost exclusively observed among old people who are also from the same social class. Although only one investigator purposely chose housing that was homogeneous by social class, the other kinds of housing typically also have this characteristic. Both public housing and private retirement residences tend to recruit people from similar class backgrounds because the financial requirements filter out people with higher incomes in one case and lower incomes in the other.

The consequences of living with other old people are also different for different individuals. First of all, the amount of social contact they want to have affects how much they will be affected by the presence of many potential friends. For those who are not particularly interested in more social ties, increasing interaction possibilities won't make much difference. People in certain social circumstances are also especially sensitive to this kind of influence. Women, the older among the old, and those who never married or who have lost a spouse are affected most strongly by having other old people near them. Members of the working class, who at any age characteristically find more friends among their neighbors than people in the middle class, also respond more dramatically to having many age-mates nearby.[2]

The second caveat concerns the relationship between closeness to age peers and morale. Morale and social contact are independently affected by age density. It must not be concluded, in other words, that older people have higher morale when they live together *because* they have more social contacts. Since older people are not at all homogeneous in terms of personality or previous life experience, age-homogeneous living arrangements affect their morale in different ways. The availability of social contacts may certainly be a source of higher morale for the older people who want social activity and who have the social skills to connect with potential friends. However, the general relationship between separate residence and morale reflects other consequences of living with people the same age: emergence of norms, definition of older neighbors as role models and reference groups, development of an age identity, and potential help in emergencies. All of these are available to individuals who do not want or cannot take advantage of, opportunities for more friends or more social activity.[3]

"Communally cohesive," "tightly-knit, homogeneous community," "vibrant community of old people," "cohesive community," are the terms used to describe old people living, respectively, in a life-care home for Sephardic Jews, a mobile home park (Idle Haven), a public housing apartment building (Merrill Court), a luxurious condominium complex (Arden).[4] Although these are not technically a sample of residential possibilities for old people, they do represent four major types of available housing. Each of these settings has been described by someone who spent many months, sometimes several years, in the kind of intensive, holistic research usually called a community study. All of them report situations that, in our terms, include strong we-feeling and distinctive social organization.

These examples of community among old people first of all reprieve Les Floralies from the status of unique case study. Their most significant contribution, however, is not simply to document that other communities of old people exist. Since community formation has obviously taken place in these settings, the major question is how and why. These cases allow us to ask whether the background and emergent factors observed in the French residence also influence community creation in these American cases. Information about each factor is not available from every study, but, with one exception, what is reported parallels the experience at Les Floralies.

Background Factors
Homogeneity

Homogeneity of the old people in terms of characteristics other than age is the background factor insistently present in every example of old-age communities.[5] Various combinations of common social class, ethnicity, marital status, sex, previous residence, association memberships, occupation, political affiliation, region of origin, or religious affiliation bolster the shared age identity. Residents of the Sephardic Home, for instance, are not only from the same ethnic group and share the same orthodox religious practices, but are often former neighbors in New York, and emigrants from the same villages in Greece or Turkey as other residents. Tenants in the mobile-home park are all white, mostly former blue-collar workers, Protestant, and former residents of the San Francisco Bay Area. In the apartment building, the old people who became the "vibrant community" are almost all widows, white, Protestants, working class, and of rural origin. A majority of the condominium owners add a common conservative political orientation to shared social class, religion, ethnicity, and previous residence.

Lack of Alternative

Many of the retired people in Idle Haven described their discovery of the park as almost a miracle. They saw themselves in danger as a racial minority in their old neighborhoods; their houses and yards were too large and too much work to maintain; many were expropriated by highways or urban renewal; the sale of their homes did not bring enough money to finance moving to a desirable area. A visit to friends or relatives in the mobile home park suggested an answer to what had seemed appallingly irresolvable problems.

These responses of gratitude, and relief at finding a place to live sound very familiar. I have heard them in life-care homes and condominiums in California as well as from French seamstresses and house painters. They are voiced again and again by old people in leisure villages as well as in public housing: "Shangri-La," "Heaven on earth," "a chance to be an asset, not a liability."

Housing is always cited as a major problem by older people and by those who work for their benefit.[6] Consider an older person in the United States, for example. The value on independence is very high; social maturity is to a great extent defined by living in an independent household. With a fixed and limited income, pinched further by inflation, confronted with the fact or prospect of failing strength and health, the older person determined to live independently is hardly faced with an abundance of choices. Another indication of the few housing alternatives older people perceive is that those who enter age-homogeneous settings seldom choose to live there because they are age-homogeneous. Being with other old people and the increased social possibilities they offer are usually greatly appreciated benefits, but not reasons for moving into these settings.[7]

With the repetitious poignancy of a Greek chorus, older residents of all kinds of separate housing explain why they came: they want to live independently; they are unable or afraid to stay where they are. Given independence and security, they want facilities for enjoyment of leisure. Public housing for older people often represents the only possibility of a decent and affordable place to live, period. For those with more resources, mobile home parks, leisure villages, and condominiums may offer the only possibility of a place to live in independence and security. Even for those few with the highest incomes, continuing to meet these two survival needs may not be easy outside of a separate setting. Waiting lists and application procedures for many specific housing situations, in all price ranges, make perceptions of limited alternatives all the more acute. The intensity of commitment to a housing solution should vary according to how many options each individual sees. In general, however, situations that allow older people to live as they want to are likely to be valued as highly as anything that is both necessary and scarce.

Investment and Irreversibility

The investment required for moving into Idle Haven is considerable. For the working class retired people who live there, it usually means selling a house in order to buy the mobile-home. There is also a surprising, at least to the uninitiated, degree of irreversibility in choosing a mobile-home park for many older people. Since park managers typically place a restriction on the age of mobile-homes which they will accept in the park, the older person who has owned a mobile-home for five years or more cannot easily move it to another park. The owner of an older mobile-home will also have great difficulty selling it, since the buyer would not necessarily be allowed to leave it in its present park, and a guaranteed place in a park is crucial to most mobile-home sales.

An average two-bedroom apartment in Arden required a $5,500 down payment and a monthly payment of $237 in 1968. This investment seems, financially at least, less irreversible than the decision to live in a mobile home park, since the condominium apartments can easily be resold. The anthropologist who studied the Arden community, however, suggested that there may be other aspects of irreversibility. She describes the residents of Arden as having cut many of their formal and informal ties with "outsiders." These might be difficult to revive for a person leaving the condominium. Since they can move more easily than people in some other settings, but probably have difficulty going "home," Arden residents may be more committed to some type of retirement housing rather than to this particular place. There is also the possibility in this kind of comparison that we are running into a measurement problem. Since the bases on which different researchers make their judgments about community are not always clear, but almost certainly not identical, the level of community at Arden may not in fact be as high as that at Idle Haven or Les Floralies.

The Sephardic Home is typical of many life-care communities that require an individual to turn over assets to the institution. Other life-care contracts require a high initial payment that is not refundable after a specified length of time. The investment in these cases is not only irreversible, but staying in the residence and living a long time are ways to be a "winner" in a kind of actuarial roulette.[8]

Material Distinctions

Furnishings in the apartments at Merrill Court were remarkable to the sociologist who worked there because of their similarity. One large floral couch, bowls of homemade artificial flowers, a Bible, Woolworth pictures, potted plants, photograph albums, and a souvenir from the old home stocked each apartment, where they were even arranged in the same way. As in any public housing for old people, the narrow range of types of apartments, and the severely limited incomes of everyone in the community contributed further to the lack of material differences in the tenants' life-styles.

Material distinctions are also limited at Idle Haven by the space restrictions, by the income range, and by the very fact that everyone lives in a mobile-home. Even in more affluent Arden, the range of apartment sizes and styles is small. The notion that too many obvious material differences among individuals living together may be an obstacle to community formation is closely related to the factor of homogeneity. Things in common, after all, must be perceived. People must feel that they have certain characteristics in common if this fact is to have any effect on community formation. Too many or too broad differences in consumption styles could easily delay or even prevent the recognition of other commonalities. Furnished apartments, mobile-home parks, public housing, or the relatively narrow gamut of types of unit in most retirement settings put a brake on this kind of "distraction" from community. Common in communities of older people is a shared understanding that material differences, with their origin in the past, are to be muted. New signals of status distinction are just as often part of these emerging shared understandings. When these are part of a new mutual map of social relations, they become an aspect of the developing community, rather than a threat to it.

Leadership

Residents with leadership skills are mentioned in all of the community studies. "The Talleyrand of the community's political life" is the description given to the leader of the counter-elite in Merrill Court. There is, of course, also an elite, made up of the formal officers of the residents club. At Arden the elected officers often acquired their leadership skills in their former roles as corporation executives. They were challenged by a Residents Association of politically more liberal homeowners demanding more open meetings, freer flow of information, and more direct election of officers.

A "gregarious, humorous, quick-witted woman," and "outgoing, organizationally able men" are among the formal and informal leaders described in Idle Haven.

At the Sephardic Home, residents serve as officers of their own synagogue and of voluntary charitable organizations paralleling those in the outside society. They also participate in less formal but intense power struggles through factions defined by kinship ties and often identified with a town of origin in Greece or Turkey.

Size

All of the communities studied have small populations. Forty-three people live in Merrill Court; 360 at Idle Haven; 180 in the Sephardic Home. Arden is the largest, with 5,011, but its residents move into their apartments in neighborhood groups of 150 to 250.

Exclusive Social Ties

The exceptional factor that operates differently at Idle Haven and the Sephardic Home than it does at Les Floralies, Arden, or Merrill Court is ties among residents before they move in. One-third of the mobile-home owners who responded to the anthropologist's questionnaire had known someone in the park before they came.[9] There were also twelve extended family households, and eleven sets of relatives living in separate units. Kinship ties and lifelong friendship networks are central to social life in the Sephardic Home.

These finds emphasize the fact that the original proposition about social exclusivity as a threat to community was derived from the study of utopias, which strive to immerse individuals in a direct rapport with the community as a whole. In most natural communities, individuals are, on the contrary, linked into the whole by just such mediating ties as kinship and friendship. The reports from Idle Haven and the Sephardic Home make it likely that the lack of preexisting social relationships among residents in the other settings was not an important aspect of community formation.

The mobile-home park and the Sephardic institution do not represent all possible degrees of already present social ties among new residents. In Idle Haven a minority has this kind of link to others in the park; at the Sephardic Home everyone is tied in this way. These seem likely to be the conditions under which preexisting social relationships will promote rather than threaten community. If a majority share this kind of tie, it may become the dominant basis of social participation, and make problematic the integration of those who are left out. When the people who share this kind of bond are in the minority it seems more likely that they will also be drawn into present social life in the new context. If one becomes a participant, the others may be pulled along. The universal continuity of social roles and relationships present in the Sephardic Home makes the question of contradiction between past and present social organization almost meaningless. An entire generation of a tightly-knit ethnic and religious community simply moves together—as it has changed neighborhoods before—into a new living arrangement, without interruption of participation in kinship, friendship or factional ties.

The degree of institutionality of an age-homogeneous setting is explicitly raised by the case of the Sephardic Home. The anthropologist who worked there argues that community exists, in spite of the institutional context, because of the ethnic, kinship, and religious ties among the residents. Looking at all the cases of community formation, including Les Floralies, the degree of institutionality appears as an important additional background factor.

There is a general hypothesis that the degree to which special settings for older people are institutions with social control over their residents has a negative relationship to social activity.[10] Spontaneous social activity is the least likely in the most institutional settings. If community formation is to take place among older people, the setting in which they are brought together should not be too institutional. Residents must feel some independence from the staff, which can happen in various ways. At the Sephardic Home, other roles and loyalties cross-cut the staff-inmate distinction. At Les Floralies, potential domination by the staff was counteracted by residents' feelings that staff members were employees who could be fired, by perceptions of them as young, inexperienced, and less competent than residents in certain domains, by identification with them as fellow workers or grandparents. At Idle Haven, residents bring informal influence to bear on the manager; and in other parks residents have organized formally in opposition to managerial policies, in one case extending their conflict to the California State Legislature. Certainly, mobile-home parks are not institutions, although they do have rules and regulations. As the manager of Idle Haven expressed it, only behavior that might disturb other park residents was her business, anything done inside the mobile-homes was not. At Arden, a residents board has control over the management firm paid to administer the condominium. Merrill Court is an apartment building with only two staff people, a recreation director and her assistant; neither lives in the building.

Age-homogeneity itself has so far been considered a kind of

background to the background factors, since it has been assumed as the context in which community creation might take place given certain other conditions. However, only half of the residents of Idle Haven are older people. Exceptionally careful research in several apartment buildings in Cleveland reinforces 50 percent as the magic number, since it was when one-half or more of the tenants were older people that the consequences of age concentration appeared.[11]

Physical Setting

The physical context will affect the impact of many other factors in community creation, as well as having its own direct effect on social interaction. Homogeneity, for example, must be visible in order to be perceived by potential community members, and consequently to have a possible effect on their feelings about each other. Physical characteristics of housing—ease of mobility, arrangement of furniture, presence of public areas—may provide this visibility, as well as directly promoting social contacts.

The dining hall at Les Floralies was crucial both to social life and to ethnographic research. Descriptions of the other situations in which old people have created communities also report effects of the physical context. In Merrill Court, a porch extended the length of all the apartments, and the elevator was in the middle of each floor. Since every resident placed a chair next to the window overlooking the porch, comings and goings were easy to observe. The recreation room and the mail room on the ground floor are the arenas for the public or "downstairs" roles.

At Idle Haven, as in many mobile-home parks, residents have a great deal of visual contact with each other, as well as meeting in common recreation and laundry rooms, on the sidewalks, and over the garden fences. Even tenants who did not participate extensively in either formal or informal relationships said they felt the park was "friendly" because they so frequently saw other people in their yards, getting their mail, doing their laundry.

Arden was designed, apparently successfully, to promote social encounters in neighborhoods that share a driveway, parking spaces, lounges, laundry rooms, bulletin boards, and walkways that intersect to bring those entering or leaving their apartments into contact.

At Victoria Plaza, high-rise public housing in San Antonio, Texas, physical characteristics of the building also stimulate social interaction and awareness of what is going on. Hallways are exterior balconies passing by the apartment windows, and there is also a Senior Center on the ground floor which residents regard as their "living room." Some complain about the lack of privacy built-in to these arrangements, but many "porch-sitters" and "lobbyists" enjoy the opportunities for observation and information gathering that they provide.[12]

Emergent Factors
Community-wide Events

Spaghetti dinners, dances, and bingo games are widely attended at Idle Haven; religious services have high participation in the Sephardic Home. The widows of Merrill Court share a daily work session, weekly potluck lunches, birthday parties every month, recreation day once a week, seasonal holiday celebrations and an annual election and installation ritual.

A role in decision-making is available in all of the communities. The Sephardic residents are responsible for the religious activities central to their social lives. They organize observances of all events on the religious calendar, and they participated in hiring the rabbi. In the condominium, residents legally run their own community; the power struggles there are between "establishment" and "opposition" groups of residents. The retired people living at Idle Haven are tenants, and consequently subject to some park regulations and to the authority of a park manager. However, the Park Association that organizes its formal social activities is controlled and financed by its members. Decisions about organization of events, rights to attend, and spending money are in the hands of its officers, who are elected by the residents often to the accompaniment of Bagnolet-style campaigns and conflicts.

The formal and informal social life of Merrill Court was created by the people who live there. They structure its activities, choose its leaders, decide what to do with the results of their work, and fight among themselves about control over the interior world of the Court as well as its relations to the outside. There are limits to how much control the old people have in the Sephardic Home or the housing project. The women at Merrill Court, for instance, tried to force the resignation of a disliked recreation director, but with the support of the Welfare Department, she stayed. Compared to the powerless position most of them would have in the wider society, however, the influence they have over what is of daily importance to them seems very significant.

Interdependence

"We take care of each other here," is the way Merrill Court residents talk about their interdependence. Friends and neighbors check on each other daily; curtains not open by mid-morning are the cue for a visit to make sure nothing is wrong. Meals were prepared, shopping done, and laundry washed and ironed for one blind resident. A look inside Merrill Court refrigerators also reveals an exchange network of food specialties. Except for the most extreme cases, such as the blind person, exchanges are reciprocal. Of course, in a less tangible way, the blind man did offer a great deal in return to his caretakers. They enjoyed being the givers and carers, and they missed him bitterly when he died.

In the mobile home park, help offered among residents includes rides to the supermarket, household or car repairs, driving an ill or injured person to the hospital, and daily visits, help with housework, and preparation of hot meals during convalescence. The publication of news about illness or deaths in the monthly newsletter, and a monthly public announcement of the people who have received get-well or condolence cards from the "Sunshine Girl" also stimulates support in times of crisis, since others contact the person in need as a result of this information. At Idle Haven, too, reciprocity is punctilious, and in a few cases, individuals extricated themselves from these relationships because they felt they could not keep up their end of the exchanges.

At Arden, neighboring is active particularly within the separate clusters of apartments. Help in illness cr emergency is the most valued kind of interdependence, and the one that people talked about the most to the anthropologist who visited them. Residents also water plants and care for pets when neighbors are away, and offer each other rides and garden equipment.

Proportion of Kinds of Social Contacts

The range of kinds of social contacts shared by members of all these communities of old people is extensive. They work, relax, fight, worship, and find romance and friendship among themselves. In Idle Haven and the Sephardic Home, they also share kinship ties. In view of the fears often expressed about age-segregation as a threat to family relations, it is important to emphasize that no study either of age-segregation or of old age communities gives any evidence that participation in a community of age peers in any way restricts relationships with relatives, particularly children.[13]

The subculture which developed in the San Francisco apartment building fostered strong family ties. The most active people at Merrill Court also had the most contact with their children. Family members who do not live at Idle Haven are often included in its activities and in the relationships which are created among park residents. Participation in park activities can be a source of increased status in the family, while the achievements of family members can provide prestige within the park. Information about the families of residents is an important element of news in the Idle Haven newspaper. At Les Floralies, other residents are often included in contacts with family, and there is no correlation between family contacts and various kinds of participation in residence social life. The residents of the Sephardic Home carry many kinship ties with them into the new environment, as they are related to other residents, and their children are often on the board, on the staff, or among the volunteer workers.

Peers and children are two distinct spheres of social and emotional contact.[14] An increase in the frequency and intensity of relationships with peers consequently does not elicit any decrease in contact or closeness with children. If anything, more satisfying relationships with peers allow old people to be less exclusively dependent upon their children, and therefore to enjoy more relaxed and less duty-bound relationships with them.[15]

Work

"Workshop" is the first entry on every morning's schedule at Merrill Court. The widows talk about being on "company time" and as they work, plan what to do when they are "free." In the mobile-home park, such roles as Sunshine Girl, newspaper editor, or chef are seen as jobs. At Arden, neighbors in about half of the "mutual" units work together to landscape their areas. Work is not specifically discussed in the report on the Sephardic Home, but it seems likely that residents perceive their organization of synagogue affairs as work.[16]

Threat

Both Idle Haven and Arden are repeatedly praised by their residents as havens from physical danger as well as from the less tangible threat of "undesirable" elements in contemporary society.

Another kind of potential threat, to the distinctiveness of a newly forming community, rather than to its individual members, is assertion inside the new setting of the status system current outside it. Successful utopian experiments, for instance, were characterized by status systems defined in terms of internally relevant attributes and participation. Importation of an outside status system should be additionally threatening to an emergent community of old people, since in industrial societies their age and their retirement assign them low positions.

Evidence from communities of older people does reveal avoidance of this double-barreled threat through definition of status in internal terms and strong resistance against attempts to make past, outside statuses too significant.

A cook, a dance band leader, and a ham radio operator who tried to use their skills for the benefit of the Idle Haven park by organizing community meals, dances, and bingo games (which require microphones and amplifiers) were so strongly sanctioned by other residents that two of these individuals left the park, the third withdrew from all activities. They were all accused of trying to fill their own pockets at the expense of other people in the park, which, in the opinion of the anthropologist who observed the events, was completely untrue. This kind of accusation is reminiscent of the label "witch" used against individuals who become too powerful in essentially egalitarian societies such as Navajo or Tiv.[17] Those who try to set themselves apart, who try to emphasize their special skills, and create new positions of power and importance based on these skills are being told, and harshly, that their behavior is undesirable in Idle Haven.

One of the aspects of park life that residents talk about most positively is the absence of "keeping up with the Joneses." Status competition which depends on past or outside experiences is a severe threat to a community of older people for two reasons: it can shatter the perceptions of homogeneity which are fundamental to community formation; and it also destroys the possibility of the new community acting as a refuge from the loser's role which is assigned to older and retired people, especially if they are also poor, in the status game of the wider society.

There were different social statuses at Idle Haven, at least as indicated by leadership roles, both formal and informal. The important difference about these kinds of roles, which seems to make them acceptable to the residents, is that they are much more universally available to everyone in the park, on the basis of what they do in the present and at Idle Haven. Although there is some sorting out by special skills (for example, the park secretary is usually someone who was a secretary, the treasurer someone with bookkeeping ability), most positions do not require such specialized skills, and there are also a large number of individuals with those skills which are required. For instance, over half the women (55.5 percent) were in clerical or sales work, which suggests many potential secretaries and bookkeepers. Friendship with the manager, and the possibility of influencing her, was an important source of informal leadership, also rooted in present participation in park social life.

Conflicts storm about who should occupy the leadership roles at Idle Haven, but there is a basic acceptance that their existence is appropriate. Sanctions are aimed not at those who are leaders, but at anyone who seems to be trying to exaggerate the difference between leaders and other residents: the dance combo director was also president of the residents' association when he was accused of trying to make a profit off the park. His sin was worse because he was in a formal office at the time he organized the offending dances.

A leader who got "out of line" by attempts to mix outside and inside status was also strongly criticized at Merrill Court. Rather than simply bringing outside status in, she acquired status inside the project, parleyed it outside, and then returned with increased prestige to her audience of age-mates. Her position as president of the Court was a source of invitations to various functions with leaders of other voluntary organizations in the town. She also received thanks and honors for the work done in the Court workshop. When these kinds of distinctions were then brought back inside the community, the "masses" complained that it wasn't fair for them to do all the work while she got all the credit. As the leader of the counter-elite summed it up: "We're all elder people here. The club president isn't a day younger than any of us. There's no reason for her to be feeling so special."

Status earned inside the world of Merrill Court is derived from work, and from holding electoral office. Everyone has the potential to be a good participant in the workshop; and there are enough offices that only four members of the residents club did not chair something during the three years of research. The undifferentiated low status generally assigned to old, poor people was also avoided in Merrill Court by its "poor dear" hierarchy. Everyone had a "poor dear" who was less healthy, older, had fewer or less successful children; the oldest and frailest in the Court had "poor dears" in nursing homes. A kind of honor was given to those who were lucky in health and family situation, and everyone had the possibility of negotiating some honor by "poor dearing" someone less fortunate.

At Arden, elected officers on the managing board have particularly high status. Leadership within its voluntary organizations is also a source of prestige; and the groups vie with each other to achieve distinction for most successful fund-raising, highest attendance figures, or most frequent use of desirable community facilities.

Social status is not explicitly discussed in the reports on the Sephardic Home to which I have access. However, it seems likely that at least some sources of status there, such as leadership in religious activities and charitable organizations, are the same as those in the Sephardic subculture of New York City. Even in the context of striking continuity which has been created at this home, however, the old people are no longer actually competing in the outside status game. The rules inside the home are parallel, but they are applied separately to the old people, who have their own synagogue and form their own voluntary groups. It is not at all clear that they would have similar opportunities for controlling these central aspects of their lives if they had to compete in the society outside the home. The apparent use of religious and charitable activities as a source of social status in the home is similar to the relationship between work and high status at Les Floralies. The general rule for status is the same as in the society outside, but the specific activity through which the rule is applied takes place inside the community and in the present tense.

In terms of the patterns of social status in embedded communities described in chapter 4, the status system at the Sephardic Home reflects the outside system rather than making it irrelevant as is the case at Les Floralies. Although this pattern does not contribute as much to definition of a community border as the reversal or irrelevance responses to outside status, it can provide the same escape from a guaranteed loser's role by offering parallel but separate paths to status.

Intense resistance to the publication of a "Who's Who" in a California condominium summed up for me the findings about social status and communities of older people. The director thought publishing a small newsletter-type "Who's Who" with brief biographies of all residents would be a stimulus to sociability and community feelings in the new condominium. Residents opposed the idea with vehement unanimity. It was obvious from listening to them that they were not opposing dissemination of information: they already had it. They were against the emphasis of differences among residents, and most emphatically against those differences which derived from the past. "We care about what somebody does here, and not about what he did before." All available information indicates that these people are speaking for older people in a wide range of communities. Where community is created, an emergent factor in the process is a status system defined in inside terms.[18] In some cases, both the principles for assigning status and the specific activities through which the principles are applied are internal and distinctive. In others, the principles come from the outside, but the activities are inside the separate residential setting. Although the double autonomy defines a sharper border around the new community, both patterns give participation in it the special value of escape from an outside system in which older, retired people are predestined to a loser's role.

Symbols

Mobile-home rather than trailer is a symbol of the shared image that Idle Haven residents want to protect. "Beatrice," wearing tight pants and diamond earrings, drinking in her room with men, is now a symbol of the undesirable community member at Merrill Court. Her neighbors are united in their disapproval of her and also in their frequent attempts to defend, by contrast, what they see as the appropriate behavior for their community. The "fruit-pie incident" at Idle Haven, and the "October Revolution" in Arden are now landmark events for making sense out of subsequent factional alignments.

Summary

As I was talking about Les Floralies once, a woman who has
studied a public housing complex for old people in Florida suddenly
interrupted me in amazement to ask, "You mean they're French?"
Since she didn't hear the beginning of the conversation, she
assumed that these people who sounded so familiar to her must be
Americans in some other public housing project. That feeling of
familiarity is close to nostalgia every time I read about the social
lives of old people in another community; I'm always surprised that
they don't speak French.

The first answer to the "so what" question—so what if old people
have created a community at Les Floralies?—is that they are not the
only ones. Other old people have also formed communities, in a
variety of settings, but through processes that include the same
factors that were important in Bagnolet. Each of these communities
of old people has been created by individuals who share many
characteristics in addition to age: ethnicity, class, religion, educational level, income, and in some cases also marital status, sex, or
occupation. They all feel they have very little alternative to these
situations, and have made a great financial and emotional investment in them. They all entered these new settings in small enough
numbers to know each other personally, found some talented
leaders, and an institutional framework that is not overpowering.
All of these old people have turned to each other for many kinds of
social needs. They are friends, lovers, and factional adversaries;
they support each other in illness and emergency; they laugh,
dance, and prepare for death together. They evaluate each other
in terms of the life they share, rather than according to the status
ladders of the outside world where they are guaranteed a place on
the bottom rungs. That outside world is seen as dangerous in many
ways: physically, financially, socially, and psychologically; the
community of age-mates is a refuge from all of these threats. Its
members value it accordingly and try to influence its future by
taking part in the decisions that affect them.

As these comparisons have also shown, there is much more work
to be done. We need to look at settings that vary in terms of all
these background and emergent factors, to isolate the effects and
importance of each one.[19] Systematic comparison of the life cycles
of various communities will also provide information about the
timing of maximum impact of different factors.[20] Old people living

near each other do not always form communities, and negative cases will be very revealing. What is it about Single Room Occupancy hotels that apparently does not promote community? What are the relative influences of the kinds of people who choose to live there, physical characteristics of the hotel, the kind and degree of threat from the outside environment?[21] What we know so far, however, is consistent: given the background and emergent factors we have identified, old people do form communities. The next question is consequently more general: What is the significance of these communities for old people in modern society?

To answer that question we must first look at the old people involved in these communities. They are numerous in western, industrial societies, and their numbers are increasing. One estimate is that 10 percent of American old people now live in separate residential settings.[22] From the range of kinds of special housing old people have moved into, and in many cases found satisfying, it is also apparent that the individuals involved are not a narrowly circumscribed category. Different social classes, ethnic groups, religious affiliations, and life styles are represented. The important requirement for community formation is not any particular identity in terms of these characteristics, but their availability as a basis for perceptions of homogeneity. In response to one widely repeated stereotype, it is important to point out that the attraction of separate housing is not limited to old people with no children; in the housing about which this information is available, half or more of the residents have children.

Although these settings may have a special appeal to old people without children, it is just as clear that this appeal is not restricted to them. As I pointed out above, I could find no evidence that living with age peers is associated with decreases in either desired or actual contact with children. It is possible, on the other hand, that satisfying relationships with peers, as well as a sense of security about financial and physical needs, make relationships with children more relaxed and mutually rewarding.

Most older people in industrial societies are not rejected by their families or isolated from them.[23] They are far more likely to lack contact with their peers, with its own distinct satisfactions. It would seem bizarre to suggest that any other age group, except perhaps extremely young children, should find all of its social participation within the immediate family, and yet this formula is frequently applied to older people. The consequences of age density for both social contacts and morale suggest that cross-generation kin relations, although highly significant, are no more sufficient to old people than to anyone else.

It is also not only the busy "joiners" who may find satisfying social lives in separate residences. Morale is affected by age density independent of interaction levels. Feelings of physical and financial security, a sense of independence, new reference groups, protection from status loss, one close friend, may all make living with other old people attractive to individuals who do not participate at all in organized activities.

The reasons why older people move into separate housing arrangements are considerably less diverse than the individuals involved. In every case where reasons for these choices are known, the twin desires for independence and security reappear. Older people often see the mobile-home park, the retirement village, or the life-care home as the only way to meet these needs. Where the history of retirement housing has been traced, the needs which old people want to have met show up in clear contrast to what many developers and planners *thought* they wanted. For instance, medical care, an essential aspect of security for older people, was seen by one Arizona builder as "advertising decrepitude."[24] He assumed that old people in good health would not want to be reminded of sickness by too many arrangements for health care in a retirement community. The old people, much closer to the realities of aging than this young business man, have since convinced many planners of retirement housing that health care is a crucial requirement in choosing retirement housing, and consequently good business.

As many older people have learned from painful experience, when medical care is not available, or if it is limited to minimal infirmary care, a person who becomes seriously ill or incapacitated will have to leave the community. The difficult search for housing, a second move, another process of social adjustment, will be required at the same time as a separation from neighbors and friends when their support is most needed. Although a move from one kind of unit to another within one residential setting may be difficult, as it emphasizes a change in physical condition, or a social loss, such as death of a spouse, it is less traumatic than a total move, and it can take place with the support of neighbors and friends.[25] Residents have demanded more extensive health facilities in already established housing, and planners have progressively included more medical care in new installations.[26]

Rural tranquility and resort-area sunshine were also assumed to be major attractions for older people considering separate housing arrangements. In the United States, for instance, the first retirement housing appeared in Arizona, Florida, and California. Even in these sunny spots, a high proportion of the older people who moved into the new housing came from close by.[27] In market surveys, others said they would be interested in special housing if it did not require moving far away from their own neighborhoods.[28] These patterns emphasize the fact that this kind of move is often not motivated by climate or geography, but by the search for independence and security, without sacrifice of closeness to family, friends and a familiar life space.

Peer relationships, improved morale, opportunities for social participation and status, as well as the possibility of community formation, are consequences of living with other old people, not typically reasons for doing so. Many of these effects are observed even when the old people did not intentionally enter an age-homogeneous setting. As communities of older people become more visible on the social scene, and as the image of the retirement residence is distinguished from the specter of the old folks home, these positive consequences may become positive reasons for recruitment into separate settings.

A powerful force for perpetuation of stereotypes about the stagnation, rejection, and isolation supposedly implicit in age-segregated housing is the attitudes of younger people. In the face of evidence that these settings have consistently positive consequences for many older people, the reasons for these negative attitudes pose an intriguing question, which derives direct practical consequences from the fact that most decisions about both private and public housing for older people are made by younger researchers, planners, and administrators.

One obvious possibility is that evidence about consequences of separate residential situations for older people does not have an impact on the attitudes of many younger people because that evidence is not well known. Negative reactions to residential separation may, in other words, simply be based on misinformation. If people realized the diversity of the old people living in these settings, the positive effects on their morale, the vitality of the communities they create, the persistence of their ties to their children, perhaps attitudes toward separate housing would change. As a social scientist writing about housing for older people, of course, I would be delighted to believe that publication of this kind of information would be sufficient to change attitudes. However, I think these negative feelings have sources far deeper than lack of information.

The violence with which reactions to "fogey farms," "geriatric ghettos," or "waiting rooms for death," are expressed is the kind which often explodes under the pressure of deep contradictions in cultural imperatives. In the United States, for example, the melting pot image of social heterogeneity is a value worn shiny with repetition if not with use. Everyday experience as well as volumes of social science research demonstrate repeatedly that individuals in fact spend much of their time, and meet the great majority of their social needs, with others who are very much like them. To state that people in the middle class are likely to find friends, sexual partners, and neighborly help in emergency among themselves will sound banal both to the person with experience in social living and to the researcher who studies it. However, a similar statement about old people, in particular if it supports a conclusion that separate residences may be desirable, evokes vociferous denunciations of segregation and rejection. Why?

Contradictions in the directions an individual receives as a member of a culture, first of all, are painful only if they are perceived. If people are not forced to confront the fact that their prized values are inconsistent with their habitual and approved behavior, they do not have a problem. If they are made to see the contradiction, their reaction may be violent. When the contradiction concerns the definition of social borders, the emergence of a new border may provide just this kind of unpleasant stimulus to recognition of inconsistencies. Separate housing for older people, which introduces an explicit, highly visible, spatial marker for the age border, forces Americans, for instance, to see this border—and its uncomfortable contradiction of values about mixing of social categories—becomes more difficult to avoid. One reason for strong reactions against residential separation for older people, in other words, has to do with the fact that it emphasizes a social border in a society whose values indicate that borders in general should be minimized. Although many barriers to social contacts across generations, as well as classes or ethnic groups, obviously exist, calling explicit attention to them arouses opposition because it stresses contradictions between the behavior which defines these barriers, and the values which deplore or deny their existence.

Response to the definition of a social border is also conditioned by the characteristic which marks it. Negative reactions will be stronger if the social characteristic used to signal the border is negatively evaluated. The difference between reactions to membership in the Episcopal church, or an exclusive country club, as markers of social borders, and reactions to retirement communities or Black separatist groups should make the point. In most western industrial societies, old age is negatively valued, to say the least.[29] In addition, the aura of sickness and scandal surrounding the U.S. nursing home industry has certainly tinged the public image of any housing for older people. When the additional tendency of most younger people to attempt strict avoidance of any recognition that they will become old is also added in, it is understandable that visible clusters of old people evoke responses ranging from discomfort to bitter caricature and rejection.

Feelings of guilt exceeding any realistic call of duty are also a possible source of reactions to residential separation of older people. Although all the research available on the subject suggests that old people in western industrial societies prefer not to live with their children, the children seem to have a hard time believing this.[30] Old people living in separate settings evoke assumptions of rejection by their children. The younger people to whom I talk about communities of the old, both in France and in the United States, almost inevitably make a reference to the shame of the rejection involved, and then move directly into a barrage of questions to me, as a presumed expert, about what they could possibly do to resolve the problems posed by their own aged mother, aunt or father-in-law. It seems to me that the rejection aimed toward special housing for old people often gains force from feelings of guilt aroused by thoughts that this might provide a solution to the questioner's own family problems. The irony is obvious. Many older people in societies whose definition of social maturity includes self-reliance, typically indicated by maintenance of a separate household, prefer not to become dependent by living with their children.[31] However, these children, because they assume the parents do want to live with them, feel guilty because they do not want to share their household, and consequently reject housing arrangements that might resolve the conflict and provide satisfying family ties for both generations.

Emotions aroused by the topic of old age are so intense for most Americans that it is difficult to discuss any prescription for the problems of aging in moderation. Reactions swing from total rejection to universal application. Although I am arguing that separate housing is not bad for all old people, I am not proposing that it is good for all old people. The casts of characters in the communities I have described should eloquently communicate the diversity among older people. Although like any category that is seen by others as a "social problem," old people are often treated as being alike, they are probably less like each other than any other age group, since in terms of personality we seem to become "more so" of whatever we were at earlier life stages. Types of housing which offer the possibility of community creation are also diverse. The evidence we already have demonstrates this, and also points out both the need and the direction for creative experimentation with different kinds of settings which could provide the factors promoting community. One of the greatest losses for many old people is the loss of choice. The ideal housing situation for the aged would consequently provide variety and the possibility of choosing.

"Just because I need help crossing the street doesn't mean I don't know where I'm going." This remark by an old woman to a young researcher is one of my favorite quotations. Older people may not only know where they are going, they may be showing where the rest of us are headed as well. Avant-garde responses to the circumstances of aging should certainly be found among old people, who are living through the process first. Any recipe they discover for continuing to live satisfying social lives in the context of societies that surround them with extraordinary obstacles, should certainly be taken very seriously, even if it contradicts assumptions and values that are difficult to let go.

What have these people discovered? Common age can become a context for community. Participation in community is an essential aspect of human social life. The entire discussion of community creation among old people is intriguing not because it distinguishes the old from other groups, but because it underlines their similarity to many other kinds of people. Friendship, love, conflict, power, laughter at "in" jokes, support in the face of common fears and sorrows, and roles to structure time and action are the stuff of everyday social life, so necessary that most of us take them profoundly for granted. To the old, they often become both scarce and precious. By preserving these possibilities for each other, older people join in a kind of communal conspiracy to continue living like human beings.

Notes

Chapter One

1. For a more complete discussion of participant observation and the research situations in which it is most appropriate, see Jennie-Keith Ross and Marc Howard Ross, "Participant Observation in Political Research," *Political Methodology* 1, no. 1 (1974): 63–88.

2. See Herbert J. Gans, *The Urban Villagers: Group and Class in the Life of Italian-Americans* (New York: The Free Press, 1962); Sheila K. Johnson, *Idle Haven: Community Building among the Working Class Retired* (Berkeley: University of California Press, 1971); Colin Turnbull, *The Forest People* (New York: Simon and Schuster, 1968).

For discussions of the decline of community in urban, industrial society, see, for example, Robert Nisbet, *Community and Power* (New York: Oxford Galaxy Books, 1962); Louis Wirth, "Urbanism as a Way of Life," *American Journal of Sociology* 44 (1938): 1–24.

3. Nisbet, *Community and Power*; Wirth, "Urbanism."

4. See Michael Young and Peter Willmott, *Family and Kinship in East London* (Baltimore: Penguin Books, 1957); Peter Townsend, *The Family Life of Old People* (London: Routledge and Kegan Paul, 1957); Ethel Shanas et. al., *Old People in Three Industrial Societies* (London: Routledge and Kegan Paul, 1968); Ethel Shanas and Gordon Streib, eds., *Social Structure and the Family: Generational Relations* (Englewood Cliffs, N.J.: Prentice-Hall, 1965); Scott Greer, *The Emerging City* (New York: John Wiley and Sons, 1962).

5. Richard L. Merritt, *Symbols of American Community, 1735–1765* (New Haven: Yale University Press, 1966); James S. Coleman and Carl J. Rosberg, *Political Parties and National Integration in Tropical Africa* (Berkeley: University of California Press, 1964); Karl Deutsch et al., *Political Community and the North Atlantic Area* (Princeton: Princeton University Press, 1957).

6. See, for example, Marc Howard Ross, *The Political Integration of Urban Squatters* (Evanston: Northwestern University Press, 1973), and Rosabeth Moss Kanter, *Commitment and Community: Communes and Utopias in Sociological Perspective* (Cambridge, Mass.: Harvard University Press, 1972).

7. M. Ross, *Political Integration*, p. 78; Kanter, *Commitment*, pp. 93–94; Karl Deutsch et al., *Political Community*; Philip Jacob and Henry Teune, "The Integrative Process: Guidelines for Analyses of the Bases of Political Integration," in *The Integration of Political Communities*, ed. Philip Jacob and James Toscano (Philadelphia: Lippincott, 1964).

8. See Irving Rosow, *Social Integration of the Aged* (New York: The Free Press, 1967).

9. M. Ross, *Political Integration*, p. 75.

10. Kanter, *Commitment*, pp. 80–81.

11. Arnold van Gennep, *The Rites of Passage* (Chicago: University of Chicago Press, 1960); Leon Festinger, *A Theory of Cognitive Dissonance* (Evanston, Ill.: Peterson and Row, 1957).

12. Kanter, *Commitment*, pp. 94–95.

13. Ibid., pp. 86–91; see also Melford Spiro, *Kibbutz* (New York: Schocken Books, 1963).

14. M. Ross, *Political Integration*, p. 79; Kanter, *Commitment*, pp. 116–20; Ernst Haas, *Beyond the Nation-State* (Stanford, Cal.: Stanford University Press, 1958).

15. M. Ross, *Political Integration*, p. 80.

16. Kanter, *Commitment*, pp. 98–99.

17. M. Ross, *Political Integration*, p. 77.

18. Sidney Verba, *Small Groups and Political Behavior* (Princeton, N.J.: Princeton University Press, 1961).

19. M. Ross, *Political Integration*, pp. 78, 164–65.

20. Kanter, *Commitment*, p. 104.

21. M. Ross, *Political Integration*, pp. 78–79, 166–67; Deutsch et al., *Political Community*.

22. Kanter, *Commitment*, pp. 95–98.

23. M. Ross, *Political Integration*, p. 76; Kanter, *Commitment*, pp. 102–3; Deutsch et al., *Political Community*.

24. Kanter, *Commitment*, pp. 108–10.

25. M. Ross, *Political Integration*, pp. 76–77, 150–51; Richard L. Merritt, *Symbols*.

Chapter Two

1. For detailed information on the CNRO, its members, and the residences, see Yves Pergeaux, *Les Realities du Troisieme Age* (Paris: Dunod, 1968), and the series of publications by the CNRO Centre de Gerontologie Sociale, *CNRO Documents d'information et de gestion*.

2. 1–2 percent of those who wanted to enter the residence were refused because they were considered too ill or were otherwise likely to have difficulty living there (for instance, because of incontinence or blindness). There were exceptions even to these limits, however, as there were several residents at Les Floralies who entered with severe handicaps: one woman was blind, another woman could barely walk, one man was a deaf-mute.

A CNRO study of individuals who were asked in a mail survey if they would like to move into a residence in the Nancy region found the following characteristics correlated with "yes" answers: proximity to the new residence, feelings of solitude, tenant vs homeowner status, living in town rather than country, living in an apartment rather than a house, low intensity of social relations, mobility, previous geographical mobility, unattached status.

Age interacted with marital status, so that widows were more interested in the home if they were older, couples and unattached men were more interested if they were younger. Choice of the most important among a list of nine services offered by the residence also varied by marital status. Couples mentioned meals, health care, financial security and rest as most important; widows chose nearness to town, freedom, and group activity. ("Retired Persons and Homes for the Elderly." *CNRO Documents d'information et de gestion* 6 [March 1968]).

3. For details of the admission process, see "Homes for Old Age People," *CNRO Documents d'information et de gestion* 3 (May 1966): 8–9.

4. Some residents also receive gifts and money from children or other relatives, but I do not have systematic information on the individuals or the amounts involved.

5. My use of the term *faction* corresponds quite closely to the definition suggested by Nicolas: Factions are conflict groups, political groups, not corporate groups; their members are recruited by a leader on diverse principles. Ralph Nicolas, "Factions: A Comparative Analysis," in *Political Systems and the Distribution of Power*, ed. Michael Banton (London: Tavistock Publishers, 1965), pp. 27–29. In contrast to Bailey's usage, however, factions in the residence do have an ideological basis. F. G. Bailey, *Stratagems and Spoils* (Oxford: Basil Backwell, 1969), p. 52. The pro- or anti-Communist orientation is a requirement for recruitment into a faction, although it may be marked in various ways and has varying degrees of significance for different individuals. Mobilization in specific conflict situations does depend on the diverse ties to leaders and core members stressed by "transactional" analysts of factions, although the benefits offered to residents are less often material than in those cases. For a review of the anthropological literature on factions, see Janet Bujra, "The Dynamics of Political Action: A New Look at Factionalism," *American Anthropologist* 75 (1973): 132–52.

6. This coding system is described in more detail in Jennie-Keith Ross and Marc Ross, "Participant Observation in Political Research," *Political Methodology* 1 (1974): 63–88.

7. Because my codings are almost always available for every resident, while response rates for each questionnaire item differ, sample sizes for statistics based on the two kinds of data, or both, will vary. In every case where questionnaire items or scores on my codings are combined in scales, these scales were created by factor analysis of the items or scores. Unless I have indicated otherwise, all correlations presented are significant at the .05 level. For comments on the usefulness of presenting significance levels for statistics derived from a total population rather than a random sample, see Hubert M. Blalock, Jr., *Social Statistics*, 2d ed. (New York: McGraw-Hill), pp. 238–39. The major advantage is the possibility of evaluating the influence of chance processes in producing an observed relationship.

8. Analysis of variance shows that sex, age, income, length of residence, and strength of political identification have no significant relationship to whether or not a person responded to the questionnaire; there is a slightly significant relationship between direction of political identification and response, with non-Communists (anti-Communists and neutrals combined) slightly more likely to respond than Communists.

Chapter Three

1. *Possession of a work role* is defined by both participation in work activities and identification by other residents as having a work role. High score indicates that, according to my observations, an individual works regularly and is clearly identified in a work role. Medium indicates that an individual works occasionally when needed, but identification with the work role is not strong. Low indicates that a person never or very rarely works. *Social status* is a scale based on scores on my rankings of individuals according to observation of their leadership roles, popularity, and visibility. A high score on *leadership* indicates that according to my observations an individual was often seen as a task, emotional, or opinion leader by other residents. A medium score indicates that an individual was sometimes seen as a leader; a low score indicates that he or she was rarely or never seen as a leader. *Popularity* scores are based on my observations of the numbers of people by whom an individual was liked and the intensity of their expression of this attitude. Individuals were scored separately on numbers and intensity, and then the scores were combined; a high on numbers and a low on intensity would produce a popularity score of medium. *Visibility* scores (high, medium, low) are based on my observations of the extent to which an individual is known in the community, either by name or by an outstanding characteristic or activity. Sources of social status and its measurement are discussed in detail in chapter 4.

2. These attitudes are measured by the following questionnaire items, to which possible responses were agree, disagree, neither: "Everyone who is able to should take a job in the residence in order to contribute to community life"; "Residents are always ready to help each other"; "People have a right to demand what they want here in the residence."

3. Of those who responded to the questionnaire item "Everyone who is able to should take a job in the residence in order to contribute to community life," 72 percent of the non-Communists agreed, 47 percent of the pro-Communists agreed. This relationship is in the same direction as my observations and interviews, although it is not statistically significant. The variable that is probably intervening is the salience of political affiliation to different individuals, but the small sample size makes controlling for salience impossible.

4. $r = .02$, $N = 121$.

5. *Formal group participation* refers to institutionalized public contact with other residents through participation in regular public groups (for example, the residents committee, the sewing club, television in the lounge, pottery class, card games). A high score indicates my observation of an individual's formal group participation about five times a week; medium score indicates participation about once a week; low score indicates rare participation or never.

6. *Frequency of leaving the residence* is a score based on my observations: high represents leaving the residence at least once a day; medium represents leaving two to six times per week; and low represents leaving once a week or less.

7. Another example of table territoriality is reported in Pamela J. Cluff

and William Campbell, "The Social Corridor: An Environmental and Behavioral Evaluation," *Gerontologist* 15 (December 1975): 516–23.

8. *Visiting other residents* is an index based on responses to two questionnaire items: (a) When was the last time you visited another resident? Within the last week? Within the last month? More than a month ago? (b) When was the last time another resident came to see you? (Same response categories.)

9. *Strength of political identification* is a score based on my observations of the extent to which an individual was identified by other residents as being aligned with either the Catholic-Socialist coalition or the Communist opposition. A high score indicates that an individual was clearly identified, medium that he or she was partially or vaguely identified, low that he or she was not identified at all. Twenty-seven percent of the residents have high scores, 46 percent medium scores, and 27 percent have low scores.

10. The correlation between political affiliation and visiting in the residence is $r = .04$, $N = 65$.

11. Because of reasons mentioned in chapter 2 (recent inquiries by the welfare agency, fear for their children's privacy, etc.), the number of responses is very low for questions about family. Statistics including these data should be read with these problems in mind.

12. The correlation between frequency of contact with friends outside the residence and frequency of visiting inside the residence is $r = -.20$ (not significant at the .05 level), $N = 40$.

Contacts with family is an index constructed from the following questionnaire items: (a) When was the last time you saw one of your children? Within the last week, during the last month, during the last year? (b) When was the last time you saw one of your grandchildren? (c) When was the last time you saw one of your sisters? (d) When was the last time you saw one of your brothers? (all with same response categories as above). The score on contacts with family is the highest (most recent) response to any of these items.

Contacts with friends outside the residence is scored on the basis of response to a questionnaire item: When was the last time you saw a friend who does not live in the residence? During the last week, during the last month, during the last year?

13. See, for example, Elaine Cumming and William E. Henry, *Growing Old: The Process of Disengagement* (New York: Basic Books, Inc., 1961).

14. See, for example, E. B. Palmore, "The Effects of Aging on Activities and Attitudes," in *Normal Aging*, ed. E. B. Palmore (Durham: Duke University Press, 1970); Robert J. Havighurst, Bernice L. Neugarten, and Sheldon S. Tobin, "Disengagement and Patterns of Aging," in *Middle Age and Aging*, ed. Bernice Neugarten (Chicago: University of Chicago Press, 1968), pp. 161–72.

15. Happiness is correlated with frequency of family contacts $r = -.13$, $N = 45$; with formal group participation, $r = -.12$, $N = 67$; with having a work role, $r = .12$, $N = 67$; with frequency of visiting with other residents, $r = -.08$, $N = 64$; with frequency of visiting with friends from outside the residence, $r = -.03$, $N = 66$. (None significant at the .05 level.)

Happiness is an index constructed from the following questionnaire items: Would you describe your life these days as very happy, fairly happy, or not very happy? In general does the life you lead now seem happier, less happy, or about the same as the life you used to lead? Does the life you lead now seem happier, less happy, or about the same as the life you led before moving into the residence? In general, is your life in the residence better than you expected, worse than you expected, or about the same as you expected?

16. For discussion of the effects of personality and previous life experience on sources of life satisfaction among older people, see Bernice L. Neugarten, Robert J. Havighurst, and Sheldon S. Tobin, "Personality and Patterns of Aging," in Neugarten, *Middle Age*, pp. 173–77; George L. Maddox, "Persistence of Life Style among the Elderly," in ibid., pp. 181–83; and Richard H. Williams and Claudine Wirth, *Lives Through the Years* (New York: Atherton Press, 1965); Robert C. Achley, *The Social Forces in Later Life* (Belmont, Cal.: Wadsworth Publishing Co., 1972), p. 37; Anne-Marie Guillemard, *La Retraite: Une Mort Sociale* (The Hague: Mouton, 1972); Arlie Russell Hochschild, "Disengagement Theory: A Critique and Proposal," *American Sociological Review* 40 (October 1975): 553–69, is a useful critique of the disengagement hypothesis and the research it has stimulated.

17. *Self-evaluation of health* is based on responses to a questionnaire item: By comparison with other people your age, do you think that your health is excellent, good, fair, or poor? Self-evaluation of health has been found to correlate well with medical evaluations. See, for example, George L. Maddox, "Some Correlates of Differences in Self-assessments of Health Status among the Elderly," *Journal of Gerontology* 17 (1962): 180–85.

18. The correlation between age and positive evaluation of health is $r = .11, N = 73$; between age and frequency of visiting inside the residence, $r = -.11, N = 64$; between age and having a work role, $r = .13, N = 120$; between age and formal group participation, $r = .05, N = 120$. (None significant at the .05 level.)

19. Michael Banton, *Roles: An Introduction to the Study of Social Relations* (London: Tavistock Publications, 1965). Other researchers have argued that maintenance of distinct roles for men and women after retirement is an important possibility offered by the organized social life of age-homogeneous communities. Cf. Susan Washburn Byrne, "Arden, an Adult Community" (Ph.D. diss., University of California, Berkeley, 1971).

20. The correlation between sex and factional affiliation is $r = .00$, $N = 126$.

21. When the relationship between political identification and visiting is reexamined controlling for sex, the correlation is raised from .32 to .38.

Chapter Four

1. See Yves Pergeaux, *Les Realities du Troisieme Age* (Paris: Dunod, 1968), pp. 9–12.

2. Problems with eliciting sociometric responses from a similar population in the United States are reported in Frances M. Carp, *A Future for the Aged* (Austin, Texas: University of Texas Press, 1966), p. 157. Researchers in three other CNRO residences had difficulty getting any rejection responses; see Pergeaux, *Les Realities*, pp. 123, 171–72; and "Residence 'La Croix-du-Gue': La Vie Collective," *CNRO Documents d'information et de gestion* 8 (December 1968):17. Sheila K. Johnson, *Idle Haven: Community-Building among the Working Class Retired* (Berkeley: University of California Press, 1971), p. 82, reports no difficulty in eliciting choices of friends, but did not ask for rejections.

3. Factor analysis of these three characteristics shows that they cluster together into one dimension, which I have labeled social status.

4. See Rose Giallombardo, *Society of Women* (New York: John Wiley and Sons, 1966).

5. See J. A. Hoestetler and G. E. Huntington, *The Hutterites in North America* (New York: Holt, Rinehart and Winston, 1967).

6. See Jennie-Keith Hill (Ross), *The Culture of Retirement* (Ph.D. diss., Northwestern University, 1968), chapter 8.

7. The evidence now available does not make it clear what factors are related to the emergence of which of these patterns. Future research might begin with examination of three factors which appear to be important: value congruence between insiders and outsiders, especially in terms of the characteristic(s) by which people are recruited into the new community; members' expectations of staying in the new community permanently or for a very long time; existence of social ties crosscutting the member/nonmember distinction. Value congruence, expectation of leaving the community, and existence of crosscutting ties should promote the reflection pattern rather than reversal or irrelevance. The distinction between these two seems to depend on more subtle variations of insider-outsider views both of the characteristic(s) marking the community border, and of the appropriateness of that border's existence. Reversal seems more likely, for instance, when insiders see the outside negatively and place a high positive value on border maintenance; irrelevance should be more likely when outsiders view insiders negatively, and insiders see border maintenance as very desirable. For more discussion of border definition and maintenance, see Jennie-Keith Ross, "Social Borders: Definitions of Diversity," *Current Anthropology* 6 (1975):53–72.

8. See, for example, Arnold M. Rose, "The Subculture of the Aging," in *Older People and their Social World*, ed. Arnold M. Rose and Warren K. Peterson (Philadelphia: F. A. Davis and Co., 1965).

9. See William Caudill, *The Psychiatric Hospital as a Small Society* (Cambridge, Mass.: Harvard University Press, 1958).

10. Robert W. Kleemeier, "Moosehaven: Congregate Living in a Community of the Retired," *American Journal of Sociology* 59 (1954): 347–51.

11. Present income is not related to social status in the residence. The distinction between those who pay for themselves in the residence and those who receive welfare is related to status: $r = .17$, $N = 124$. However, when this relationship is re-examined, controlling for strength of political identification, the characteristic which explains most of the variance in social status, it is reduced to $r = .08$. See the last four sections of this

chapter for discussion of the relationship between strength of political identification and social status.

12. E. P. Friedman, "Age, Length of Institutionalization and Social Status in a Home for the Aged," *Journal of Gerontology* 22 (1967): 474–77.

13. Controlling for strength of political identification reduces the correlation between visiting inside the residence and social status from $r = .34$, $N = 65$, to $r = .19$, $N = 65$ (not significant at the .05 level). Controlling for strength of political identification raises the correlation between formal group participation and social status from $r = .25$, $N = 121$, to $r = .28$, $N = 121$. The correlation between possession of a work role and social status is also raised by controlling for strength of political identification, from $r = .34$, $N = 121$, to $r = .37$, $N = 121$.

14. *Importance of residence* is a score (high, medium, or low) based on my observation of the subjective salience of the community to an individual, as indicated by his or her tendency to make social judgments in internal terms, to express strong loyalty or criticism, to show strong affect or commitment to the community in any way. When the relationship between social status and importance of the residence to the individual is re-examined, partialling for the effect of strength of political identification, the relationship is weaker, but still significant: $r = .48$, $N = 122$, reduced from $r = .61$, $N = 122$.

Chapter Five

1. Clyde Kluckhohn, "Myth and Ritual," *Harvard Journal of Theology* 35 (1942): 45–79.

2. David L. Gutmann, "The Hunger of Old Men," *Transaction* 9 (1971): 55–66.

3. Descriptions of collective responses to death in age-homogeneous settings can be found in Victor W. Marshall, "Socialization for Impending Death in a Retirement Village," *American Journal of Sociology* 80 (1975): 1124–44; Arlie Russell Hochschild, *The Unexpected Community* (Englewood Cliffs, N. J.: Prentice-Hall, 1973), pp. 79–87; and Robert W. Kleemeier, "Moosehaven: Congregate Living in a Community of the Retired," *American Journal of Sociology* 59 (1954): 347–51.

4. See Max Gluckman, "Gossip and Scandal," *Current Anthropology* 4 (1963): 307–16, for discussion of the functions of gossip as a form of social control in small communities.

Chapter Six

1. Frances M. Carp also suggests that criticism does not indicate unhappiness. She thinks that freedom to voice complaints may be a requisite for good morale. See Frances M. Carp, *A Future for the Aged* (Austin: University of Texas Press, 1966), pp. 171–72.

2. Arnold van Gennep, *The Rites of Passage* (Chicago: University of Chicago Press, 1960).

3. Howard S. Becker, "Personal Change in Adult Life," in *Middle Age and Aging*, ed. Bernice Neugarten (Chicago: University of Chicago Press, 1968), pp. 148–56.

4. Irving Rosow, *Social Integration of the Aged* (New York: The Free Press, 1967).

Chapter Seven

1. Herbert Danzger, "A Quantified Description of Community Conflict," *American Behavioral Scientist* 12 (1968): 11; E. E. Schattschneider, *The Semi-Sovereign People* (New York: Holt, Rinehart and Winston, 1960), pp. 16, 40. James Coleman, *Community Conflict* (New York: The Free Press, 1957), pp. 10–11.

2. Murray Edelman, *The Symbolic Uses of Politics* (Urbana, Illinois: University of Illinois Press, 1964); David Cassady, "Taxi-Cab Rate War," *Journal of Conflict Resolution* 1 (1957): 364–68; R. L. Crain, E. Katz, and D. E. Rosenthal, *The Politics of Community Conflict* (New York: Bobbs-Merrill Company, Inc., 1969), esp. p. 10.

3. Coleman, *Community Conflict*, pp. 11–12.

4. Ibid., p. 21.

5. Michael Barkun, *Law Without Sanctions* (New Haven: Yale University Press, 1968), pp. 36–58; J. Burton, *Conflict and Communication* (New York: The Free Press, 1969), pp. 60–87; Coleman, *Community Conflict*, pp. 22, 17; William Gamson, "Rancorous Conflict in Community Politics," *American Sociological Review* 31 (1966): 71–81; Max Gluckman, *Politics, Law and Ritual in Tribal Society* (Chicago: Aldine, 1965), pp. 109–16; Muzafer Sherif, *Inter-group Conflict and Co-operation: Robber's Cave Experiment* (Norman, Okla.: University of Oklahoma Institute of Group Relations, 1961).

6. Schattschneider, *Semi-Sovereign People*, pp. 3–4. Matthew Crenson, *The Unpolitics of Air Pollution* (Baltimore: Johns Hopkins University Press, 1971), pp. 69–73.

7. Burton, *Conflict and Communication*, pp. 48–59; Robert Dubin, "Industrial Conflict and Social Welfare," *Journal of Conflict Resolution* 1 (1957): 179–99; Joseph S. Himes, "The Functions of Racial Conflict," *Social Forces* 45 (1966): 1–10.

8. Georg Simmel, *Conflict and the Web of Group-Affiliations* (New York: The Free Press, 1964), pp. 48–50.

9. Coleman, *Politics of Community Conflict*, pp. 3–4.

Chapter Eight

1. Leadership is not easily classified as a background or emergent factor, since it might be either or both. I have resolved this question in terms of my specific case, since at Les Floralies the leadership skills of several individuals were an important background factor in community formation.

2. Rosabeth Moss Kanter, *Commitment and Community: Communes and Utopias in Sociological Perspective* (Cambridge, Mass.: Harvard University Press, 1972), p. 99.

3. Marc Howard Ross, *Political Integration of Urban Squatters* (Evanston, Ill.: Northwestern University Press, 1973), p. 77.

4. *Loyalty to residence* is an index constructed from the following questionnaire items: Everyone who is able to should take a job in the residence in order to contribute to the life in community. Agree, disagree, neither. People who have a tendency to criticize the residence are basically ingrates. Agree, disagree, neither.

5. Kanter, *Commitment*, p. 93.

6. M. Ross, *Political Integration*, pp. 136–38; Karl Deutsch, et al.,

Political Community and the North Atlantic Area (Princeton: Princeton University Press, 1957).

7. Factional conflict is reported in research on other communities of older people; see, for example, Susan Washburn Byrne, "Arden, an Adult Community," (Ph.D. diss, University of California, Berkeley, 1971); Arlie Russell Hochschild, *The Unexpected Community* (Englewood Cliffs, N.J.: Prentice-Hall, 1973; Sheila K. Johnson, *Idle Haven: Community-Building among the Working Class Retired* (Berkeley, Calif.: University of California Press, 1971). Jacobs has pointed out that although conflict among older people is often seen as inappropriate or annoying, especially by relatives and administrators, it is a source of excitement and integration into the community for old people just as for people of other ages. See Ruth Harriet Jacobs, "One-Way Street: an Intimate View of Adjustment to a Home for the Aged," *Gerontologist* 9 (1969): 268–75.

Chapter Nine

1. For documentation and discussion of the relationships between age density and social interaction and morale, see the following: Zena Smith Blau, "Structural Constraints on Friendships in Old Age," *American Sociological Review* 21 (1956): 198–203; Eunice Boyer, "Health Perception in the Elderly: Its Cultural and Social Aspects," paper presented in the Symposium on Aging, American Anthropological Association, San Francisco, Calif., 74th Annual Meeting, 1975; G. L. Bultena and Vivian Wood, "The American Retirement Community: Bane or Blessing?" *Journal of Gerontology* 24 (April 1969): 209–17; Frances M. Carp, *A Future for the Aged* (Austin: University of Texas Press, 1966); Maurice B. Hamovitch, "Social and Psychological Factors in Adjustment in a Retirement Village," in *The Retirement Process*, ed. Frances M. Carp (Washington, D.C.: U.S. Department of Health, Education, and Welfare, 1966); G. C. Hoyt, "The Life of the Retired in a Trailer Park," *American Journal of Sociology* 59 (1954): 347–51; Mark Messer, "The Effects of Age Groupings on Organizational and Normative Systems of the Elderly," Seventh International Congress of Gerontology, *Proceedings*, vol. 6 (Vienna: Wiener Medizinishchen Akademie), pp. 253–58; idem., "The Possibility of an Age-concentrated Environment Becoming a Normative System," *Gerontologist* 7 (1967): 247–51; George S. Rosenberg, *Poverty, Aging and Social Isolation* (Washington, D.C.: Bureau of Social Science Research, Inc., 1967), cited in Matilda White Riley and Anne Foner, *Aging and Society*, vol. 1 (New York: Russell Sage Foundation, 1968), p. 569; Irving Rosow, *Social Integration of the Aged* (New York: The Free Press, 1967); M. Seguin, "Opportunity for Peer Socialization in a Retirement Community," *Gerontologist* 13 (1973): 208–14; G. L. Bultena, "Structural Effects on the Morale of the Aged: A Comparison of Age-Segregated and Age-Integrated Communities," in *Late Life: Communities and Environmental Policy*, ed. Jaber F. Gubrium (Springfield, Ill.: Charles C. Thomas, 1974), pp. 18–31; Susan Sherman, "Patterns of Contacts for Residents of Age-Segregated and Age-Integrated Housing," *Journal of Gerontology* 30 (1975):103–7; K. K. Schooler, "The Relationship between Social Interaction and Morale of the Elderly as a Function of Environmental Charac-

teristics," *Gerontologist* 9 (1969): 25–29; Joseph D. Teaff, M. Powell Lawton, and Diane Carlson, "Impact of Age Integration of Public Housing Projects Upon Elderly Tenant Well-Being," paper presented to the Gerontological Society, Miami Beach, Florida, 26th Annual Meeting, 1973.

The ineffectiveness of spatial integration as a stimulus to social integration of older people is discussed in the following: Johanna F. Alger, *Activity Patterns and Attitudes Toward Housing of Families in Specially Designed Apartments for Aged Living in Ten New York City Projects* (Ithaca, New York: Cornell University Housing Research Center, 1959); Arlie Russell Hochschild, *The Unexpected Community* (Englewood Cliffs, N.J., 1973), p. 29; Leonard Rosenmayr and Eva Kockeis, "Family Relations and Social Contacts of the Aged in Vienna," in *Aging Around the World*, vol. 1, ed. Clark Tibbitts, et al. (New York: Columbia University Press, 1962); G. L. Bultena, "Age-Grading in the Social Interaction of an Elderly Male Population," *Journal of Gerontology* 23 (1968): 539–43.

2. Characteristics of individuals most sensitive to the effects of age density are discussed in Boyer, "Health Perception"; Rosow, *Social Integration*; Susan R. Sherman, "Mutual Assistance and Support in Retirement Housing," *Journal of Gerontology* 30 (July 1975): 479–84.

3. Messer, "Effects of Age Groupings," and "Possibility of an Age-concentrated Environment"; Teaff et al., "Impact of Age Integration." M. Powell Lawton, "The Relative Impact of Congregate and Traditional Housing on Elderly Tenants," *Gerontologist* 16 (1976): 237–42, discusses the different effects of different types of age-homogeneous housing on both morale and social interaction.

4. Susan Washburn Byrne, "Arden, an Adult Community" (Ph.D. diss., University of California, Berkeley, 1971); Giselle Hendel-Sebestyen, "Total Institution and Community: A Necessary Contradiction?" Paper presented to the American Anthropological Association, New York City, New York, 1971, and cited with permission of the author; Hochschild, *Unexpected Community*; Sheila K. Johnson, *Idle Haven: Community-Building among the Working Class Retired* (Berkeley, Calif.: University of California Press, 1971).

5. Homogeneity in terms of characteristics other than age is also discussed in Boyer, "Health Perception"; Robert W. Kleemeier, "Moosehaven: Congregate Living in a Community of the Retired," *American Journal of Sociology* 59 (1954): 347–51; H. Proppe, "Housing for the Retired and Aged in Southern California: An Architectural Commentary," *Gerontologist* 8 (1968): 176–79; Rosow, *Social Integration*; Irving Rosow, *Socialization to Old Age* (Berkeley, Calif.: University of California Press, 1974), pp. 160–61; and Joseph F. Sheley, "Mutuality and Retirement Community Success: an Interactionist Perspective in Gerontological Research," *International Journal of Aging and Human Development* 5 (1974): 71–80; Anne-Marie Guillemard, *Réunion des Chercheurs en Gerontologie Sociale* (Paris: Caisse National d'Assurance Vieillesse des Travailleurs Salariés, 1975), p. 43.

6. See, for example, "Housing," in *Toward a National Policy on Aging*, vol. 2, Final Report of the 1971 White House Conference on Aging (Washington, D.C.: U.S. Government Printing Office, 1971), pp. 29–36.

7. Hamovitch, "Social and Psychological Factors"; Susan R. Sherman,

"The Choice of Retirement Housing among the Well-Elderly," *International Journal of Aging and Human Development* 2 (1971): 118–38; Linda Winiecke, "The Appeal of Age Segregated Housing to the Elderly Poor," *International Journal of Aging and Human Development* 4 (1973): 293–306; Claudette Collot and Hannelore LeBris, "Les Aspirations au Logement de Retraité, *CNRO Documents d'information et de gestion* 30 (1975).

8. See, for example, Victor W. Marshall, "Game-analyzable Dilemmas in Retirement Village Living," *International Journal of Aging and Human Development* 4 (1973): 285–91.

9. Although the original residents of Merrill Court were strangers to each other, when vacancies occur now, residents try to "speak for" their friends, which may further encourage sociability (Hochschild, *Unexpected Community*, p. 12).

10. Robert W. Kleemeier, "The Use and Meaning of Time in Special Settings: Retirement Communities, Homes for the Aged, Hospitals and Other Group Settings," in *Aging and Leisure*, ed. Robert W. Kleemeier (New York: Oxford University Press, 1961), pp. 273–308.

11. Rosow, *Social Integration*, p. 75. Another study examined the relationships among life satisfaction, interaction levels, and community age structure in natural settings, where older people had lived for many years in communities whose population ranged from 3 to 36 percent elderly. These researchers reported that although interaction with age peers was related to life satisfaction, the percentage of older people in a community was not related to life satisfaction, to total interaction, or to interaction with age peers. Their findings underscore the importance of the 50 percent "take-off" level for effects of age density. See Karen A. Conner and Edward A. Powers, "Structural Effects and Life Satisfaction Among the Aged," Journal Paper #J–75586 of the Iowa Agricultural and Home Economics Experiment Station, Ames, Iowa, Project #1871.

Research in a noncongregate setting where older people (over 60) formed a majority of the population revealed that under these circumstances they controlled formal organizations and had high levels of social contacts with age peers, and for both reasons acquired social approval and personal satisfaction. See Gordon K. Aldridge, "Informal Social Relationships in a Retirement Community," *Marriage and Family Living* 21 (1959): 70–72.

12. Boyer, "Health Perception"; Carp, *Future for the Aged*, pp. 101, 111, 114; Cluff, "Social Corridor"; Robert Sommer and H. Ross, "Social Interaction on a Geriatric Ward," *International Journal of Social Psychology* 4 (1958): 128–33; Edward P. Friedman, "Spatial Proximity and Social Interaction in a Home for the Aged," *Journal of Gerontology* 21 (1966): 566–71; and M. Powell Lawton and Bonnie Simon, "The Ecology of Social Relationships in Housing for the Elderly," *Gerontologist* 8 (1968): 108–15, also discuss the influence of spatial arrangements on social interaction.

13. Sherman, "Patterns of Contacts," reports that interaction with children is similar for residents of age-segregated housing and for a control group, if distance from children is held constant. See also Hochschild, *Unexpected Community*, pp. 88–111.

14. See Rosow, *Social Integration*, p. 315, for a summary of his findings on the independence of kin and friendship contacts; and also, Gary D.

Hampe and Audie L. Blevins, Jr., "Primary Group Interaction of Residents in a Retirement Hotel," *International Journal of Aging and Human Development* 6 (1975): 309–20.

15. Hochschild, *Unexpected Community*, pp. 88–111; Mark Messer, "Age Grouping and the Family Status of the Elderly," *Sociology and Social Research* 52 (1968): 271–79; Yonina Talmon, "Aging in Israel, a Planned Society," in *Middle Age and Aging*, ed. Bernice Neugarten (Chicago: University of Chicago Press, 1968), p. 465; M.-F. Fichet, "Logement et Troisieme Age," *Gerontologie* 4 (1971): 10.

16. Kleemeier, "Moosehaven," discusses the importance of work in this retirement community.

17. Paul Bohannan, "Extra-Processual Events in Tiv Political Institutions," *American Anthropologist* 60 (1958): 1–12; Clyde Kluckhohn, *Navajo Witchcraft* (Boston: Beacon Press, 1944).

18. Internal sources of status are also reported in Jerry Jacobs, *Fun City: An Ethnographic Study of a Retirement Community* (New York: Holt, Rinehart and Winston, 1974); Ernest W. Burgess, "Social Relations, Activities and Personal Adjustment," *American Journal of Sociology* 59 (1954): 352–60; and E. P. Friedman, "Age, Length of Institutionalization and Social Status in a Home for the Aged," *Journal of Gerontology* 22 (1967): 474–77.

19. Preliminary analysis of data from a multi-ethnic public housing project in Florida suggests that friendship pairs and cliques form within each of three ethnic groups, although they are also linked by brokers, dyadic friendships, and some isolated individuals who participate in informal activities of an ethnic group other than their own. Interesting from the point of view of the emergence of internal principles of social organization is the fact that physical distance seems to be at least as important as, and perhaps more important than, ethnicity in setting limits for friendship formation. This research was generously described to me by Randy Kandel, assistant professor of anthropology at Florida International University, who is conducting the investigation jointly with Marion Heider, RN.

20. Irving Rosow, in his comments on Hamovitch, "Social and Psychological Factors," suggests that there is a life cycle of retirement communities, in which the first twelve to eighteen months are characterized by high activity, extensive interaction, and mutual aid. Several of the studies referred to here were done well after this "honeymoon phase," and in several cases included revisits. They document the persistence of high levels of interaction and reciprocal help: Hochschild, *Unexpected Community*; Marshall, "Socialization to Impending Death"; Johnson, *Idle Haven*; Carp, *Future for the Aged*; and Frances M. Carp, "Impact of Improved Housing on Morale and Life Satisfaction," *Gerontologist* 15 (1975): 511–15.

21. The lack of community in SRO's has been described to me in a personal communication by Paul Bohannan. It is also reported in J. Stephens, "Society of the Alone: Freedom, Privacy, and Utilitarianism as Dominant Norms in the SRO," *Journal of Gerontology* 30 (1975): 230–35. J. H. Shapiro, in "Single-room Occupancy," *Social Work* 11 (1966): 24–33,

on the other hand, describes an SRO in which tenants are extensively and intimately involved with each other. There were only six isolated individuals in the buildings. The others belonged to "well-defined, matriarchal quasi-families" whose members visited constantly in the "mothers' " room. Shapiro suggests that this unusual degree of solidarity may have been promoted by a relatively stable population, prominent negative publicity about the building, and a threat of eviction.

22. Sheila K. Johnson, "Growing Old Alone Together," *New York Times Magazine*, Nov. 11, 1973, p. 40.

23. Cf. Ethel Shanas, Peter Townsend, Dorothy Wedderburn, Henning Friis, Poul Milhoj, and Jan Stenouwer, *Old People in Three Industrial Societies* (New York: Atherton Press, 1968); Ethel Shanas and Gordon F. Streib, eds., *Social Structure and the Family: Generational Relations* (Englewood Cliffs, N.J.: Prentice-Hall, 1965); Peter Townsend, *The Family Life of Old People* (London: Routledge and Kegan Paul, 1957).

24. *Business Week*, April 4, 1964, p. 130.

25. Marshall, "Socialization to Impending Death."

26. An extremely complete survey of housing for older and retired people in California illustrates this shift. In 1964, 9 percent of the "Fixed Dwelling Unit" sites—non-licensed housing for older and retired people (i.e., not boarding homes or nursing homes)—had medical facilities present or under construction. Fifty percent of the planned sites in this category would include a clinic and/or a doctor, 32 percent a pharmacy, and 21 percent a hospital. See R. P. Walkley, Wiley P. Mangum, Susan Sherman, Suzanne Dodds, and Daniel M. Wilner, *Retirement Housing in California* (Berkeley: Diablo Press, 1966), p. 65.

Calvin Trillen, "Wake Up and Live," *The New Yorker* 40 (April 1964): 120–72, describes the efforts of residents in one early retirement community (Sun City, Arizona) to obtain medical care that was not originally provided. Residents of "Arden" repeatedly requested a private home health care service which they now have (Byrne, "Arden"). The most popular complaint at "Fun City" is the absence of adequate medical facilities (Jacobs, *Fun City*, p. 33).

27. See, for example, Johnson, *Idle Haven*, p. 62; Jacobs, *Fun City*, p. 48; Leland Frederick Cooley and Lee Morrison Cooley, *The Retirement Trap* (New York: Doubleday, 1965), p. 30.

28. A market survey in which 80 percent of the older respondents said they did not want to change locations, but 50 percent felt their homes were not "suitable for retirement," is reported in *Business Week*, April 15, 1961, p. 48. Such directories as those published regularly by the National Council on Aging, the Dartnell Corporation (*1001 Places to Live When You Retire*), and George Stromme (*Resort/Retirement Facilities Register*) show a very even distribution of establishments in various regions of the United States.

29. See, for example, Donald O. Cowgill, "A Theory of Aging in Cross-Cultural Perspective," in Donald O. Cowgill and Lowell D. Holmes, eds., *Aging and Modernization* (New York: Appleton-Century-Crofts, 1972), pp. 1–13; Simone de Beauvoir, *La Vieillesse* (Paris: Gallimard, 1970).

30. Although most Americans feel that older people and their children should not share a household, in one national survey the respondents most likely to say children should be responsible for their parents were children with living parents; their parents were the most likely to feel the government should take care of them. See Ethel Shanas, *The Health of Older People: A Social Survey* (Cambridge, Mass.: Harvard University Press, 1962), p. 28. The older people most likely to live with their children in America are widows. Since they consistently have the lowest incomes in their age category, they have the least possibility of choosing other living arrangements but are in fact likely to think it is preferable for older people to live independently. See Marilyn Langford, *Community Aspects of Housing the Aged* (Ithaca, N.Y.: Cornell University Center for Housing and Environmental Studies, 1962), p. 28, and also Cowgill, "Theory of Aging," p. 253. Rosenmayr and Kockeis, "Family Relations," also report the preference of older people in Vienna for what they call "intimacy par distance." J. M. Richardson makes similar observations about older people in Scotland in *Age and Need, A Study of Older People in North East Scotland* (Edinburgh: Livingston, 1964), p. 60.

31. For a discussion of the impact of values about dependency on aging in America, see Margaret Clark, "Cultural Values and Dependency in Later Life," in Cowgill and Holmes, *Aging and Modernization*, pp. 263–74.

Bibliography

Aldridge, Gordon K. "Informal Social Relationships in a Retirement Community." *Marriage and Family Living* 21 (1959):70–72.

Alger, Johanna F. *Activity Patterns and Attitudes toward Housing of Families in Specially Designed Apartments for Aged Living in Ten New York City Projects*. Ithaca, NY: Cornell University Housing Research Center, 1959.

Atchley, Robert C. *The Social Forces in Later Life*. Belmont, Cal.: Wadsworth Publishing Co., 1972.

Bailey, Frederick G. *Strategies and Spoils*. Oxford: Basil Blackwell, 1969.

Banton, Michael. *Roles: An Introduction to the Study of Social Relations*. London: Tavistock Publications, 1965.

Barkun, Michael. *Law without Sanctions*. New Haven: Yale University Press, 1968.

Becker, Howard S. "Personal Change in Adult Life." In *Middle Age and Aging*, edited by Bernice Neugarten, pp. 148–56. Chicago: University of Chicago Press, 1968.

Beyer, Glenn H., and Nierstrasz, F. H. J. *Housing the Aged in Western Countries*. Amsterdam: Elsevier, 1967.

Blalock, Hubert M. *Social Statistics*. 2d ed. New York: McGraw-Hill, 1972.

Blau, Zena Smith. *Old Age in A Changing Society*. New York: New Viewpoints, 1973.

————. "Structural Constraints on Friendship in Old Age." *American Sociological Review* 21 (1956):198–203.

Bohannan, Paul. "Extra-Processual Events in Tiv Political Institutions." *American Anthropologist* 60 (1958):1–12.

Bujra, Janet M. "The Dynamics of Political Action: A New Look at Factionalism." *American Anthropologist* 75 (1973):132–52.

Bultena, G, L. "Age-grading in the Social Interaction of an Elderly Male Population." *Journal of Gerontology* 23 (1968):539–43.

————. "Relationship of Occupational Status to Friendship Ties in Three Planned Retirement Communities." *Journal of Gerontology* 24 (1969):461–64.

————. "Structural Effects on the Morale of the Aged: A Comparison of Age-Segregated and Age-Integrated Communities." In *Late Life: Communities and Environmental Policy*, edited by Jaber F. Gubrium. Springfield, Ill.: Charles C. Thomas, 1974, pp. 18–31.

Bultena, G. L., and Wood, Vivian. "The American Retirement Community: Bane or Blessing?" *Journal of Gerontology* 24 (1969):209–17.

Burgess, Ernest W. "Social Relations, Activities, and Personal Adjustment." *American Journal of Sociology* 59 (1954):352–60.

Burton, J. *Conflict and Communication*. New York: Free Press, 1969.

Business Week, April 15, 1961, p. 48; April 4, 1964, p. 130.

Butaud, J.-P., and Pons-Vignon, B. "Les Retraités face aux residences." *CNRO documents d'information et de gestion*, vol. 6 (1968).

Byrne, Susan Washburn. "Arden: An Adult Community." Ph.D. dissertation, University of California, Berkeley, 1971.

Carp, Frances M. *A Future for the Aged*. Austin: University of Texas Press, 1966.

———. "Impact of Improved Housing on Morale and Life Satisfaction." *Gerontologist* 15 (1975):511–15.

Cassady, David. "Taxi-Cab Rate War." *Journal of Conflict Resolution* 1 (1957):364–68.

Caudill, William. *The Psychiatric Hospital as the Small Society*. Cambridge, Mass.: Harvard University Press, 1958.

Clark, Margaret. "Cultural Values and Dependency in Later Life." In *Aging and Modernization*, edited by D. O. Cowgill and L. D. Holmes, pp. 263–74. New York: Appleton-Century-Crofts, 1972.

Clark, Margaret, and Anderson, Barbara. *Culture and Aging*. Springfield, Ill.: Charles C. Thomas, 1967.

Cluff, Pamela J., and Campbell, William. "The Social Corridor: An Environmental and Behavioral Evaluation." *Gerontologist* 15 (1975):516–23.

Coleman, James. *Community Conflict*. New York: Free Press, 1957.

Coleman, James, and Rosberg, Carl J. *Political Parties and National Integration in Tropical Africa*. Berkeley: University of California Press, 1964.

Collot, Claudette. "Les Attitudes des personnes agées en habitat collectif." *Revue de gerontologie d'expression Française* 3 (1972): 32–36.

———. "La Vie collective: Solutions ou palliatifs." *Revue Française de gerontologie*, vol. 17 (1971).

Collot, Claudette, and Le Bris, Hannelore. "Les Aspirations au logement de retraité." *CNRO documents d'information et de gestion*, vol. 30 (July 1975).

Conner, Karen A., and Powers, Edward A. "Structural Effects and Life Satisfaction among the Aged." Journal paper no. J–75586 of the Iowa Agricultural and Home Economics Experiment Station, Ames, Iowa, Project no. 1871.

Cooley, Leland Frederick, and Cooley, Lee Morrison. *The Retirement Trap*. New York: Doubleday, 1965.

Cowgill, D. O. "A Theory of Aging in Cross-Cultural Perspective." In *Aging and Modernization*, edited by D. O. Cowgill and L. D. Holmes, pp. 1–13. New York: Appleton-Century-Crofts, 1972.

Crain, R. L.; Katz, E.; and Rosenthal, D. E. *The Politics of Community Conflict*. New York: Bobbs-Merrill, 1969.

Crenson, Matthew. *The Unpolitics of Air Pollution*. Baltimore: Johns Hopkins University Press, 1971.

Cumming, Elaine, and Henry, William E. *Growing Old: The Process of Disengagement*. New York: Basic Books, 1971.

Danzger, Herbert. "A Quantified Description of Community Conflict." *American Behavioral Scientist* 12 (1968):9–14.

de Beauvoir, Simone. *La Vieillesse*. Paris: Gallimard, 1970.

de Moussac, Olivier. "Les Residences pour anciens du batiment." *Revue Française de gerontologie* 13 (1967):15–20.

Deutsch, Karl, et al. *Political Community and the North Atlantic Area*. Princeton: Princeton University Press, 1957.

Donfut, C., and Faucherand, C. "Les Personnes agées et la vie communautaire: Essai de comparison." *Revue Française de gerontologie* 15 (1969):35–8.

Dubin, Robert. "Industrial Conflict and Social Welfare." *Journal of Conflict Resolution* 1 (1957):179–99.

Edelman, Murray. *The Symbolic Uses of Politics*. Urbana: University of Illinois Press, 1964.

Ehrlich, I. F. "Life Styles among Persons 70 Years and Older in Age-Segregated Housing." *Gerontologist* 12 (1972):27–31.

Ferraud, D. "Premier bilan medical à la Residence pour Anciens de la Buissonière." *Revue Française de gerontologie* 15 (1969):103–10.

Festinger, Leon. *A Theory of Cognitive Dissonance*. Evanston, Ill.: Row, Peterson, 1957.

Fichet, M.-F. "Logement et troisième age." *Gerontologie* 4 (1971): 10.

Friedman, Edward P. "Age, Length of Institutionalization, and Social Status in a Home for the Aged." *Journal of Gerontology* 22 (1967):474–77.

―――. "Spatial Proximity and Social Interaction in a Home for the Aged." *Journal of Gerontology* 21 (1966):566–71.

Gamson, William. "Rancorous Conflict in Community Politics. *American Sociological Review* 31 (1966):71–81.

Gans, Herbert J. *The Urban Villagers: Group and Class in the Life of Italian-Americans*. New York: Free Press, 1962.

Giallombardo, Rose. *Society of Women*. New York: John Wiley and Sons, 1966.

Gluckman, Max. "Gossip and Scandal." *Current Anthropology* 4 (1963):307–16.

Greer, Scott. *The Emerging City*. New York: John Wiley and Sons, 1962.

Gubrium, Jaber F. *Living and Dying at Murray Manor*. New York: St. Martin's Press, 1975.

Guillemard, Anne-Marie. "Comments." In *Réunion des chercheurs en gerontologie sociale*. p. 43. Paris: Caisse Nationale d'Assurance Vieillesse des Travailleurs Salariés, 1975.

_____. *La Retraite: Une Mort sociale*. The Hague: Mouton, 1972.

Guttman, David. "The Hunger of Old Men." *Trans-Action* 9 (1971):55–66.

Haas, Ernst. *Beyond the Nation-State*. Stanford, Cal.: Stanford University Press, 1958.

Hamovitch, Maurice B. "Social and Psychological Factors in Adjustment in a Retirement Village." In *The Retirement Process*, edited by F. Carp. Washington: Department of Health, Education, and Welfare, 1966.

Hampe, Gary D., and Blevins, Audie L., Jr. "Primary Group Interaction of Residents in a Retirement Hotel." *International Journal of Aging and Human Development* 6 (1975):309–20.

Havighurst, Robert J.; Neugarten, Bernice L.; and Tobin, Sheldon S. "Disengagement and Patterns of Aging." In *Middle Age and Aging*, edited by Bernice Neugarten, pp. 161–72. Chicago: University of Chicago Press, 1968.

Hendel-Sebestyen, Giselle. "Total Institution and Community: A Necessary Contradiction?" Paper presented to the American Anthropological Association, New York, 1971.

Hess, Beth. "Friendship." In *Aging and Society*. Vol. 3, *A Sociology of Age Stratification*, edited by Matilda White Riley et al, pp. 357–93. New York: Russell Sage Foundation, 1972.

Himes, Joseph S. "The Functions of Racial Conflict." *Social Forces* 45 (1966):1–10.

Hochschild, Arlie Russell. "Disengagement Theory: A Critique and Proposal." *American Sociological Review* 40 (1975):553–69.

_____. *The Unexpected Community*. Englewood Cliffs, N. J.: Prentice-Hall, 1973.

Hoestetler, J. A., and Huntington, G. E. *The Hutterites in North America*. New York: Holt, Rinehart and Winston, 1967.

Hoyt, G. C. "The Life of the Retired in a Trailer Park." *American Journal of Sociology* 59 (1954):347–51.

Jacob, Philip, and Teune, Henry. "The Integrative Process: Guidelines for Analyses of the Bases of Political Integration." In *The Integration of Political Communities*, edited by Philip Jacob and James Toscano. Philadelphia: Lippincott, 1964.

Jacobs, Jerry. *Fun City: An Ethnographic Study of a Retirement Community*. New York: Holt, Rinehart and Winston, 1974.

Jacobs, Ruth Harriet. "One-Way Street: An Intimate View of Adjustment to a Home for the Aged." *Gerontologist* 9 (1969): 268–75.

Johnson, Sheila K. "Growing Old Alone Together." *New York Times Magazine*, November 11, 1973, p. 40.

_____. *Idle Haven: Community Building among the Working Class Retired*. Berkeley: University of California Press, 1971.

Kanter, Rosabeth Moss. *Commitment and Community: Communes and Utopias in Sociological Perspective*. Cambridge, Mass.: Harvard University Press, 1972.

Kleemeier, Robert W. "Moosehaven: Congregate Living in a Community of the Retired." *American Journal of Sociology* 59 (1954):347–51.

_____. "The Use and Meaning of Time in Special Settings: Retirement Communities, Homes for the Aged, Hospitals and Other Group Settings." In *Aging and Leisure*, edited by Robert Kleemeier. New York: Oxford University Press, 1961.

Kluckhohn, Clyde. "Myth and Ritual." *Harvard Journal of Theology* 35 (1942):42–79.

_____. *Navajo Witchcraft*. Boston: Beacon Press, 1944.

Knockkaert, R. "Bilan medical d'une residence de la CNRO." *Revue de gerontologie d'expression Française* 3 (1972):55–9.

Langford, Marilyn. *Community Aspects of Housing the Aged*. Ithaca, N.Y.: Cornell University Center for Housing and Environmental Studies, 1962.

Lawton, M. Powell. "Ecology and Aging." In *The Spatial Behavior of Older People*, edited by L. A. Pastalan and D. H. Carson. Ann Arbor: University of Michigan Press, 1970.

_____. "The Relative Impact of Congregate and Traditional Housing on Elderly Tenants." *Gerontologist* 16 (1976):237–42.

Lawton, M. Powell, and Simon, Bonnie. "The Ecology of Social Relationships in Housing for the Elderly." *Gerontologist* 8 (1968):108–15.

Lemon, B. W., et al. "An Exploration of the Activity Theory of Aging: Activity Types and Life Satisfaction among In-Movers to a Retirement Community." *Journal of Gerontology* 27 (1972): 511–23.

Maddox, George L. "Persistence of Life Style among the Elderly." In *Middle Age and Aging*, edited by Bernice Neugarten, pp. 181–83. Chicago: University of Chicago Press, 1968.

_____. "Some Correlates of Differences in Self-assessments of Health Status among the Elderly." *Journal of Gerontology* 17 (1962):180–85.

Manil, P. "La Tolerance dans la cohabitation dans un home de vieillards." *Revue de gerontologie d'expression Française* 17 (1970):31–44.

Marshall, Victor W. "Game Analysable Dilemmas in Retirement Village Living." *International Journal of Aging and Human Development* 4 (1973):285–91.

_____. "Socialization for Impending Death in a Retirement Village." *American Journal of Sociology* 80 (1975):1124–44.

Merritt, Richard L. *Symbols of American Community, 1735–1765*. New Haven: Yale University Press, 1966.

Messer, Mark. "Age Grouping and the Family Status of the Elderly." *Sociology and Social Research* 52 (1968):271–79.

_____. "The Effects of Age-Groupings on Organizational and Normative Systems of the Elderly." In Seventh International Congress of Gerontology, *Proceedings*, vol. 6, pp. 253–58. Vienna: Wiener Medizinischen Akademie, 1966.

_____. "The Possibility of an Age-Concentrated Environment Becoming a Normative System." *Gerontologist* 7 (1967):247–51.

Nicolas, Ralph. "Factions: A Comparative Analysis." In *Political Systems and the Distribution of Power*, edited by Michael Banton, pp. 27–29. London: Tavistock Publishers, 1965.

Nisbet, Robert. *Community and Power*. New York: Oxford Galaxy Books, 1962.

Pacaud, Suzanne, and Chapé, M. "Les Rapports sociaux dans la vie communautaire: etude sociometrique dans un service hosptalier." *Revue Francaise de gerontologie* 11 (1965):359–98.

Pacaud, Suzanne, and Lahalle, M. O. *Attitudes, comportements, opinions des personnes agées dans le cadre de la famille moderne*. Paris: Centre National de la Recherche Scientifique, 1969.

Paillat, Paul. *Sociologie de la vieillesse*. Paris: Presses Universitaries de France, 1963.

Palmore, E. B. "The Effects of Aging on Activities and Attitudes." In *Normal Aging*, edited by E. B. Palmore. Durham, N.C.: Duke University Press, 1970.

Pergeaux, Yves. *Réalitiés du troisième âge*. Paris: Dunod, 1968.

Proppe, H. "Housing for the Retired and Aged in Southern California: An Architectural Commentary." *Gerontologist* 8 (1968):176–79.

"Residence 'La Croix-de-Gué': La Vie collective." *CNRO documents d'information et de gestion*, vol. 8 (December 1968).

"Retired Persons and Homes for the Elderly." *CNRO documents d'information et de gestion*, vol. 6 (March 1968).

Richardson, J. M. *Age and Need: A Study of Older People in North East Scotland*. Edinburgh: Livingston, 1964.

Riley, Matilda White, and Foner, Anne. *Aging and Society*. Vol. 1, *A Research Inventory*. New York: Russell Sage Foundation, 1968.

Riley, Matilda White; Johnson, Marilyn; and Foner, Anne. *Aging and Society*. Vol. 3, *A Sociology of Age Stratification*. New York: Russell Sage Foundation, 1972.

Rose, Arnold M. "The Subculture of the Aging." In *Older People and their Social World*, edited by Arnold M. Rose and Warren K. Peterson. Philadelphia: F. A. Davis, 1965.

Rosenberg, George S. *Poverty, Aging, and Social Isolation*. Washington: Bureau of Social Science Research, 1967.

———. *The Worker Grows Old*. San Francisco: Jossey-Bass, 1970.

Rosenmayr, L., and Kockeis, Eva. "Family Relations and Social Contacts of the Aged in Vienna." *Aging around the World*, vol. 1, edited by Clark Tibbitts et al. New York: Columbia University Press, 1962.

Rosow, Irving. *Social Integration of the Aged*. New York: Free Press, 1967.

———. *Socialization to Old Age*. Berkeley: University of California Press, 1974.

Ross, Jennie-Keith. "The Culture of Retirement." Ph.D. dissertation, Northwestern University, 1968.

———. "Learning to Be Retired: Socialization into a French Retirement Residence." *Journal of Gerontology* 29, no. 2 (1975): 211–23.

———. "Life Goes On: Social Organization in a French Retirement Residence." In *Late Life: Recent Readings in the Sociology of Aging*, edited by Jaber F. Gubrium. Springfield, Ill.: Charles C. Thomas, 1974.

———. "Social Borders: Definitions of Diversity." *Current Anthropology* 16 (1975): 53–72.

———. "Successful Aging in a French Retirement Residence." In *Successful Aging: Proceedings of the Duke University Center for the Study of Gerontology Conference on Successful· Aging*. Durham, N.C.: Duke University Press, 1974.

Ross, Jennie-Keith, and Ross, Marc Howard. "Participant Observation in Political Research." *Political Methodology* 1 (1974): 63–88.

Ross, Marc Howard. *The Political Integration of Urban Squatters*. Evanston, Ill.: Northwestern University Press, 1973.

Schattschneider, E. E. *The Semi-Sovereign People*. New York: Holt, Rinehart and Winston, 1960.

Schooler, K. K. "The Relationship between Social Interaction and Morale of the Elderly as a Function of Environmental Characteristics." *Gerontologist* 9 (1969):25–29.

Seguin, M. "Opportunity for Peer Socialization in a Retirement Community." *Gerontologist* 13 (1973):208–14.

Shanas, Ethel, et al. *Old People in Three Industrial Societies*. London: Routledge and Kegan Paul, 1968.

Shanas, Ethel, and Streib, Gordon. *Social Structure and the Family: Generational Relations*. Englewood Cliffs, N.J.: Prentice-Hall, 1965.

Shapiro, J. H. "Single-Room Occupancy." *Social Work* 11 (1966): 22–33.

Sheley, Joseph F. "Mutuality and Retirement Community Success." *International Journal of Aging and Human Development* 5 (1974):71–80.

Sherif, Muzafer. *Inter-Group Conflict and Co-operation: Robber's Cave Experiment*. Norman, Okla.: University of Oklahoma Institute of Group Relations, 1961.

Sherman, Susan. "The Choice of Retirement Housing among the Well-Elderly." *Aging and Human Development* 2 (1971):118–38.

_____. "Mutual Assistance and Support in Retirement Housing." *Journal of Gerontology* 30 (1975):479–84.

_____. "Patterns of Contacts for Residents of Age-Segregated and Age-Integrated Housing." *Journal of Gerontology* 30 (1975): 103–7.

Simmel, Georg. *Conflict and the Web of Group Affiliations*. New York: Free Press, 1964.

Sommer, Robert, and Ross, H. "Social Interaction on a Geriatric Ward." *International Journal of Social Psychology* 4 (1958): 128–33.

Spiro, Melford. *Kibbutz*. New York: Schocken Books, 1963.

Stephens, J. "Society of the Alone: Freedom, Privacy, Utilitarianism as Dominant Norms in the SRO." *Journal of Gerontology* 30 (1975):230–35.

Talmon, Yonina. "Aging in Israel, a Planned Society." In *Middle Age and Aging*. ed. Bernice Neugarten. Chicago: University of Chicago Press, 1968.

Teaff, J.; Lawton, M. Powell; and Carlson, Diane. "Impact of Age Integration of Public Housing Projects upon Elderly Tenant Well-Being." Paper presented to the Gerontological Society, 26th Annual Meeting, Miami Beach, Fla., 1973.

Townsend, Peter. *The Family Life of Old People*. London: Routledge and Kegan Paul, 1957.

Trillen, Calvin. "Wake Up and Live." *The New Yorker*, April 1964, pp. 120–72.

Turnbull, Colin. *The Forest People*. New York: Simon and Schuster, 1968.

van Gennep, Arnold. *The Rites of Passage*. Chicago: University of Chicago Press, 1960.

Verba, Sidney. *Small Groups and Political Behavior*. Princeton, N.J.: Princeton University Press, 1961.

Walkley, R. P., et al. *Retirement Housing in California*. Berkeley: Diablo Press, 1966.

White House Conference on Aging. "Housing." In *Toward a National Policy on Aging*, vol. 2. Washington: Government Printing Office, 1971.

Williams, Richard, and Wirths, Claudine. *Lives through the Years*. New York: Atherton Press, 1965.

Winiecke, Linda. "The Appeal of Age-Segregated Housing to the Elderly Poor." *International Journal of Aging and Human Development* 4 (1973):293–306.

Wirth, Louis. "Urbanism as a Way of Life." *American Journal of Sociology* 44 (1938):1–24.

Young, Michael, and Willmott, Peter. *Family and Kinship in East London*. Baltimore: Penguin Books, 1957.

Index

outside contacts, 77–79; and
political identity, 81–82; and
previous roles, 79–80; and
seniority, 80; sources of, 75–84;
and work, 40
Symbols: factor in community
formation, 15; at Les Floralies,
171–73, 175; in other age-homogeneous settings, 191

Territoriality, 21–22, 24–26; in
dining hall, 21–23; on floors, 24–
25
Territory, as aspect of community,
5–8, 151
Threat: factor in community forma-

tion, 13; at Les Floralies, 169–71,
175; in other age-homogeneous
settings, 188–91.

Visibility, as aspect of social status,
68–75; measurement of, 71

We-feeling, 86–88, 153–55; as
aspect of community, 5–6
Work, 35–42; and attitudes about
residence, 41; and factions, 41–
42; factor in community formation, 13, 163–65; in other age-
homogeneous settings, 187; and
social status, 40